NASCAR NEXTEL CUP SERIES 2007

2007 NASCAR NEXTEL CUP SERIES AWARDS CEREMONY

WALDORF=ASTORIA, NEW YORK, N.Y.
NOVEMBER 30, 2007

DEDICATION

WILLIAM C. FRANCE JR.
Pioneer, Innovator, Friend
1933-2007

UMI PUBLICATIONS STAFF

Chairman and Publisher:
Ivan Mothershead

President:
Bill Seaborn

Vice President and Associate Publisher:
Rick Peters

Controller:
Lewis Patton

National Advertising Sales Director:
Paul Kaperonis

Business Development:
C. Ivan Mothershead IV

Managing Editor:
Ward Woodbury

Art Director/Publication Design:
Brett Shippy

Treasurer and Director of Customer Services:
Mary Flowe

Executive Secretary and Customer Services Representative:
Renee Wedvick

ACKNOWLEDGEMENTS

NASCAR NEXTEL CUP SERIES 2007

UMI Publications is pleased to present "NASCAR NEXTEL Cup Series 2007," the official chronicle of the NASCAR NEXTEL Cup Series season. It will be remembered as an incredible year filled with milestones and great accomplishments, all of them included in the pages of this book for you to enjoy for years to come.

Congratulations to Jimmie Johnson, Chad Knaus and the entire No. 48 team from Hendrick Motorsports. With a late-season surge of unparalleled success, Johnson rallied over the second half of the Chase for the NASCAR NEXTEL Cup with four consecutive wins to overtake his teammate and friend, Jeff Gordon, and successfully defend his NASCAR NEXTEL Cup Series crown. Congratulations also to Rick Hendrick. In addition to winning his seventh NASCAR NEXTEL Cup Series championship as a team owner, his four race teams put on an amazing display of power and skill over the 2007 season, driving to Victory Lane a combined 18 times in half of the 36 points races on the season schedule.

Just as winning in NASCAR takes great teamwork, so does creating the NASCAR NEXTEL Cup Series Yearbook. We'd like to take a moment to thank those on the "team" who work so hard to make this effort possible.

To our friends at NASCAR, we offer our gratitude and appreciation. Thanks especially to Brian France, Mike Helton, Jim Hunter, Paul Brooks, Liz Schlosser, Jennifer White, Herb Branham, John Farrell, Mike Forde and Heather Greene for their help and guidance throughout the year.

We would also like to express our heartfelt thanks to our friends at Sprint, who help make this book possible. To Tim Kelly, Dean Kessel, Tom Murphy and Paul Saleh, as well as Liz Aitken at Octagon Marketing, we thank you for your support and outstanding service to this effort.

No story such as this would be complete without exceptional imagery to bring it to life. Therefore, we would like to recognize the hard-working and gifted photographers who make it possible. Special thanks to the staff of CIA Stock Photography — Don Grassmann, Ernie Masche, Gary Eller, Tom Copeland, Andrew Copley, Jennifer Grassmann, Mike Simmons and McKenzie Hubbard — along with our friends at Action Sports Photography — Walter Arce, Tina Snyder, Tami Kelly-Pope, Matt Thacker, Russell LaBounty, Alan Smith, Jared Tilton, Geoff Burke and Tiffany Tiger — for providing us with some of the very best photography available anywhere. We thank them all for their extreme talents and tireless efforts.

Most of all, we'd like to thank you, the fans of NASCAR NEXTEL Cup Series racing, for your support over the years. We're proud to say that NASCAR has the greatest fans of any sport. This book is for you, and we hope you enjoy it as much as we enjoyed bringing it to you.

Proudly produced and printed in the U.S.A.

ISBN # 0-943860-39-3

FOREWORD

T he 2007 season will undoubtedly be remembered as a showcase for hard-charging race winners.

Prior to the season, we adjusted both the point-earning system and the Chase for the NASCAR NEXTEL Cup format to increase the importance of winning races. Drivers in the NASCAR NEXTEL Cup Series responded to the "emphasis on winning" by trying harder than ever to do just that.

The result was Jimmie Johnson winning ten times – including four times consecutively during the Chase – and successfully defending his series championship, edging out his Hendrick Motorsports teammate Jeff Gordon, who won six races.

And, for the fourth consecutive year, the four-year-old Chase format produced a championship battle that wasn't decided until the season's last race, at Homestead-Miami Speedway.

What a year it was, starting with one of the most thrilling Daytona 500s ever as Kevin Harvick nipped Mark Martin by only 0.20 seconds. That was the closest Daytona 500 finish recorded since the advent of electronic scoring.

The excitement built from there.

The first twenty-six races prior to the ten-race Chase was dominated by Gordon, but he shared the spotlight. Harvick won the NASCAR NEXTEL All-Star Challenge. Casey Mears got his first series victory in one of the series' major events, the Coca-Cola 600. Martin Truex mounted a mid-season charge with his first series win, at Dover, going on to qualify for the Chase. Juan Pablo Montoya got his inevitable breakthrough, winning the road-course race at Infineon Raceway en route to Raybestos Rookie of the Year honors. Tony Stewart won at his favorite track, Indianapolis. And Clint Bowyer emerged as the season's surprise, making the Chase and then winning the first Chase race – which also happened to be his first win in the series.

NASCAR drivers, teams and tracks also established the foundation for the future, working together to make the safety-oriented Car of Tomorrow a reality. Thus, we no longer need to call it the "COT." These days, it's the "new car."

There are so many highlights to reflect on, as evidenced by the stories and photos from the past season in these pages of UMI's 2007 NASCAR NEXTEL Cup Series Yearbook.

Enjoy.

Best regards,

Brian France
NASCAR Chairman/CEO

"What a year it was, starting with one of the most thrilling Daytona 500s ever as Kevin Harvick nipped Mark Martin by only 0.20 seconds. That was the closest Daytona 500 finish recorded since the advent of electronic scoring."

CONTENTS

2007 SEASON PREFACE

*O*ptimism abounded as the 2007 NASCAR NEXTEL Cup Series season approached in the days leading to Speedweeks at Daytona International Speedway. Change was in the air, and all of it pointed to a sport that was in very fine health and continuing to grow.

For the first time, NASCAR's premier series welcomed a foreign-based manufacturer in Toyota. With several successful seasons of NASCAR Craftsman Truck Series competition already under their belts, the folks at Toyota were ready to begin fielding stock cars, and their arrival was no halfhearted effort.

Equipped with three multi-car teams, Toyota arrived on the scene with seven drivers set to pilot Camrys during the year. Bill Davis Racing, which had worked closely with Toyota in their development leading up to the season, enlisted veteran drivers Jeremy Mayfield and Dave Blaney. Michael Waltrip Racing, formed during 2006 in anticipation of Toyota's debut, prepared three teams for action with drivers Michael Waltrip, former NASCAR NEXTEL Cup Series champion Dale Jarrett, and rookie David Reutimann. The third organization, Team Red Bull, was new to the sport but brought with them considerable experience in various other forms of professional racing. Brian Vickers, formerly with Hendrick Motorsports, and A.J. Allmendinger, of open-wheel notoriety, arrived ready to take the Red Bull colors into action.

Those at Toyota Racing Development (TRD) were not disillusioned about the task ahead of them. "I think everyone understands the mountain we have to climb," said Lee White, TRD senior vice president, "and the most important thing is for everyone to keep improving. That is one of the fundamental characteristics of Toyota as a company."

(Left) Tony Stewart poses for publicity photos at Daytona International Speedway, one of the many tasks drivers perform at the beginning of each new season. Stewart's thoughts, though, were on the race track, where he hoped to capture his third NASCAR NEXTEL Cup Series championship.

After a few years of development, the Car of Tomorrow was set to debut in 2007. Wider, taller, and with new aerodynamic features such as the front air splitter seen here, the car would present a challenge for all teams.

Making the transition from open-wheel racing to stock cars along with Allmendinger was Juan Pablo Montoya. His highly-anticipated entrance to the sport brought with it a sound international following, garnered from his days in Formula One. Driving for team owner Chip Ganassi, with whom Montoya had already won the Indianapolis 500 and an open-wheel championship, Montoya's engaging personality yet fiercely-competitive spirit was welcomed with open arms by the entire NASCAR community.

Everyone would be competing under a point system that had undergone a few changes to be implemented at the start of the 2007 season. In an effort to place more emphasis on winning, an additional five points would be awarded to the victor of each event. Further, each win would have a significant impact for those drivers competing in the Chase for the NASCAR NEXTEL Cup. As before, the last 10 races of the season

Colombian-born Juan Pablo Montoya prepares for his run at Raybestos Rookie of the Year honors, driving a Dodge for Chip Ganassi Racing with Felix Sabates. An Indy 500 winner, open-wheel champion and Formula One star, Montoya readily admitted that learning to compete with the world's best stock car drivers would be a new and welcome challenge.

(Above) Team Red Bull approached the season ready to hit the ground running with the No. 83 Toyota driven by Brian Vickers, and its sister car, the No. 84 Camry with newcomer and open-wheel star A.J. Allmendinger.

(Right) After a brief semi-retirement, veteran Ricky Rudd signed on to drive a full season for Robert Yates Racing, after Dale Jarrett left the team to drive Toyotas for Michael Waltrip. Rudd began the season with 875 career starts and 23 victories over 30 years of **NASCAR NEXTEL Cup Series** competition.

would comprise the championship fight, with the top 12 drivers — up from 10 as in the previous two years — after the season's first 26 events eligible to compete for the title. This year, however, the points for all 12 contenders would be set at 5000, with an additional 10 points added to each driver's total for every win achieved up to that point in the season.

A new challenge faced all teams with the introduction of the Car of Tomorrow (COT), set to be phased in over the 2007 season. The COT, a completely new design created to enhance safety, generate more competition and reduce costs, was scheduled for use at all tracks less than 1.5 miles in length, both road courses and with restrictor plates at Talladega Superspeedway late in the season. It would see its debut at Bristol Motor Speedway in the fifth race of the year, with at least 16 other events to follow. There were unknowns about the car that would take some getting used to for drivers and teams, but clearly, the COT was the way of the future.

(Above) Team owner Joe Gibbs (left) began the season with full confidence in his driver, Denny Hamlin (right). The reigning Raybestos Rookie of the Year, Hamlin embarked on his sophomore season after winning twice in 2006 and finishing third in the final point standings.

(Left) Rookie driver David Ragan was a popular subject of interviews as the new season drew near. Ragan, who was set to run for rookie titles in both the NASCAR NEXTEL Cup Series and the NASCAR Busch Series, had big shoes to fill, taking over the No. 6 Ford driven for many years by Mark Martin.

(Above) Jimmie Johnson arrived on the scene looking forward to defending his NASCAR NEXTEL Cup Series championship in his sixth full season of competition.

(Below) As he approached the final year of his contract with DEI, everything surrounding Dale Earnhardt Jr. was buzzing. While his team did everything they could to prepare him for a run at the title, speculation ran rampant about what his future might hold.

Looking over the list of entries as the season approached revealed more teams prepared to run the complete schedule than at any time in recent memory. There were at least eight brand-new, full-time efforts, signaling that competition on the track would be hotly contested on a weekly basis. In addition to new teams, the sport welcomed at least seven new primary sponsors, as corporate leadership continued to recognize the opportunities offered through the NASCAR NEXTEL Cup Series.

The usual swapping of drivers and crew chiefs among various teams during the off-season was evident when activities began at Daytona. But most of the talk about who would be driving for which team focused on the future plans of one man. Dale Earnhardt Jr., the sport's most popular driver, was about to begin the final year of his contract with Dale Earnhardt Inc., the company founded by his father, seven-time NASCAR NEXTEL Cup Series champion Dale Earnhardt, and Teresa Earnhardt.

Negotiations were already underway as the new season began, as were countless scenarios generated by the press regarding where Earnhardt Jr. might end up. He, however, was focused on driving and winning. A new season lay ahead, which meant a new opportunity to capture the NASCAR NEXTEL Cup Series championship he so badly wanted to win.

Would this be his year? Or would Jeff Gordon finally win his fifth series title? Could Tony Stewart put together another late-season charge to capture his third championship? Or would this be a year for youth, when young talents such as Kasey Kahne or Denny Hamlin emerged?

One thing was sure: everyone would have to deal with reigning champion Jimmie Johnson, who, after finishing fifth, second, second and fifth in his first four seasons, finally broke through in 2006 to take his first title. Johnson and crew chief Chad Knaus had established themselves as the team to beat, and knocking them off that pedestal was sure to be a formidable task for anyone and everyone.

All slates were clean. There were 36 races to be run over a 10-month season. And although many were able, when all was said and done only one driver would have the right to hoist the trophy and declare himself NASCAR NEXTEL Cup Series champion. ◂▪▪

NASCAR NEXTEL CUP SERIES CHAMPION

JIMMIE JOHNSON

(Left) Carrying the champion's flag after the Ford 400, Jimmie Johnson smokes the tires one last time in 2007. Including this burnout to celebrate winning the championship, Johnson was able to perform this ritual 11 times during the season.

Partners and friends. As a driver-crew chief combination over six full seasons, Jimmie Johnson (right) and Chad Knaus accumulated an astounding record of 33 wins, 86 top fives and 134 top 10s in 219 starts, never finishing lower than fifth in the final point standings.

O n these pages one year ago, I stated how proud I was to have won the NASCAR NEXTEL Cup Series championship, especially for this race team. How proud I was of what we accomplished as a team, how we had matured as a team, and how we pulled together as a team over an entire season to win the championship that had eluded us for a couple of years.

I have to say that this year, having won back-to-back titles, I'm even more proud of what we've been able to achieve. Winning one championship in this sport is extremely hard to do given the level of competition we face each week. It would have been so easy to be satisfied after finally winning our first championship, to let up a little bit. When you win the championship, the whole team deserves to enjoy the moment and let it soak in. They were able to do that, and I was able to do that.

But what is so impressive with our team is that we still opened up the 2007 season winning races right out of the box. We didn't lose anything over the off-season. Everyone stepped up with the single focus to get even better as a team and repeat as champions. All the teams work hard, and everybody's doing all that they can, but our guys found a little extra this year. I'm really thankful for the effort that everybody put in. We went out and beat the best in the business, so I'm very, very proud of what we've accomplished.

Some people might get the wrong idea about being so proud of what we've done. There are some responsibilities that come with being the champion, and I feel that taking the professional approach that I do, wanting to represent the sport and sponsors in the right manner, is what I should do and need to do. But I also think that to be a good champion, it's important to carry yourself in a way that lets people see how excited and how happy a driver and team are to be in that position. They've worked hard for it, and when they carry themselves in a way that shows they're proud to be champions, it makes a difference. We're going to smile all year long and try to represent this sport in a very positive manner.

Crew members escort the No. 48 Chevrolet through the garage area as they prepare for weekend competition. Arriving each week with superbly-prepared cars and equipped with a "let's win" attitude, the reigning champions were a threat to reach Victory Lane everywhere they went.

So much credit for what we've been able to do has to go to Rick Hendrick. Every year our team is together, we're stronger. We learn from the past season and try to recognize and improve on our weak points. As each year goes by and the core of the team stays together, we're able to make it better. It's tough to keep a team together, especially when it's on top, and if a guy has an opportunity to improve his position, then I certainly understand. I had to make choices along the way, and I encourage our guys to do the same if an opportunity is there. But one of the things Rick Hendrick does so well is create a family atmosphere at Hendrick Motorsports, and I think people think long and hard about leaving. I think that is something that is not very com-

(Above) The No. 48 pit crew performed like champions all season, helping their driver post 10 wins. It was the first time any driver won more than eight times in a season since 1998, nine years before, when Jeff Gordon posted 13 victories.

(Left) Jimmie Johnson (left) and crew chief Chad Knaus discuss setups in the garage. Johnson says the key to their successful relationship is that, above all else, they believe in one another.

(Right) Coexisting in the 24-48 shop at Hendrick Motorsports, the teams of Jimmie Johnson and Jeff Gordon draw from all of the same resources. It showed on the track in 2007; they combined for 16 wins and battled for the title right down to the final race of the year.

(Below) More than teammates, Jeff Gordon (left) and Jimmie Johnson have developed a strong friendship over the years. It was Gordon who brought the young talent to the attention of Rick Hendrick, and Gordon who invested his own money to help establish the No. 48 team.

mon in other shops. It's an important factor in the strength of all our teams, and it's a real tribute to Mr. Hendrick.

A lot of people have asked me about the middle of the season when our finishes dropped off after we had such a strong start, winning four of the first 10 races. The real truth of the matter is that we just had some bad luck. Our performances were stronger than what we posted. We had tire problems at Indy, Chicago and Dover, but a lot of what went on in the summer was that we just had some bad racing luck. We were frustrated and couldn't understand why we had a stretch of luck that we couldn't get rid of. But the important thing is that we never lost our focus. We finally shook

that bad luck and got back to our winning ways at Fontana and Richmond, just as the Chase was about to start.

People also wonder if we did anything differently at the end of the season when we were finishing so well. We really didn't change our approach. The thing about our team is that we keep that "let's win every week" mentality. Our approach is really the same from Daytona all the way to Homestead. I feel that we do a good job of balancing taking advantage of opportunity with being reckless. We go out and get everything we can, and we try to do that without taking a lot of unnecessary risks. That's really the way we operate, and we just do a good job of that in general.

One thing that really did help us at the end of the season, though, was qualifying well. It's something we had been trying to address for a long time. We felt we were losing so much in track position and on pit-stall selection, that we were making the events harder on ourselves than we needed to. For whatever reason this year we did a much better job, and then we got real hot in qualifying at the end of the season, which was a very welcome thing for our qualifying program.

I can say that the Atlanta win, our second in the Chase, was really because we qualified well. That gave us a good pit-stall pick. Being down at the end of pit road, where we could see what the rest of the field was doing, allowed us to switch from a four-tire stop late in the race, which is what we were planning, to a two-tire stop. Taking just two tires gave us the track position that led to us winning the race.

Making great calls like that one is just one of the reasons Chad Knaus is such an awesome crew chief. I can't imagine working with anyone else at this point. Sure, we've certainly had different points of view throughout the season and throughout our careers together. But I think those times really strengthen the relationship, same as it does with friendships. When you get tested and you get frustrated and you can

(Right) A picture of focus and intensity, Jimmie Johnson gathers his thoughts before rolling off the line in the final event of 2007. Johnson says, "I like to keep myself in check. I always stay hungry and fear that something is going to go wrong. I try to stay hungry that way."

(Below) For the second straight year, Jimmie Johnson hoists the coveted NASCAR NEXTEL Cup Series trophy amidst a grand celebration at Homestead-Miami Speedway.

> **" I'm really thankful for the effort that everybody put in. WE WENT OUT AND BEAT THE BEST IN THE BUSINESS, so I'm very, very proud of what we've accomplished."**

your mind to someone, I think it grows the relationship, and we've certainly been through those times. It comes with life and working with someone. But the foundation of our relationship is that we've always believed in each other, and that's really what makes it work so well.

I want to take this opportunity to thank everyone at Hendrick Motorsports. Without them, none of this could happen. Everyone there is focused on winning championships and giving us all the tools we need to go out on the track and do our jobs. They are just really great people, all 560 of them, and I want to make sure they know how much I appreciate everything they do.

I also want to thank Rick Hendrick and Jeff Gordon for believing in me and giving me the chance to be in this position. We've had an amazing run; a great time together. Friendships and relationships within our organization have grown, as well as the respect we have for one another. I look forward to the future and the really great times we have ahead of us.

More than anyone, I want to thank the fans for their support over the years. Even if you're not a Jimmie Johnson fan, the most important thing is your enthusiasm for the sport of NASCAR racing. It has sustained this sport since the beginning, and the continued growth and support shown by the fans is what fuels us to compete to the best of our abilities each and every week.

As for our team, I think we're just really hitting our stride. I think that we have a lot of good years ahead of us and we'll be fighting for more championships and certainly winning more races as the years go by. Hopefully, we'll be a three-time champion in the near future. 🏁

Jimmie Johnson
2007 NASCAR NEXTEL Cup Series Champion

DAYTONA 500

DAYTONA INTERNATIONAL SPEEDWAY

When the smoke cleared — literally — Kevin Harvick had barely edged Mark Martin by a scant two-hundredths of a second in their side-by-side battle to the line to gain victory in the 49th running of The Great American Race, while crumpled race cars littered the tri-oval behind them.

That scene was the culmination of months of preparation by teams and drivers for the festivities that annually kick off the season — at least on the race track. This year, by the time the NASCAR NEXTEL Cup Series team haulers rolled into the World Center of Racing, the drama was well underway courtesy of the motorsports media.

The hot topic already on the table as engines roared to life for the first time was the status of Dale Earnhardt Jr., who was about to enter the final year of his contract with DEI, the company founded by his late father and run by the younger Earnhardt's stepmother, Teresa.

Negotiations between driver and DEI executives were already underway — and going quite nicely, according to the series' most popular personality. And although "Junior" insisted his desire was to remain with the team — and seize a controlling interest in the company — stories continued to abound in the press speculating about life at DEI without its favorite son.

Thankfully, such talk dwindled as the 2007 roster of cars and drivers took to the asphalt in preparation for the week's full schedule of on-track competition.

First up was the annual Budweiser Shootout at Daytona, a 70-lap Saturday night sprint for nothing more than a barrelful of cash and bragging rights for, at least, the next several days. Dale Jarrett gave the folks from newcomer Toyota a huge morale boost by pulling the No. 1 position in a blind draw to determine the starting grid among the 21 Budweiser Pole Award winners from 2006 and former champions of the special event.

After the field shook itself out, Kyle Busch took control before the midpoint of the race and led 35 consecutive laps, clearly signaling his intent to walk away with the winner's share of the $1 million-plus purse. Included in that span was the night's first caution that brought the field to pit road with 17 laps left to run.

Taking two tires and enough fuel to complete the 175-mile distance, Busch returned to the track still with the lead. In Tony Stewart's pit, crew chief Greg Zipadelli surmised that four tires would be enough to negate Busch's advantage and sent his driver back into action shod with fresh Goodyears on all four corners of the orange-and-white Chevrolet.

That, as it turned out, made the difference, as Stewart pressured Busch before closing in on the bumper of the No. 5 Monte Carlo in Turn 1 with seven laps to go. Already a tad loose as he pushed his car to the limit, Busch felt the back end slide up the track as Stewart lifted the air from behind, then dove to the inside to wrest the point for the last time on the way to his third career victory in the annual event.

David Gilliland, who started 13th in his first race on the 2.5-mile superspeedway, took the opportunity to use it as a learning experience under the tutelage of veteran crew chief Todd Parrott. And he did just that, staying out of trouble and settling in behind Stewart in the closing laps to finish a very respectable, if not impressive, second in the race, while Busch, Jimmie Johnson and Harvick rounded out the top five.

Although Sunday's qualifying session would decide only the starting front row for the Daytona 500, much was at stake. According to the rules, the top 35 cars in 2006 owner points were guaranteed a place in the starting field. In addition, one provisional spot was reserved for a former series champion. That left only seven available starting positions to be contested among approximately 25 drivers, with three of those seven to be decided by times and speeds posted during the qualifying round.

Kevin Harvick starts the victory celebration after edging Mark Martin at the line to win the 2007 Daytona 500.

When asked, many competitors cited the Fords from Robert Yates Racing as some of the fastest on the track during practice, and that notion was verified when Gilliland turned momentum gained the night before into a hot lap at 186.320 mph to capture the pole position for Daytona 500. It was the second pole of Gilliland's brief, 16-race career, the other coming at Talladega late in the 2006 season. Gilliland's Yates Racing teammate, Ricky Rudd, celebrated his return to the sport after a one-year hiatus and

BUDWEISER SHOOTOUT
at Daytona
February 10, 2007

Fin. Pos.	St. Pos.	Car No.	Driver	Laps	Laps Led	Status
1	14	20	Tony Stewart	70	11	Running
2	13	38	David Gilliland	70		Running
3	19	2	Kurt Busch	70	6	Running
4	8	48	Jimmie Johnson	70		Running
5	20	29	Kevin Harvick	70	11	Running
6	10	01	Mark Martin	70	0	Running
7	6	5	Kyle Busch	70	39	Running
8	4	83	Brian Vickers	70	2	Running
9	12	31	Jeff Burton	70		Running
10	2	10	Scott Riggs	70	1	Running
11	7	21	Ken Schrader	70		Running
12	3	60	Boris Said	70		Running
13	5	16	Greg Biffle	70		Running
14	17	8	Dale Earnhardt Jr.	70		Running
15	15	9	Kasey Kahne	70		Running
16	18	19	Elliott Sadler	70		Running
17	21	11	Denny Hamlin	70		Running
18	1	44	Dale Jarrett	70		Running
19	16	37	Bill Elliott	70		Running
20	9	12	Ryan Newman	46		Engine
21	11	24	Jeff Gordon	31		Electrical

posted the second-fastest lap of the session to reserve his place on the all-Yates front row for Sunday's main event.

Others who got an emotional boost in qualifying were the Ganassi cars of David Stremme (third fastest) and Juan Pablo Montoya (fourth fastest), with rookie David Ragan turning the fifth-fastest time for Roush-Fenway Racing in the No. 6 Ford.

Boris Said, Sterling Marlin and Johnny Sauter locked up their places in the starting field by turning the fastest laps among those not already having a reserved seat for the Daytona 500. That left only four open spots for the main event, with two to be decided in each of the Gatorade Duel 130s scheduled for Thursday.

As if tensions weren't already high enough, five teams entered a whole new realm of anxiety following post-qualifying inspection. The cars of both Scott Riggs and Elliott Sadler from Evernham Motorsports were found to have hollowed-out bolts used to attach the rear spoiler to the car, a modification

GATORADE DUEL No.1
February 15, 2007

Fin. Pos.	St. Pos.	Car No.	Driver	Laps	Laps Led	Status
1	9	20	Tony Stewart	63	37	Running
2	11	8	Dale Earnhardt Jr.	63		Running
3	26	31	Jeff Burton	63	9	Running
4	1	38	David Gilliland	63	8	Running
5	7	11	Denny Hamlin	63		Running
6	20	07	Clint Bowyer	63		Running
7	10	1	Martin Truex Jr.	63		Running
8	31	55	Michael Waltrip	63	6	Running
9	6	25	Casey Mears	63		Running
10	24	21	Ken Schrader	63		Running
11	5	48	Jimmie Johnson	63		Running
12	3	60	Boris Said	63		Running
13	27	49	Mike Bliss	63		Running
14	4	70	Johnny Sauter	63		Running
15	8	36	Jeremy Mayfield	63		Running
16	14	16	Greg Biffle	63		Running
17	23	78	Kenny Wallace	63		Running
18	25	44	Dale Jarrett	63		Running
19	28	30	Stanton Barrett	63		Running
20	21	37	Bill Elliott	63		Running
21	29	72	Brandon Whitt	63		Running
22	12	43	Bobby Labonte	63		Running
23	30	58	James Hylton	63		Running
24	16	45	Kyle Petty	63		Running
25	13	66	Jeff Green	58		Accident
26	15	4	Ward Burton	56		Accident
27	22	41	Reed Sorenson	50		Engine
28	2	6	David Ragan	44	3	Accident
29	19	84	A.J. Allmendinger	23		Accident
30	18	22	Dave Blaney	23		Transmission
31	17	7	Robby Gordon	22		Accident

GATORADE DUEL No.2
February 15, 2007

Fin. Pos.	St. Pos.	Car No.	Driver	Laps	Laps Led	Status
1	4	24	Jeff Gordon	60	1	Running
2	18	2	Kurt Busch	60	6	Running
3	2	40	David Stremme	60	4	Running
4	6	5	Kyle Busch	60	31	Running
5	29	17	Matt Kenseth	60		Running
6	8	18	J.J. Yeley	60		Running
7	23	99	Carl Edwards	60		Running
8	13	12	Ryan Newman	60		Running
9	21	13	Joe Nemechek	60		Running
10	17	96	Tony Raines	60		Running
11	28	09	Mike Wallace	60		Running
12	5	14	Sterling Marlin	60		Running
13	11	26	Jamie McMurray	60		Running
14	16	01	Mark Martin	60		Running
15	15	15	Paul Menard	60		Running
16	30	9	Kasey Kahne	60		Running
17	19	34	Kevin Lepage	60		Running
18	27	74	Derrike Cope	60		Running
19	12	39	Regan Smith	60		Running
20	24	71	Frank Kimmel	60		Running
21	10	19	Elliott Sadler	60		Running
22	1	88	Ricky Rudd	60		Running
23	25	04	Eric McClure	60		Running
24	26	27	Kirk Shelmerdine	60		Running
25	22	10	Scott Riggs	59		Running
26	20	83	Brian Vickers	49		Accident
27	9	23	Mike Skinner	35		Engine
28	7	00	David Reutimann	33		Electrical
29	14	29	Kevin Harvick	25		Rear End
30	3	42	Juan Pablo Montoya	24	18	Suspension

"AS IF TENSIONS WEREN'T ALREADY HIGH ENOUGH, five teams entered a whole new realm of anxiety following post-qualifying inspection.**"**

deemed in violation of the rules. As a result, team managers Rodney Childers (Riggs) and Josh Browne (Sadler) were suspended for two weeks, fined $25,000 each, and 25-point penalties were levi

It got worse for Ray Evernham when his third car, Kasey Kahne's No. 9 Dodge, failed inspection due to an illegal aerodynamic modification. He wasn't alone, however, as the Ford of Matt Kenseth failed under the same ruling. Kahne's team manager, Kenny Francis, along with Robbie Reiser, crew chief for Kenseth, were subsequently sent home for four weeks, fined $50,000 apiece, and both teams were hit with 50-point penalties.

But all of that paled in comparison to the shock waves created when inspectors discovered a foreign substance in the intake manifold of Michael Waltrip's Toyota. Manifold and car were impounded immediately and, three days later, NASCAR announced that due to their determination that the substance was a fuel additive, a record $100,000 fine and 100-point penalty (second highest in history to a 151-point penalty issued to Jeremy Mayfield in 2000, also for a fuel violation) had been levied against both driver Michael Waltrip and car owner Buffy Waltrip. In addition, crew chief David Hyder and Bobby Kennedy, vice president of competition for Michael Waltrip Racing, were suspended indefinitely.

With Waltrip's qualifying time disallowed, he was forced to join the ranks of those who needed to race their way into the starting lineup for the Daytona 500 via

(Left) Team owners Michael Waltrip (top) and Ray Evernham ran into early trouble when their cars failed post-qualifying inspection. All three of Evernham's entries were declared noncompliant, while a "foreign substance" found in the fuel system of Waltrip's Toyota resulted in serious penalties.

(Below) Sweet! The Candy Cars driven by David Gilliland (right) and veteran Ricky Rudd nailed down both front-row starting positions for Robert Yates Racing.

At age 72, James Hylton attempted to make the Daytona 500 driving a Chevrolet with an engine provided by Richard Childress. Hylton, who started 16 ARCA races in 2006, missed the show after a 23rd place in his Gatorade Duel.

(Above) Juan Pablo Montoya (left) illustrates his technique for turning left for fellow series rookie and open-wheel star A.J. Allmendinger.

(Right) Dale Earnhardt Jr. got bumped and spun in his Gatorade Duel but recovered and rallied to a hard-fought second-place finish.

(Left) In his first NASCAR NEXTEL Cup Series action, A.J. Allmendinger (84) tangles with Robby Gordon during their Gatorade Duel. The incident ended Allmendinger's bid to make the Daytona 500.

Thursday's Gatorade Duel 150s. Driving teammate David Reutimann's backup Toyota, Waltrip lined up at the back of the field in the first Duel and began his quest. An early caution played into Waltrip's hands and, by remaining on the track while most others pitted, his No. 55 was listed atop the leader board when the race resumed. Swift-running Stewart and Earnhardt Jr. hooked up quickly to draft past Waltrip's Toyota, but as they did, Waltrip clipped Earnhardt's Chevrolet and sent him spinning down the backstretch.

Both former teammates recovered, with Earnhardt rallying to a strong second place behind Stewart, who continued to show dominating strength by leading 37 laps, including the final 13, on his way to the win. Waltrip drove to a hard-fought eighth place — good enough to grab a starting spot for Sunday's race — while Boris Said's 12th-place finish boosted David Reutimann into the Daytona 500 field.

In the second Duel 150, Jeff Gordon put on a late-race surge from 13th place on the final restart with just seven laps remaining and barely cleared both Kyle and Kurt Busch through Turns 3 & 4 on the final lap to take the win by mere 0.187-second margin. Joe Nemechek in the No. 13 entry from Ginn Racing and Mike Wallace, driving for Phoenix Racing, finished ninth and 11th, respectively, to gain entrance into Sunday's main event.

The first three-quarters of the Daytona 500 were, for all intents and purposes, uncharacteristically calm, interrupted once when Boris Said spun down the backstretch 18 laps into the race, and again on Lap 80 for Kyle Petty's accident in Turn 2.

Gilliland led from the pole and stayed out front for the fist 18 laps before Kurt Busch and Stewart took over. Between them, the two former champions led all but four of the next 135 laps and established themselves as the class of the field.

Stewart took his first lead from Busch on Lap 49 and held it for 30 laps until the second caution flew. But a problem in the pits, including a penalty for exiting too fast, dropped Stewart to 40th for the Lap-84 restart. Determined as ever, Stewart worked his way back through the field and regained the lead from Busch on Lap 150. Busch battled back over the next three laps until Stewart bobbled coming off Turn 4 with Busch tight

(Above) The U.S. Armed Forces helped provide an impressive pre-race ceremony on opening day of the 2007 NASCAR NEXTEL Cup Series season.

(Right, Above) The command center for Matt Kenseth's No. 17 Ford comes fully equipped with all the latest electronics, including dual HDTV monitors.

(Right) David Gilliland (38) battles with Matt Kenseth (17) with Ryan Newman (12) riding in Kenseth's draft. Gilliland led the first 18 laps, stayed out of trouble and took home a solid eighth place in his first Daytona 500.

on his bumper. With Stewart forced to check up, Busch had nowhere to go and the two leaders crashed to bring out the day's third caution. Both cars were done for the day.

Three more multi-car accidents interrupted the action over the final 40 laps, the last when Earnhardt Jr., Jamie McMurray and Ricky Rudd tangled on the backstretch. With

(Above) In one of the wildest endings in Daytona 500 history, Kevin Harvick (29) barely edged Mark Martin in a green-white-checkered finish. Martin had led the previous 26 laps, but Harvick made up six positions in two laps and got a huge boost from Matt Kenseth to eke out the huge win.

(Left) Chaos erupted as the field approached the finish line with multiple cars scattering throughout the tri-oval. Clint Bowyer managed to beat Juan Pablo Montoya (42) for 18th place while sliding on his roof.

RACE RESULTS

NASCAR NEXTEL Cup Series Race No. 1 — February 18, 2007
Daytona International Speedway

DAYTONA 500

Fin. Pos.	Start Pos.	Car No.	Driver	Team	Laps	Laps Led	Status
1	34	29	Kevin Harvick	Shell/Pennzoil Chevrolet	202	4	Running
2	26	01	Mark Martin	U.S. Army Chevrolet	202	26	Running
3	7	31	Jeff Burton	Cingular Wireless Chevrolet	202		Running
4	22	09	Mike Wallace	Miccosukee Resorts Chevrolet	202		Running
5	35	6 #	David Ragan	AAA Ford	202		Running
6	30	19	Elliott Sadler	Dodge Dealers/UAW Dodge	202		Running
7	28	9	Kasey Kahne	Dodge Dealers/UAW Dodge	202		Running
8	1	38	David Gilliland	M&M's Ford	202	18	Running
9	18	13	Joe Nemechek	CertainTeed/Ginn Resorts Chevrolet	202		Running
10	42	24	Jeff Gordon	DuPont Chevrolet	202		Running
11	6	40	David Stremme	Coors Light Dodge	202		Running
12	12	18	J.J. Yeley	Interstate Batteries Chevrolet	202		Running
13	33	41	Reed Sorenson	Target Dodge	202		Running
14	23	60	Boris Said	SoBe No Fear Energy Drink Ford	202		Running
15	39	7	Robby Gordon	Jim Beam Ford	202		Running
16	41	70	Johnny Sauter	Yellow Transportation/Haas Chevrolet	202		Running
17	38	14	Sterling Marlin	Waste Management Chevrolet	202		Running
18	11	07	Clint Bowyer	Jack Daniel's Chevrolet	202		Running
19	36	42 #	Juan Pablo Montoya	Texaco/Havoline Dodge	202		Running
20	17	25	Casey Mears	National Guard/GMAC Chevrolet	202		Running
21	27	43	Bobby Labonte	Cheerios/Betty Crocker Dodge	202		Running
22	43	44	Dale Jarrett	UPS Toyota	202		Running
23	14	99	Carl Edwards	Office Depot Ford	202		Running
24	8	5	Kyle Busch	CARQUEST/Kellogg's Chevrolet	202	4	Running
25	25	16	Greg Biffle	Ameriquest Ford	202		Running
26	2	88	Ricky Rudd	Snickers Ford	202		Running
27	10	17	Matt Kenseth	DEWALT Ford	202	6	Running
28	9	11	Denny Hamlin	FedEx Express Chevrolet	201		Running
29	13	1	Martin Truex Jr.	Bass Pro Shops/Tracker Boats Chev.	201	13	Running
30	15	55	Michael Waltrip	NAPA Auto Parts Toyota	200		Running
31	24	26	Jamie McMurray	Crown Royal Ford	195		Accident
32	5	8	Dale Earnhardt Jr.	Budweiser Chevrolet	195		Accident
33	20	96	Tony Raines	DLP HDTV Chevrolet	195		Running
34	37	22	Dave Blaney	Caterpillar Toyota	186		Parked
35	19	21	Ken Schrader	Little Debbie Snack Cakes Ford	185		Accident
36	31	66	Jeff Green	Best Buy/HAAS Automation Chevrolet	181		Running
37	32	10	Scott Riggs	Valvoline/Stanley Tools Dodge	179		Running
38	16	12	Ryan Newman	Alltel Dodge	175	1	Engine
39	21	48	Jimmie Johnson	Lowe's Chevrolet	173		Accident
40	40	00 #	David Reutimann	Domino's Toyota	173		Accident
41	4	2	Kurt Busch	Miller Lite Dodge	166	95	Running
42	29	45	Kyle Petty	Wells Fargo Dodge	160		Running
43	3	20	Tony Stewart	The Home Depot Chevrolet	152	35	Accident

\# Raybestos Rookie of the Year Contender.

NASCAR NEXTEL CUP SERIES TOP 12

(After 1 Race)

Pos.	Driver	Points
1	Kevin Harvick	190
2	Mark Martin	175
3	Jeff Burton	165
4	Mike Wallace	160
5	David Ragan	155
6	David Gilliland	147
7	Joe Nemechek	138
8	Jeff Gordon	134
9	David Stremme	130
10	J.J. Yeley	127
11	Elliott Sadler	125
12	Reed Sorenson	124

just three laps to go in the scheduled 200-lap distance, NASCAR threw the red flag, forcing a green-white-checkered finish for the second consecutive year.

Mark Martin sat at the head of the pack, having assumed the lead under the day's fifth caution on Lap 176. And while Martin pondered his strategy for the final two-lap shootout, Harvick, who had just charged from 30th place to seventh in less than 20 laps after having a hole in his front grille repaired, radioed to his crew: "We're going to win this thing. … Tell the '17' (Kenseth) to stick with me, I'm going to run to the front and we're going to win it."

Martin's plan was simple. His only thought as he led the field under green for the last time was to protect the inside line and keep the Chevrolet of Kyle Busch behind him.

"I knew that we were in good shape being on the inside line when I had Kyle behind me, because he had been so strong," Martin said.

It was working perfectly for Martin as the field took the white flag and roared into Turn 1 for the last time. As he headed down the backstretch, Martin weaved desperately back and forth, parlaying every attempt to advance by the hard-charging Busch, while on the outside, Kevin Harvick hugged the wall with Kenseth glued to his bumper.

"We were just going so much faster than they were," Harvick explained later. "… I was coming like a freight train I guess you could say, and we were up against the wall. At that point it was take all you can take … and there wasn't any give."

As the field climbed the Turn-3 banking, Martin dropped low as Harvick, recipient of a huge boost from Kenseth, pulled even on his right. The pair rolled off Turn 4 and onto the short chute with the checkers in sight, door-to-door, trading the advantage back and forth as they headed for the line.

Suddenly and with victory in sight, Martin slowed a bit as his pusher, Busch, lost control and spun.

"I had no idea what happened behind me," Martin said. "I looked up and Kyle was gone."

With that, Harvick edged ahead to the slightest of margins to snatch the victory, while chaos erupted behind him as the field barreled down the frontstretch.

Among those caught up in the incident were Kenseth, Gilliland, Greg Biffle and Clint Bowyer, who crossed the finish line in 18th place while sliding on his roof.

Perhaps Harvick said it best while reflecting back on the second-closest finish in Daytona 500 history: "It was the wildest thing I've been part of in a long time."

AUTO CLUB 500

CALIFORNIA SPEEDWAY

As drivers and crew members returned home after 12 grueling days of Speedweeks that was capped off by the biggest race of the year, the Daytona 500, they barely had time to catch their breath as team haulers pulled away for the east-to-west cross-country trek to the Los Angeles area and sparkling California Speedway.

With just one race in the books, some teams already had one eye turned toward the point standings, taking what they either gained or lost at Daytona as a factor in what needed to be done over the next four races. Beginning at Martinsville, the sixth event on the 2007 schedule, the top 35 in points would enjoy a guaranteed starting spot in the field each week, and with close to 50 teams planning to race the full schedule, competition for the remaining positions on the starting grid would become fierce.

For some, penalties handed out at Daytona put them behind the eight-ball early on. Among them were Matt Kenseth and Scott Riggs, both of whom lost 50 points for rule infractions before finishing in the bottom half of the field at Daytona. As a result, Kenseth and Riggs fell to 40th and 42nd in the standings, respectively.

Others notables such as Jeremy Mayfield, Ward Burton, Mike Bliss, Kenny Wallace and Red Bull Toyota teammates Brian Vickers and A.J. Allmendinger failed to make the field at Daytona and hoped to get things rolling in the right direction with strong efforts at California.

Worse off was Michael Waltrip. Despite finishing 30th in the Daytona 500, his 100-point penalty left him in last place in the standings with a point total of -27 and an uphill battle as he toiled with his three-car effort bearing the Toyota nameplate.

Everyone was eager to get things going at California, the first "normal" race weekend that offered a regular schedule of events while using non-restrictor-plate cars. Kevin Harvick, still riding the emotional wave generated with his Daytona 500 victory, was especially anxious to see if he could continue the winning momentum on a track that had, in the past, been somewhat of a trouble spot for him and his team.

Kenseth, on the other hand, could look at the two-mile oval with confidence based on his record of success, with three NASCAR Busch Series wins in addition to six top 10s in 10 career NASCAR NEXTEL Cup Series starts, including his status as the defending event champion.

Kenseth proved he hadn't lost his touch at the track by taking the win in the NASCAR Busch Series race on Saturday and, despite qualifying 25th for the Auto Club 500, marched directly to the front on Sunday, catching and passing pole-winner Jeff Gordon, front-row starter Kasey Kahne and race-leader Kyle Busch within the first 30 laps to take his first lead of the day.

In all, Kenseth led seven times for an event-high 133 laps, but as the race entered its final stages, it was Jimmie Johnson holding a solid advantage after taking the point on Lap 200 and looking like the man to beat.

That all changed when the day's eighth caution flew for debris with just 23 laps to go, bringing the field to the pits to prepare for the final sprint to the finish. Arriving first on pit road, Johnson's crew bobbled, while Kenseth's team, under the direction of interim crew chief Chip Bolin, clicked off a perfect stop and sent their driver back into action with the lead, while Johnson fell to fifth for the restart.

"Our car was real good on a short run, and the first three or four laps [after the restart] I was able to put a pretty huge distance up there," Kenseth said of his ability to open up a lead. But as the laps wound down, Kenseth could see Harvick's bright yellow-and-red Chevrolet closing steadily from behind.

"He (Harvick) was a little quicker every lap, and with seven or eight to go, I don't know," Kenseth said. "I really thought we were going to lose when the '29' was running us down."

TOP 10 QUALIFIERS

1. **JEFF GORDON**
   38.765 SEC. 185.735 MPH

2. **KASEY KAHNE**
   38.810 SEC. 185.519 MPH

3. **MARK MARTIN**
   38.814 SEC. 185.500 MPH

4. **KEVIN HARVICK**
   38.830 SEC. 185.424 MPH

5. **DALE EARNHARDT JR.**
   38.834 SEC. 185.405 MPH

6. **CLINT BOWYER**
   38.960 SEC. 184.805 MPH

7. **MARTIN TRUEX JR.**
   39.009 SEC. 184.573 MPH

8. **JEFF BURTON**
   39.058 SEC. 184.341 MPH

9. **JUAN PABLO MONTOYA**
   39.084 SEC. 184.219 MPH

10. **CASEY MEARS**
    39.098 SEC. 184.153 MPH

Brian Vickers brings his Red Bull Toyota to a stop on California's pit road. With a solid 15th-place qualifying effort, Vickers granted Team Red Bull their Series debut and wrapped it up with Toyota's first-ever top-10 finish.

Among the celebrities on hand in Southern California were movie star Kevin Costner (left) and singer Sammy Hagar (right). Hagar may not be able to drive 55, but he was right at home with the NASCAR crowd.

(Below) Jeff Gordon's Chevrolet burps some excess fuel on a quick, late-race stop. Gordon, who won his 58th career Budweiser Pole Award, led just two laps in the race but stayed among the leaders and came home in second place.

But as Harvick closed in with a mere handful of laps remaining, Bobby Labonte and David Reutimann got together and smacked the Turn-4 wall, bringing the race to a halt with only five laps left to run.

With the track cleaned off during a brief red flag, Kenseth brought the field around for one final restart ahead of Harvick, Jeff Burton, Gordon and Johnson. But as the field rolled off the fourth turn and headed toward the final green flag, Harvick peeled off toward pit road with a flat left-front tire.

(Above) A dejected Budweiser crew rolls their car and driver, Dale Earnhardt Jr., behind the wall. Earnhardt qualified fifth and looked fast in the race, but his engine was not up to the task and detonated after just 74 laps.

(Right) Kurt Busch is upbeat while on camera with Dick Berggren in the California garage. He bounced right back from a disappointing wreck at Daytona after leading the most laps with a good, clean seventh-place effort, tops for the Dodge Boys.

Kenseth escaped cleanly on the restart, while Burton spun his tires, allowing Gordon and Johnson to scoot past and battle for the runner-up position, while Kenseth drove off to a 0.679-second margin for his 15th career victory.

Gordon took second ahead of Johnson and Burton, while Mark Martin rounded out

Matt Kenseth completes the weekend sweep. His 15th career NASCAR NEXTEL Cup Series victory came on the heels of a NASCAR Busch Series win the day before.

(Right) Kevin Harvick launches back into action after a stop under green. Harvick, going for two in a row, was tracking down race-leader Kenseth late in the race before a flat tire deflated his chances.

RACE RESULTS

NASCAR NEXTEL Cup Series Race No. 2 — February 25, 2007
California Speedway

AUTO CLUB 500

Fin. Pos.	Start Pos.	Car No.	Driver	Team	Laps	Laps Led	Status
1	25	17	Matt Kenseth	Carhartt/DEWALT Ford	250	133	Running
2	1	24	Jeff Gordon	DuPont Cromax Pro Chevrolet	250	2	Running
3	23	48	Jimmie Johnson	Lowe's Chevrolet	250	31	Running
4	8	31	Jeff Burton	Cingular Wireless Chevrolet	250	18	Running
5	3	01	Mark Martin	U.S. Army Chevrolet	250	1	Running
6	6	07	Clint Bowyer	Jack Daniel's Chevrolet	250	2	Running
7	18	2	Kurt Busch	Miller Lite Dodge	250		Running
8	11	20	Tony Stewart	Home Depot Chevrolet	250	28	Running
9	12	5	Kyle Busch	CARQUEST/Kellogg's Chevrolet	250	9	Running
10	15	83	Brian Vickers	Red Bull Toyota	250		Running
11	17	11	Denny Hamlin	FedEx Freight Chevrolet	250		Running
12	19	12	Ryan Newman	Mobil 1 Dodge	250		Running
13	29	18	J.J. Yeley	Interstate Batteries Chevrolet	250		Running
14	26	13	Joe Nemechek	CertainTeed/Ginn Resorts Chevrolet	250		Running
15	13	16	Greg Biffle	Ameriquest Ford	250	2	Running
16	39	6 #	David Ragan	AAA Insurance So. Cal. Ford	250		Running
17	4	29	Kevin Harvick	Shell/Pennzoil Chevrolet	250	3	Running
18	31	70	Johnny Sauter	Best Buy/Yellow Transportation Chevrolet	249		Running
19	24	40	David Stremme	Coors Light Dodge	249		Running
20	22	15 #	Paul Menard	Menards/Quaker State Chevrolet	249		Running
21	42	7	Robby Gordon	Jim Beam Ford	249		Running
22	37	45	Kyle Petty	Wells Fargo Dodge	249	1	Running
23	41	96	Tony Raines	DLP HD TV Chevrolet	249		Running
24	38	19	Elliott Sadler	Dodge Dealers/UAW Dodge	248		Running
25	40	38	David Gilliland	M&M's Ford	248		Running
26	9	42 #	Juan Pablo Montoya	Texaco/Havoline Dodge	248		Running
27	34	88	Ricky Rudd	Snickers Ford	248		Running
28	28	43	Bobby Labonte	Cheerios/Betty Crocker Dodge	248		Running
29	21	99	Carl Edwards	Office Depot/SBON Ford	247		Running
30	16	66	Jeff Green	Yellow Transportation Chevrolet	247		Running
31	10	25	Casey Mears	National Guard/GMAC Chevrolet	246		Running
32	43	44	Dale Jarrett	UPS Toyota	246		Running
33	33	00 #	David Reutimann	Domino's Toyota	239		Accident
34	32	37	John Andretti	Camping World Dodge	220		Electrical
35	27	14	Sterling Marlin	Panasonic Chevrolet	198		Electrical
36	36	21	Ken Schrader	Little Debbie Snack Cakes Ford	160		Engine
37	35	26	Jamie McMurray	Crown Royal Ford	134		Engine
38	2	9	Kasey Kahne	Dodge Dealers/UAW Dodge	129	20	Engine
39	14	22	Dave Blaney	Caterpillar Toyota	112		Engine
40	5	8	Dale Earnhardt Jr.	Budweiser Chevrolet	74		Engine
41	30	10	Scott Riggs	Stanley Tools/Valvoline Dodge	16		Accident
42	7	1	Martin Truex Jr.	Bass Pro Shops Chevrolet	14		Engine
43	20	41	Reed Sorenson	Target/Energizer Dodge	7		Accident

\# Raybestos Rookie of the Year Contender.

NASCAR NEXTEL CUP SERIES TOP 12
(After 2 Races)

Pos.	Driver	Points	Behind	Change
1	**Mark Martin**	**335**	—	+1
2	Jeff Burton	330	-5	+1
3	Jeff Gordon	309	-26	+5
4	Kevin Harvick	307	-28	-3
5	David Ragan	270	-65	—
6	Clint Bowyer	264	-71	+11
7	Joe Nemechek	259	-76	—
8	J.J. Yeley	251	-84	+2
9	Kyle Busch	239	-96	+14
10	David Stremme	236	-99	-1
11	David Gilliland	235	-100	-5
12	Matt Kenseth	232	-103	+28

> ## "He (Harvick) was a little quicker every lap, and with seven or eight to go, I don't know … I really thought we were going to lose when the '29' was running us down."

the top five and took over the early-season lead in the points.

Clint Bowyer finished sixth, completing an impressive day for Richard Childress Racing, marred slightly by Harvick's late misfortune that dropped him to a lead-lap 17th place at the finish despite having one of the fastest cars of the day.

Tony Stewart led four times for 28 laps but got a speeding penalty entering pit road on Lap 158 and went from a 2.2-second lead to 18th on the lead lap before rallying to finish eighth. Brian Vickers took 10th place to post the first top 10 for Toyota. ◢◣◢

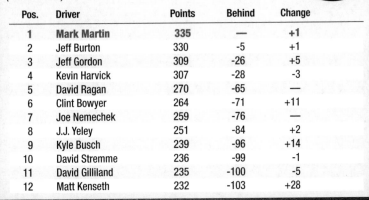

UAW-DAIMLERCHRYSLER 400

LAS VEGAS MOTOR SPEEDWAY

*A*rare weekend off for the NASCAR NEXTEL Cup Series after the California race gave some drivers a chance to join the NASCAR Busch Series in its third visit to the Autodromo Hermanos Rodriguez road course in Mexico City. Among them was NASCAR rookie Juan Pablo Montoya, who proved that although he was still learning the nuances of hustling a heavy stock car around ovals, he was no stranger to road racing — or controversy. After tangling with and dispensing of his Chip Ganassi teammate, fellow road racer Scott Pruett, the Columbia native drove to an extremely popular victory to become the first Hispanic driver to win a major NASCAR event.

Montoya was still the talk of the town when he arrived in Las Vegas for the UAW-DaimlerChrysler 400. This would be his first opportunity to compete on the 1.5-mile super speedway nestled in the Nevada desert, but in some ways, he was on more equal footing with his veteran counterparts than one might think.

Everyone was getting their first crack at a Las Vegas Motor Speedway that had undergone substantial change since the series' last visit in March 2006. In addition to the brand new Neon Garage, featuring a multi-tiered viewing area that allows fans to look down into the work stalls through windows from above, pit road was moved 150 feet closer to the frontstretch grandstands, while the racing surface was completely reconstructed. Banking in the turns was increased from a moderate 12 degrees to an aggressive 20 degrees, while the old surface was taken up entirely and replaced with a new layer of asphalt.

Testing at the facility during the off-season produced blazingly fast speeds, prompting NASCAR to request a harder left-side tire compound from Goodyear to guard against excessive wear. As an extra measure of safety, NASCAR also mandated a smaller, 13-gallon fuel cell for the event to force more frequent pit stops so crews could monitor tire conditions throughout the race.

While some teams struggled, the Dodge Boys from the shops of Ray Evernham and Chip Ganassi got the new layout whipped in short order. Kasey Kahne ripped off a fast lap at 184.856 mph to obliterate his own track qualifying record set in 2004 by nearly 10 mph to take the pole. He was followed by David Stremme, Elliott Sadler and Montoya. Jeff Burton broke up the Dodge party by placing his Chevrolet fifth on the starting grid, but he was followed by Scott Riggs and Reed Sorenson, giving the two Dodge organizations six of the top seven starting positions for the 400-miler.

One team somewhat miffed when they took to the track early in the weekend was the "48" of Jimmie Johnson and crew chief Chad Knaus. Down on speed in practice, Johnson, winner of the last two events at Las Vegas, could manage only the 23rd-fastest lap in qualifying. And that's when Johnson and Knaus began to prove why they have the NASCAR NEXTEL Cup championship.

"Nobody had any new tire data to work with," Johnson explained. "When that happens, we always smile and think, 'All right, this is a chance for us to step up and figure things out before other teams do.'

"So it was really between Chad and I to talk through the issues and the sensations I was having, and we do a good job with that."

By race time under sunny skies and 70-degree temperatures, Johnson and Knaus had what they felt was the right setup for the day. Helped by three cautions in the first 20 laps while others found themselves slipping and sliding on the new track surface, Johnson marched through traffic, dodging bullets along the way. And when the third caution brought the leaders to pit road on Lap 22, Johnson took his first lead of the day.

By the completion of green-flag stops before Lap 100, Johnson had stretched his lead to a commanding 6.5 seconds, clearly showing he and Knaus had hit on something that would be hard to beat — or so they thought.

TOP 10 QUALIFIERS

1. **KASEY KAHNE**
   29.212 SEC. 184.856 MPH

2. **DAVID STREMME**
   29.317 SEC. 184.193 MPH

3. **ELLIOTT SADLER**
   29.368 SEC. 183.874 MPH

4. **JUAN PABLO MONTOYA**
   29.478 SEC. 183.187 MPH

5. **JEFF BURTON**
   29.512 SEC. 182.976 MPH

6. **SCOTT RIGGS**
   29.530 SEC. 182.865 MPH

7. **REED SORENSON**
   29.537 SEC. 182.822 MPH

8. **STERLING MARLIN**
   29.585 SEC. 182.525 MPH

9. **JOE NEMECHEK**
   29.627 SEC. 182.266 MPH

10. **KURT BUSCH**
    29.667 SEC. 182.020 MPH

Kasey Kahne readies for a round of practice after notching his 13th career pole and his second-straight front-row start. Trying to bounce back from a poor finish at California, Kahne struggled in the race before his car broke loose and hit the wall with a handful of laps remaining.

"THE NASCAR NEXTEL CUP SERIES
YEARBOOK 2007

(Left) Among the renovations at Las Vegas is the beautiful new Neon Garage that gives fans several vantage points to view race teams at work.

(Right) There's no lack of entertainment in Las Vegas, and this year's pre-race festivities included the unique showmanship of Blue Man Group.

(Below) Fresh off a NASCAR Busch Series win in Mexico City, Juan Montoya (42) looks for a hole between Jimmie Johnson (48) and Joe Nemechek. Montoya had a fast lap in qualifying to start fourth, but the rigors of a 400-miler took its toll and resulted in a 22nd-place finish, two laps down.

Johnson led 61 of the first 107 laps until the day's fifth caution, during which he left his pit before the crew could retrieve a tire that had rolled outside the box. The resulting pass-through penalty dropped Johnson to 25th on the restart.

"When I have a great race car like that, I can work traffic and take my time," Johnson said. And once again, he began carefully picking his way back through the field.

(Above) Jimmie Johnson (48) didn't qualify that well, but he and crew chief Chad Knaus made all the right moves and Johnson easily distanced himself from everyone while running up front.

(Left) Fully protected from the hazards of handling fuel, one of Juan Pablo Montoya's crewmen tweaks his equipment before going into action.

(Far Right) Jimmie Johnson made it three straight in the Nevada desert and jumped a whopping 11 positions to fourth place in the point standings.

RACE RESULTS

NASCAR NEXTEL Cup Series Race No.3 — March 11, 2007
Las Vegas Motor Speedway

UAW-DaimlerChrysler 400

Fin. Pos.	Start Pos.	Car No.	Driver	Team	Laps	Laps Led	Status
1	23	48	Jimmie Johnson	Lowe's Chevrolet	267	89	Running
2	36	24	Jeff Gordon	DuPont/Nicorette Chevrolet	267	111	Running
3	17	11	Denny Hamlin	FedEx/Kinko's Chevrolet	267		Running
4	37	17	Matt Kenseth	DEWALT Ford	267	1	Running
5	14	01	Mark Martin	U.S. Army Chevrolet	267	15	Running
6	13	99	Carl Edwards	Office Depot Ford	267	3	Running
7	25	20	Tony Stewart	Home Depot Chevrolet	267		Running
8	39	12	Ryan Newman	Alltel Dodge	267	1	Running
9	12	5	Kyle Busch	Kellogg's/Carquest Chevrolet	267	4	Running
10	33	26	Jamie McMurray	Crown Royal Ford	267		Running
11	28	8	Dale Earnhardt Jr.	Budweiser Chevrolet	267	1	Running
12	26	1	Martin Truex Jr.	Bass Pro Shops Chevrolet	267	2	Running
13	42	43	Bobby Labonte	Cheerios/Betty Crocker Dodge	267	3	Running
14	3	19	Elliott Sadler	Dodge Dealers/UAW Dodge	267	17	Running
15	5	31	Jeff Burton	Cingular Wireless Chevrolet	267	4	Running
16	18	16	Greg Biffle	Ameriquest/3M Ford	266		Running
17	38	7	Robby Gordon	Robby Gordon Motorsports Ford	266		Running
18	24	18	J.J. Yeley	Interstate Batteries Chevrolet	266	1	Running
19	27	96	Tony Raines	DLP HDTV Chevrolet	266		Running
20	2	40	David Stremme	Coors Light Dodge	266		Running
21	21	38	David Gilliland	M&M's Ford	265		Running
22	4	42 #	Juan Pablo Montoya	Texaco/Havoline Dodge	265		Running
23	6	10	Scott Riggs	Auto Value/Valvoline Chevrolet	265		Running
24	15	78	Kenny Wallace	Furniture Row Chevrolet	265		Running
25	29	66	Jeff Green	Samsung Four Seasons of Hope Chev.	265		Running
26	10	2	Kurt Busch	Miller Lite Dodge	265		Running
27	20	29	Kevin Harvick	Shell/Pennzoil Chevrolet	265		Running
28	22	45	Kyle Petty	Wells Fargo Dodge	265		Running
29	41	21	Jon Wood	Air Force Ford	264		Running
30	40	88	Ricky Rudd	Snickers Ford	264		Running
31	7	41	Reed Sorenson	Target Dodge	263		Running
32	19	15 #	Paul Menard	Menards/Johns Manville Chevrolet	263		Running
33	43	44	Dale Jarrett	UPS Toyota	263		Running
34	8	14	Sterling Marlin	Waste Management Chevrolet	251	1	Engine
35	1	9	Kasey Kahne	Dodge Dealers/UAW Dodge	251	13	Accident
36	16	07	Clint Bowyer	Jack Daniel's Chevrolet	239	1	Running
37	35	6 #	David Ragan	AAA Ford	236		Running
38	9	13	Joe Nemechek	CertainTeed Chevrolet	156		Accident
39	32	70	Johnny Sauter	Yellow Transportation Chevrolet	147		Running
40	34	25	Casey Mears	National Guard/GMAC Chevrolet	141		Running
41	31	80	Aric Almirola	Joe Gibbs Driven Chevrolet	46		Accident
42	11	22	Dave Blaney	Caterpillar Toyota	17		Accident
43	30	4	Ward Burton	State Water Heaters Chevrolet	15		Accident

Raybestos Rookie of the Year Contender.

NASCAR NEXTEL Cup Series TOP 12
(After 3 Races)

Pos.	Driver	Points	Behind	Change
1	**Mark Martin**	495	—	—
2	Jeff Gordon	489	-6	+1
3	Jeff Burton	453	-42	-1
4	Jimmie Johnson	406	-89	+11
5	Matt Kenseth	397	-98	+7
6	Kevin Harvick	389	-106	-2
7	Kyle Busch	382	-113	+2
8	Denny Hamlin	374	-121	+10
9	J.J. Yeley	365	-130	-1
10	Elliott Sadler	236	-153	+6
11	David Stremme	339	-156	-1
12	David Gilliland	335	-160	-1

By Lap 140, Johnson had worked his way back into the top 10, but while tracking down leaders Gordon and Burton, he brushed the wall while testing the high line.

"I think I bent something," Johnson explained. "The car started hopping and bouncing under a heavy load through the corner, and I had a tight condition in the center of the turn.

"I apologized on the radio that I killed our chances of winning this thing. But Chad said, 'Don't give up and don't even say that.' ... I thought we had a third- or fourth-place car, but Chad made some great adjustments to get it right."

And right it was, as Johnson set sail once again, tracking down the leaders and passing Burton to take control with 28 laps to go. Johnson held off teammate Gordon (who led a race-high 111 laps) on the final restart with 10 to go and drove away to a 2.795-second margin at the finish to secure his third straight Las Vegas win and the 24th of his career. In so doing, Johnson notched the milestone 150th NASCAR NEXTEL Cup Series victory for Hendrick Motorsports. ◢◣◢

KOBALT TOOLS 500

ATLANTA MOTOR SPEEDWAY

One week and a few thousand miles removed from victory at Las Vegas Motor Speedway, Jimmie Johnson picked up right where he left off — at the front.

Although Ryan Newman captured the pole at Atlanta Motor Speedway, he fell to the rear of the field due to an engine change. That moved third-fastest qualifier Johnson to the inside of the front row, where he led 43 starters under the green flag to begin the KOBALT Tools 500 on a cool but sunny Sunday afternoon in Hampton, Ga.

Followed by Hendrick Motorsports teammates Jeff Gordon and Kyle Busch, Johnson immediately set sail on the lightning-fast, 1.54-mile oval. By the time 20 laps passed, Johnson had already opened up a healthy three-and-a-half-second lead, sending notice to anyone desiring to win that they would have to deal with him first.

That was fine by Tony Stewart, who, after starting 13th, steadily closed in on the race leaders and took over the point for the first time on Lap 42, shortly after the first of six cautions during the day.

And so the tone was set. Johnson — going for two wins in a row — and Stewart — winner in the series' most recent visit to Atlanta five months prior — were destined to battle this one out. Between them, they led 256 of the 325-lap distance, Johnson was strong over the long haul, while Stewart proved quicker on short runs.

TOP 10 QUALIFIERS

1. **RYAN NEWMAN**
   28.707 SEC. 193.124 MPH

2. **ELLIOTT SADLER**
   28.891 SEC. 191.894 MPH

3. **JIMMIE JOHNSON**
   28.907 SEC. 191.787 MPH

4. **MARK MARTIN**
   28.909 SEC. 191.774 MPH

5. **JEFF GORDON**
   28.918 SEC. 191.715 MPH

6. **BOBBY LABONTE**
   28.928 SEC. 191.648 MPH

7. **DAVID STREMME**
   28.949 SEC. 191.509 MPH

8. **KYLE BUSCH**
   28.950 SEC. 191.503 MPH

9. **MIKE BLISS**
   29.011 SEC. 191.100 MPH

10. **SCOTT RIGGS**
    29.039 SEC. 190.916 MPH

(Left) Ryan Newman smoked the competition in qualifying but went from first to last on the starting grid when his Dodge required a new motor.

After a rough start to the season, Carl Edwards (99) tries to build on his sixth place at Las Vegas. Hunting him down are Clint Bowyer on Edwards' left and Casey Mears (25) on his right, with Juan Pablo Montoya (42) coming from behind. Montoya fared best with his first top-five finish followed by Bowyer in sixth and Edwards in seventh.

(Above) Members of the United States Army dropped in on Atlanta Motor Speedway, part of pre-race activities often seen at tracks owned by Bruton Smith.

(Left) Elliott Sadler (right) goofs around with Team Director Josh Browne, back for his second event after serving a two-race suspension stemming from a rule violation at Daytona. The pair clicked right away with a third-place qualifying effort at Las Vegas followed by the second-fastest lap at Atlanta.

(Right) Shooting for his third straight top 10, Kyle Busch hits the pits in one of the quicker cars in the race. His effort was sidelined, though; a tire problem and a pit miscue when his car fell off the jack dropped him three laps down.

(Below) The DEI Chevrolets of Dale Earnhardt Jr. (8) and Martin Truex Jr. (1) run together on Atlanta's frontstretch. Truex scored the company's first top 10 of the season with an eighth-place finish, while late-race adjustments to Earnhardt's car caused him to fade to 14th.

With multiple cautions over the final 100 laps, the advantage went to Stewart, who darted to the front on restarts and led in large chunks. As the race wound toward its conclusion, Stewart had things seemingly in hand on the way to another dominant Atlanta victory. Until, that is, the sixth and final caution flag flew for debris with less than 15 laps remaining.

All the leaders pitted for final adjustments and a splash of fuel, including Johnson, who was running second at the time. With only a handful of laps to go, crew chief Chad Knaus ordered an adjustment to free up the car in hopes of giving Johnson a shot at Stewart in the final sprint to the checkered flag.

Matt Kenseth beat Johnson out of the pits and lined up second behind Stewart, with Juan Pablo Montoya (in the midst of a strong performance) fourth and Jeff Burton fifth with 11 laps to go.

Tony Stewart (20) and Jimmie Johnson (48) clearly were the drivers to beat and wound up settling things between themselves. Following a late-race restart, Johnson takes the inside on Stewart after tracking him down, and established the position he needed to score his second straight win.

RACE RESULTS

NASCAR NEXTEL Cup Series Race No.4 — March 18, 2007
Atlanta Motor Speedway

KOBALT TOOLS 500

Fin. Pos.	Start Pos.	Car No.	Driver	Team	Laps	Laps Led	Status
1	3	48	Jimmie Johnson	Lowe's/KOBALT Tools Chevrolet	325	135	Running
2	13	20	Tony Stewart	The Home Depot Chevrolet	325	121	Running
3	21	17	Matt Kenseth	DEWALT Ford	325	11	Running
4	32	31	Jeff Burton	Cingular Wireless Chevrolet	325	2	Running
5	16	42 #	Juan Pablo Montoya	Texaco/Havoline Dodge	325		Running
6	15	07	Clint Bowyer	DirecTV Hot Pass Chevrolet	325	2	Running
7	14	99	Carl Edwards	Office Depot Ford	325		Running
8	18	1	Martin Truex Jr.	Bass Pro Shops/Tracker Boats Chev.	325		Running
9	11	41	Reed Sorenson	Target Dodge	325	1	Running
10	4	01	Mark Martin	U.S. Army Chevrolet	325		Running
11	17	2	Kurt Busch	Miller Lite Dodge	325	14	Running
12	5	24	Jeff Gordon	DuPont Chevrolet	325	30	Running
13	7	40	David Stremme	Coors Light Dodge	325		Running
14	22	8	Dale Earnhardt Jr.	Budweiser Chevrolet	325		Running
15	37	26	Jamie McMurray	IRWIN Industrial Tools Ford	325		Running
16	6	43	Bobby Labonte	Cheerios/Betty Crocker Dodge	325	1	Running
17	19	13	Joe Nemechek	Ginn Resorts Chevrolet	325		Running
18	2	19	Elliott Sadler	Dodge Dealers/UAW Dodge	325	1	Running
19	30	11	Denny Hamlin	FedEx Ground Chevrolet	324		Running
20	39	7	Robby Gordon	Motorola Digital Audio Players Ford	324		Running
21	9	49	Mike Bliss	ZoneLoans.com Dodge	324		Running
22	20	18	J.J. Yeley	Interstate Batteries Chevrolet	324		Running
23	1	12	Ryan Newman	Alltel Dodge	324		Running
24	28	14	Sterling Marlin	Panasonic Plasma HDTV Chevrolet	324		Running
25	36	29	Kevin Harvick	Shell/Pennzoil Chevrolet	324	1	Running
26	42	88	Ricky Rudd	Snickers Ford	323		Running
27	35	22	Dave Blaney	Caterpillar Toyota	323	1	Running
28	34	25	Casey Mears	National Guard/GMAC Chevrolet	323		Running
29	26	70	Johnny Sauter	Best Buy Chevrolet	323		Running
30	27	38	David Gilliland	M&M's Ford	323		Running
31	23	15 #	Paul Menard	Menards/Quaker State Chevrolet	323		Running
32	8	5	Kyle Busch	Kellogg's/Carquest Chevrolet	322		Running
33	38	6 #	David Ragan	AAA Ford	322		Running
34	40	45	Kyle Petty	National Tire & Battery Dodge	322		Running
35	41	66	Jeff Green	Yellow Transportation Chevrolet	322		Running
36	43	44	Dale Jarrett	UPS Toyota	320		Running
37	29	21	Ken Schrader	Little Debbie Snack Cakes Ford	318		Running
38	33	96	Tony Raines	DLP HDTV Chevrolet	318		Running
39	12	9	Kasey Kahne	Dodge Dealers/UAW Dodge	306		Running
40	24	00 #	David Reutimann	Domino's Toyota	295		Running
41	25	16	Greg Biffle	Jackson Hewitt Ford	280		Running
42	31	83	Brian Vickers	Red Bull Toyota	227	5	Accident
43	10	10	Scott Riggs	Stanley Tools/Valvoline Dodge	221		Engine

Raybestos Rookie of the Year Contender.

NASCAR NEXTEL CUP SERIES TOP 12

(After 4 Races)

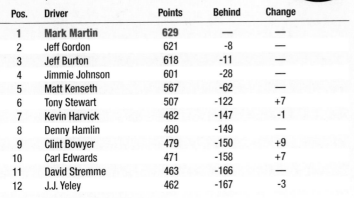

Pos.	Driver	Points	Behind	Change
1	**Mark Martin**	**629**	—	—
2	Jeff Gordon	621	-8	—
3	Jeff Burton	618	-11	—
4	Jimmie Johnson	601	-28	—
5	Matt Kenseth	567	-62	—
6	Tony Stewart	507	-122	+7
7	Kevin Harvick	482	-147	-1
8	Denny Hamlin	480	-149	—
9	Clint Bowyer	479	-150	+9
10	Carl Edwards	471	-158	+7
11	David Stremme	463	-166	—
12	J.J. Yeley	462	-167	-3

As before, Stewart jumped to the early advantage while Johnson quickly moved around Kenseth and set his sights on the orange-and-white No. 20, reducing the gap with each trip around the speedway.

"I was shocked with the grip and the closing rate," Johnson recalled of his run at the leader.

Stewart moved his line up the track to pick up more speed and give Johnson some room on the inside, and with just over three laps to go, Johnson made his move. Rolling off Turn 4, Johnson pulled alongside Stewart as they headed down the frontstretch. They crossed the line side-by-side, with Stewart just in front, and headed toward the first turn.

"I was running out of laps, so I drove it further in [to Turn 1] than I should have," Johnson explained. "But it stuck, and I got up beside Tony."

Johnson edged ahead and appeared to have Stewart cleared, but as they came off Turn 2 the sparks began to fly.

"At that point I was clear and kind of focused on the exit, where I was going to drift the car out to hit the throttle," Johnson continued. "It's wide open."

But Stewart surged on the high side coming off the turn and closed up on Johnson, who, unaware that Stewart had pulled up, squeezed Stewart to the outside when he tried to shut the door. That forced Stewart to brush the wall as the pair rolled out of the turn and onto the backstretch.

"Late off the corner, Tony had a good run on the outside," Johnson said. "When I heard he was there, it was just too late for me to adjust and I certainly squeezed him into the wall and didn't leave him a lot of room. It wasn't intentional."

Intentional or not, Johnson took the lead and opened a 1.311-second margin over Stewart, who recovered to finish second.

"I never expected him (Johnson) to do that," Stewart said later. "He had a faster car. He's probably going to get around us anyway, but I'd like to have seen him give me more room to race him for it."

Kenseth settled into third place in the closing laps, while Burton took fourth after passing Montoya, who scraped the wall on the final restart.

"I thought I had Jimmie on the outside," Montoya said of his attempt to challenge Johnson as he came off Turn 4. "I had a great run until I ran out of room. ... We damaged the fender and Jeff (Burton) passed me."

Still, Montoya's fifth-place finish capped an outstanding run that had him in the hunt throughout most of the latter half of the race.

"The best result before this was 19th," Montoya said, "so I think we're going in the right direction." ▰▰▰

FOOD CITY 500

BRISTOL MOTOR SPEEDWAY

As if any race at Bristol Motor Speedway weren't enough of a spectacle all on its own, this edition of the Food City 500 encompassed issues that made it one of the most significant events on the early 2007 NASCAR NEXTEL Cup Series schedule.

First of all, this was the much anticipated debut of the Car of Tomorrow (COT), and although there were many tests during the new car's development over the previous year or so, this weekend marked the first time the COT would compete with plenty of money and all-important points on the line.

For some teams, gaining as many of those points as possible was absolutely critical. So far, the final owner point standings from 2006 had been used to determine which teams had a guaranteed place in the starting fields. Beginning with the next event, at Martinsville, the 2007 standings would be used, making this, the fifth race of the season, the last chance to solidify a position among the top 35 in owner points and be assured of making the starting lineup each week rather than having to rely on qualifying speeds.

Several teams found themselves dangerously close to the "bubble" and desperately needed a good performance this week at Bristol. Headed into the weekend, Jeff Green sat squarely in the 35th position, with Kyle Petty 34th, just five points ahead of Green, and Dale Jarrett, best of the Toyotas so far, four points ahead of Petty in 33rd place. On the outside looking in were DEI rookie Paul Menard, nine points behind Green in 36th place, and the biggest surprises at this point in the season, Kasey Kahne, who sat 37th in owner points, 15 behind Green, and his Evernham teammate Scott Riggs, who was struggling in 42nd place, a whopping 70 points away from the 35th-place cutoff position.

One thing certain to happen in the point standings was that Mark Martin would be replaced as the leader. After finishing second at Daytona and then taking over the point lead the following week at California, Martin maintained his position on top but was under a constant barrage of questions about whether he had reconsidered his plan to run a partial schedule. Despite his strong start, Martin said from the beginning of the year he would turn the wheel of his No. 01 Chevrolet over to rookie Regan Smith at Bristol. And he did just that, missing a NASCAR NEXTEL Cup Series race for the first time since 1987 and giving the youngster the opportunity to make his series debut.

Joining Smith for his first-ever series start was A.J. Allmendinger, who qualified his Team Red Bull Toyota for the first time this season, as did Jeremy Mayfield, driving another Toyota for Bill Davis Racing.

Green, Kahne and Riggs all got their bids to move up in the points off to a promising start with top-10 qualifying runs. But none of them could beat red-hot Jeff Gordon, who grabbed his second Budweiser Pole Award of the young season. On the strength of two runner-up finishes, at California and Las Vegas, Gordon had already jumped to second place in points, and with five career wins at Bristol, he saw this as a golden opportunity to take the top spot in the standings that would be vacated by Martin at day's end.

Maybe because drivers were somewhat tentative with the new COT, the season's first short-track race was not the knock-down, drag-out affair it can sometimes be. Fourth-best qualifier Tony Stewart drove around Gordon on Lap 7 and threatened to turn the event into his own private show. Stewart led all but 31 of the first 288 laps in purely dominant fashion until fuel-pump issues sidelined his effort and squelched any chance at a decent finish.

With Stewart out of the running, teammate Denny Hamlin took over, hinting that the folks at Joe Gibbs Racing may have gotten the jump on figuring out the COT.

TOP 10 QUALIFIERS

1. **JEFF GORDON**
   15.295 SEC. 125.453 MPH

2. **KASEY KAHNE**
   15.312 SEC. 125.313 MPH

3. **ELLIOTT SADLER**
   15.328 SEC. 125.183 MPH

4. **TONY STEWART**
   15.336 SEC. 125.117 MPH

5. **JAMIE MCMURRAY**
   15.362 SEC. 124.906 MPH

6. **JIMMIE JOHNSON**
   15.372 SEC. 124.824 MPH

7. **DAVE BLANEY**
   15.379 SEC. 124.768 MPH

8. **SCOTT RIGGS**
   15.380 SEC. 124.759 MPH

9. **JEFF GREEN**
   15.397 SEC. 124.622 MPH

10. **DENNY HAMLIN**
    15.403 SEC. 124.573 MPH

There are no bad seats at Bristol, but some are better than others. Among the very best are those in this suite along the frontstretch, where fans take in the action during Saturday's NASCAR Busch Series event, precursor to Sunday's Food City 500.

A key feature of the Car of Tomorrow is standardization, as evidenced by this one-size-fits-all, full-length matrix of templates that lowers onto the body as a single unit. Teams arrived at Bristol a day earlier than usual to ease the inspection process for the new car's debut.

Hamlin seemed well in control, leading in large chunks of 109 and 68 laps when he came up on Jimmie Johnson, who was sliding across the track after a tire problem sent him up and into the wall with only 15 laps to go.

Anticipating the 14th caution of the day, Hamlin slowed his pace behind Johnson, which gave ever-alert Kyle Busch enough time — and room — to sweep past and into the lead before the track officially went to yellow.

(Left) Dale Earnhardt Jr. (8) challenges Jeff Gordon (24) on the outside through Bristol's steep-banked turns. Earnhardt finally broke the top 10 with a seventh-place finish and jumped nine positions in points to 17th, while Gordon's third top-three finish boosted him to No. 1 in the standings.

(Right) Kyle Busch (5) edges Jeff Burton at the line to put his name on record as the first COT winner.

(Below) Dale Jarrett (44) gets hit by David Gilliland in an incident that brought out the second of 15 cautions on Lap 44. It started when Jarrett got tagged by Matt Kenseth and went spinning into the wall. Gilliland became a victim with nowhere to go.

RACE RESULTS

NASCAR NEXTEL Cup Series Race No.5 — *March 25, 2007*
Bristol Motor Speedway

FOOD CITY 500

Fin. Pos.	Start Pos.	Car No.	Driver	Team	Laps	Laps Led	Status
1	20	5	Kyle Busch	CARQUEST/Kellogg's Chevrolet	504	29	Running
2	29	31	Jeff Burton	Cingular Wireless Chevrolet	504		Running
3	1	24	Jeff Gordon	DuPont Chevrolet	504	6	Running
4	40	29	Kevin Harvick	Shell/Pennzoil Chevrolet	504	9	Running
5	11	16	Greg Biffle	Jackson Hewitt Ford	504		Running
6	9	66	Jeff Green	Best Buy/Garmin Chevrolet	504		Running
7	31	8	Dale Earnhardt Jr.	Budweiser Chevrolet	504		Running
8	18	07	Clint Bowyer	Jack Daniel's Chevrolet	504		Running
9	5	26	Jamie McMurray	Crown Royal Ford	504		Running
10	16	25	Casey Mears	National Guard/GMAC Chevrolet	504		Running
11	38	17	Matt Kenseth	Arby's/DEWALT Ford	504		Running
12	32	99	Carl Edwards	Office Depot Ford	504		Running
13	33	40	David Stremme	Energizer/Coors Light Dodge	504		Running
14	10	11	Denny Hamlin	FedEx Express Chevrolet	504	177	Running
15	25	83	Brian Vickers	Red Bull Toyota	504	1	Running
16	6	48	Jimmie Johnson	Lowe's Chevrolet	503		Running
17	19	49	Mike Bliss	Obovo.com Dodge	503		Running
18	14	4	Ward Burton	State Water Heaters/Food City Chev.	502		Running
19	2	9	Kasey Kahne	Dodge Dealers/UAW Dodge	501		Running
20	26	45	Kyle Petty	Marathon Motor Oil Dodge	501		Running
21	27	78	Kenny Wallace	Furniture Row Chevrolet	501		Running
22	28	43	Bobby Labonte	Cheerios/Betty Crocker Dodge	501		Running
23	7	22	Dave Blaney	Caterpillar Toyota	501		Running
24	17	96	Tony Raines	DLP HDTV Chevrolet	501		Running
25	12	01	Regan Smith	U.S. Army Chevrolet	501		Running
26	41	6 #	David Ragan	AAA Ford	501		Running
27	3	19	Elliott Sadler	Dodge Dealers/UAW Dodge	500	5	Running
28	15	21	Ken Schrader	Little Debbie Snack Cakes Ford	500		Running
29	42	2	Kurt Busch	Miller Lite Dodge	499	10	Running
30	21	14	Sterling Marlin	Waste Management Chevrolet	499		Running
31	8	10	Scott Riggs	Valvoline/Stanley Tools Dodge	498		Running
32	36	42 #	Juan Pablo Montoya	Texaco/Havoline Dodge	497		Running
33	34	7	Robby Gordon	Robby Gordon Off Road Wheels Ford	493		Running
34	23	36	Jeremy Mayfield	360 OTC Toyota	486	1	Running
35	4	20	Tony Stewart	The Home Depot Chevrolet	479	257	Running
36	37	18	J.J. Yeley	Interstate Batteries Chevrolet	475	9	Running
37	13	1	Martin Truex Jr.	Bass Pro Shops/Tracker Boats Chev.	475		Running
38	24	88	Ricky Rudd	Pedigree Ford	453		Accident
39	22	12	Ryan Newman	Alltel Dodge	449		Accident
40	43	84 #	AJ Allmendinger	Red Bull Toyota	413		Running
41	35	38	David Gilliland	M&M's Ford	48		Accident
42	30	44	Dale Jarrett	UPS Toyota	42		Accident
43	39	41	Reed Sorenson	Target Dodge	21		Accident

\# Raybestos Rookie of the Year Contender.

NASCAR NEXTEL CUP SERIES TOP 12

(After 5 Races)

Pos.	Driver	Points	Behind	Change
1	Jeff Gordon	791	—	+1
2	Jeff Burton	788	-3	+1
3	Jimmie Johnson	716	-75	+1
4	Matt Kenseth	697	-94	+1
5	Kevin Harvick	647	-144	+2
6	Kyle Busch	639	-152	+8
7	Mark Martin	629	-162	-6
8	Clint Bowyer	621	-170	+1
9	Denny Hamlin	606	-185	-1
10	Carl Edwards	598	-193	—
11	David Stremme	587	-204	—
12	Tony Stewart	575	-216	-6

David Ragan guaranteed a rousing race finish when he looped his Ford down the frontstretch just as the white flag was ready to unfurl. Busch, Gordon and Jeff Burton lined up at the head of the field for the green-white-checkered restart, and Burton immediately jumped to the outside of Gordon and seized second place with his eyes squarely on Busch's No. 5. By the time they rounded Turn 4 to take the white flag, Burton was glued to Busch's bumper, looking for an opening — any opening — to challenge for the win.

"Obviously, I could have used the bumper and moved him out of the way and won the race," Burton said afterwards, "but I try not to do that. ... He (Busch) drives really hard, but he's always raced me with respect, so that's the way I race him."

Burton did find enough room coming off the fourth turn to drop to the inside and pull alongside Busch, but came up a mere 0.064-second short as Busch posted the fourth victory of his NASCAR NEXTEL Cup Series career. ◢◣◢

GOODY'S COOL ORANGE 500

MARTINSVILLE SPEEDWAY

Mark Martin stuck to his guns and sat out the race at Bristol, which allowed Jeff Gordon, Jeff Burton, Jimmie Johnson and Matt Kenseth all to move up one notch in the point standings. With his runner-up finish to Kyle Busch, Burton closed to just three points behind Gordon, whose third place at Bristol marked his third top-three finish over the season's first five events and put him on top of the points. Despite troubles at Bristol that halted his win streak at two, Johnson moved from fourth to third place in points, one spot ahead of Kenseth.

With a solid fourth-place Bristol finish, Kevin Harvick picked up two spots and was listed fifth ahead of Bristol's biggest gainer, Busch, whose win on the Tennessee half-mile vaulted him eight positions, from 14th to sixth.

Martin fell from first to seventh (where he would not stay long considering he was sitting out again at Martinsville), a drop in the standings equal to that of Tony Stewart, who fell from sixth to 12th after a dominating run turned bad with a malfunctioning fuel pump.

More important to some than the change in position at the top of the points was the activity around the all-important 35th position in owner points — the cutoff for having a guaranteed place in the starting field beginning this week in the season's sixth race. Jeff Green put together an outstanding sixth-place run at Bristol, good enough to propel him out of the 35th position and up to 28th. Ironically, that was a swap in positions with Green's teammate, Johnny Sauter, who failed to qualify at Bristol and fell from 28th to 35th.

Kasey Kahne had one of the fastest cars at Bristol, running in the top five for most of the race, until a cut tire dropped him three laps down. He recovered for a top-20 finish (19th) and managed to move from 37th to 34th in owner points in his first race back with Team Director Kenny Francis following his four-race suspension.

The only driver to fall out of the top 35 at Bristol was Dale Jarrett, who dropped from 33rd all the way to 39th place after a tangle with Kenseth ended his day early. However, Jarrett still had two more champion's provisionals he could use in future events.

As far as the Car of Tomorrow, the jury was still out — at least as far as most drivers were concerned. Everyone realized that, as short tracks, Bristol and Martinsville served as good venues for drivers to begin to get the feel of the new machine, and all agreed that upcoming races at longer tracks like Richmond, Phoenix and Darlington would be better proving grounds.

Johnson and Gordon gave the COT — specifically its bumpers — a true test in the Goody's Cool Orange 500, showing a major difference between the COT and the cars used earlier in the season, when a driver could finesse his adversary out of the way to make a race-winning pass.

Johnson had difficulty finding a setup he liked and qualified 20th for the race, prompting crew chief Chad Knaus to confer with Gordon's team after their third-fastest effort behind Jamie McMurray and pole-winner Denny Hamlin. Knaus promptly replaced the existing setup on the No. 48 car with the one Gordon was using, a move that showed fruitful as Johnson worked his way into the top 10 over the first 100 laps of the race.

Johnson, Gordon, Hamlin and Dale Earnhardt Jr. controlled the action, leading all but 33 of the 500-lap event. Earnhardt looked poised to capture his first win of the season, leading a race-high 137 laps until rain temporarily put a halt to the action near the 350-lap mark. After a 30-minute delay, however, Earnhardt's car did not respond as well, and although he was no longer in contention for the win, Earnhardt soldiered on to his first top-five finish of the young season.

TOP 10 QUALIFIERS

1. **DENNY HAMLIN**
   19.911 SEC. 95.103 MPH

2. **JAMIE MCMURRAY**
   19.942 SEC. 94.955 MPH

3. **JEFF GORDON**
   19.964 SEC. 94.851 MPH

4. **KEN SCHRADER**
   20.012 SEC. 94.623 MPH

5. **J.J. YELEY**
   20.025 SEC. 94.562 MPH

6. **KEVIN HARVICK**
   20.028 SEC. 94.548 MPH

7. **TONY STEWART**
   20.035 SEC. 94.515 MPH

8. **DALE EARNHARDT JR.**
   20.042 SEC. 94.482 MPH

9. **CARL EDWARDS**
   20.058 SEC. 94.406 MPH

10. **JOHNNY SAUTER**
    20.064 SEC. 94.378 MPH

Denny Hamlin hinted he had a good grip on the Car of Tomorrow with a strong run at Bristol. He confirmed it by winning his fifth career Budweiser Pole Award at Martinsville, leading the race three times for 125 laps and finishing a stout third for his second top three of the season.

(Above) Six races into the season, things were beginning to come together for Jamie McMurray's No. 26 effort. He posted the second-fastest lap in qualifying and grabbed his third top-10 finish, cracking the top 12 in points in the process.

(Left) After failing to make the field at Las Vegas and Bristol, David Reutimann qualified fast enough at Martinsville to put his No. 00 Camry on the starting grid, one of five Toyotas to make the race.

(Right) Fighting for a place among the top 35 in owner points, Scott Riggs helped himself by finishing eighth at Martinsville, his first top 10 of the season.

On a great call, Johnson pitted for fresh tires and enough fuel to go the distance before the race resumed under green, and as the leaders began to pit, Johnson moved up to second place behind his Hendrick teammate, Busch. Shod with fresher tires, Johnson easily moved around Busch and took his first lead of the day on Lap 388.

With 52 laps remaining, Gordon took second place and closed in on Johnson, intent on capturing his eighth career Martinsville win. Hounding Johnson from behind with what appeared to be a faster car, Gordon tried time and again to seize the lead. He was able to gain inside position under braking while entering the turns, only to see Johnson pull even on the outside through the corners and recapture his lead on the straightaways.

> ## "
> ## THAT WAS THE HARDEST DRIVING I HAVE EVER DONE.
> Then to have my bumper beat off by my teammate in a way that didn't jeopardize either one of us, that was a really class act by Jeff.
> "

(Above) Jeff Gordon (24) and Jimmie Johnson (48) put on one whale of a show over the final 10 laps — and learned a lot about the Car of Tomorrow in a real-time test of big-league short-track competition.

(Left) When all was said and done, Gordon's front bumper showed precious little damage considering the abuse it took against the rear of Johnson's Chevrolet.

(Right) Rear tire changer Tim Ladyga welcomes Jimmie Johnson back to pit road after Johnson held on — literally — over the closing laps to win for the third time in the season's first six events.

RACE RESULTS

GOODY'S COOL ORANGE 500

Fin. Pos.	Start Pos.	Car No.	Driver	Team	Laps	Laps Led	Status
1	20	48	Jimmie Johnson	Lowe's Chevrolet	500	113	Running
2	3	24	Jeff Gordon	DuPont Chevrolet	500	92	Running
3	1	11	Denny Hamlin	FedEx Express Chevrolet	500	125	Running
4	14	5	Kyle Busch	Kellogg's/Carquest Chevrolet	500	10	Running
5	8	8	Dale Earnhardt Jr.	Budweiser Chevrolet	500	137	Running
6	19	31	Jeff Burton	Cingular Wireless Chevrolet	500		Running
7	7	20	Tony Stewart	The Home Depot Chevrolet	500	11	Running
8	26	10	Scott Riggs	Valvoline/Stanley Tools Dodge	500		Running
9	2	26	Jamie McMurray	IRWIN Industrial Tools Ford	500		Running
10	33	17	Matt Kenseth	USG Sheetrock/DEWALT Ford	500	1	Running
11	21	07	Clint Bowyer	Jack Daniel's Chevrolet	500		Running
12	12	2	Kurt Busch	Miller Lite Dodge	500		Running
13	17	88	Ricky Rudd	Snickers Ford	500		Running
14	24	12	Ryan Newman	Alltel Dodge	500		Running
15	27	6 #	David Ragan	AAA Ford	500		Running
16	23	42 #	Juan Pablo Montoya	Texaco/Havoline Dodge	500		Running
17	9	99	Carl Edwards	Office Depot Ford	500		Running
18	28	41	Reed Sorenson	Target Dodge	500		Running
19	4	21	Ken Schrader	Little Debbie Snack Cakes Ford	500		Running
20	11	96	Tony Raines	DLP HDTV Chevrolet	500		Running
21	37	14	Sterling Marlin	Panasonic Plasma HDTV Chevrolet	500		Running
22	42	45	Kyle Petty	Marathon Motor Oil Dodge	499		Running
23	5	18	J.J. Yeley	Interstate Batteries Chevrolet	499		Running
24	18	19	Elliott Sadler	Dodge Dealers/UAW Dodge	498	10	Running
25	41	9	Kasey Kahne	Dodge Dealers/UAW Dodge	498		Running
26	36	01	Regan Smith	U.S. Army Chevrolet	498		Running
27	30	13	Joe Nemechek	Ginn Resorts/CertainTeed Chevrolet	497		Running
28	38	44	Dale Jarrett	UPS Toyota	496		Running
29	15	1	Martin Truex Jr.	Bass Pro Shops/Tracker Boats Chev.	496	1	Running
30	39	49	Mike Bliss	OBOVO.com Dodge	493		Running
31	10	70	Johnny Sauter	Yellow Transportation/Haas CNC Chev.	493		Running
32	34	16	Greg Biffle	Jackson Hewitt Ford	492		Running
33	43	00 #	David Reutimann	Domino's Toyota	491		Running
34	25	7	Robby Gordon	Robby Gordon Motorsports Ford	490		Running
35	29	40	David Stremme	Coors Light Dodge	490		Running
36	32	66	Jeff Green	Best Buy Chevrolet	487		Running
37	22	22	Dave Blaney	Caterpillar Toyota	485		Running
38	40	84 #	AJ Allmendinger	Red Bull Toyota	483		Running
39	16	38	David Gilliland	M&M's Ford	469		Rear Gear
40	13	36	Jeremy Mayfield	360 OTC Toyota	451		Running
41	6	29	Kevin Harvick	Shell/Pennzoil Chevrolet	445		Running
42	35	25	Casey Mears	National Guard/GMAC Chevrolet	371		Running
43	31	43	Bobby Labonte	Cheerios/Betty Crocker Dodge	265		Running

Raybestos Rookie of the Year Contender.

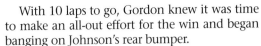

NASCAR NEXTEL CUP SERIES TOP 12

(After 6 Races)

Pos.	Driver	Points	Behind	Change
1	**Jeff Gordon**	966	—	—
2	Jeff Burton	938	-28	—
3	Jimmie Johnson	906	-60	—
4	Matt Kenseth	836	-130	—
5	Kyle Busch	804	-162	+1
6	Denny Hamlin	776	-190	+3
7	Clint Bowyer	751	-215	+1
8	Tony Stewart	726	-240	+4
9	Carl Edwards	710	-256	+1
10	Kevin Harvick	687	-279	-5
11	Dale Earnhardt Jr.	677	-289	+6
12	Jamie McMurray	650	-316	+6

With 10 laps to go, Gordon knew it was time to make an all-out effort for the win and began banging on Johnson's rear bumper.

"I hit him hard," Gordon admitted. "I hit him really hard and got him way out of shape. ... Without putting him all the way up into the wall, I couldn't get clear enough of him where he wasn't going to come back and run into the back of me — and that's not how I want to race my teammate. I felt like he did what he needed to do."

"I don't know how he could have hit me much harder," Johnson countered. "The way these bumpers line up, I just literally put my head up against the headrest and would just wait for it, because I knew it was coming and that it was coming real hard."

So the two friends and teammates battled to the finish, with Johnson able to fend Gordon off and take his third win of the season by a fender.

"That was amazing there at the end," Johnson said. "That was the hardest driving I have ever done. Then to have my bumper beat off by my teammate in a way that didn't jeopardize either one of us, that was a really class act by Jeff." ◢◣◢

SAMSUNG 500

TEXAS MOTOR SPEEDWAY

W ith all the distractions over the previous weeks — including the introduction of the Car of Tomorrow; two consecutive short-track races that ended in exciting side-by-side finishes; Dale Earnhardt Jr. clawing his way toward the top 10 amidst speculation regarding his contract status at DEI; the resurgence of Mark Martin who, after taking a firm hold of the early-season point standings, stuck to his word and vacated the No. 01 Chevrolet at Bristol and Martinsville; and the struggles of several teams, most noticeably the Toyotas along with Kasey Kahne — it almost went unnoticed that Hendrick Motorsports was quickly putting the clamps on the competition.

By the time the NASCAR NEXTEL Cup Series arrived at Texas Motor Speedway for the season's seventh event, Hendrick drivers Jimmie Johnson and Kyle Busch had swept the previous four consecutive races, while Jeff Gordon marched solidly into the No. 1 slot in the point standings. In fact, those three Hendrick teams were nearly dominating the series, posting a total of 10 top-five and 12 top-10 finishes over the past five races. Headed to Texas, they sat first, third (Johnson) and fifth (Busch) in the points.

Consistent with his demeanor, Jeff Burton was quietly effective over that same time span. Other than a 15th-place finish at Las Vegas, Burton finished no worse than sixth (Martinsville) this season. Had it not been for his battle for victory with Kyle Busch over the closing laps at Bristol — a gentlemanly challenge that fell just short and generated as much praise as criticism for its lack of fireworks — Burton may have been completely under the radar. But as he pulled into Texas Motor Speedway, Burton found himself second in the point standings, just 28 behind Gordon, and headed to a track where he had already tasted the victory champagne in its inaugural event in 1997.

QUALIFYING RAINED OUT

(Left) Jeff Burton lets the Texas bubbly fly. The contest covered 500 miles; Burton led only one — the last.

The fans had yet to sit when a multi-car accident on Lap 3 sent David Ragan (6) and Ricky Rudd (88) on this tangled slide across the frontstretch grass. The incident, triggered when Ragan and J.J. Yeley got together coming off Turn 4, collected Casey Mears as well.

THE DAY'S FIFTH CAUTION appeared on Lap 240 when Juan Pablo Montoya and Tony Stewart (apparently already perturbed at Montoya for a move he made during a previous restart) both claimed the same piece of Turn-2 real estate ...

In the 11 races run at Texas since Burton's victory, no driver had been able to make a return visit to Victory Lane. That streak would not stand, however, as Burton pulled off a last-lap pass on Matt Kenseth and stretched it to a 0.410-second margin of victory to win for the 19th time in his NASCAR NEXTEL Cup Series career.

Burton started the race on the front row next to Gordon, as the field was set according to owner points after inclement weather, including nearby tornadoes, washed out qualifying two days earlier on Friday the 13th.

Gordon was the dominant driver over the first half of the race, leading 146 of the first 153 laps before giving way to Dale Earnhardt Jr. To the delight of the Texas crowd, the red No. 8 stayed out front for 93 of the next 95 trips around the 1.5-mile super speedway and appeared to be a contender. But with just under 100 laps to go, the complexion of the race took a bizarre turn.

(Left) David Stremme (40) posts a solid effort in Texas, good enough to earn his first career top-10 finish. It also boosted him back into the top 12 in points after falling out for the first time this season following a poor finish a week earlier at Martinsville.

(Below) Ready to get back to work, Mark Martin (left) confers with crew chief Ryan Pemberton at Texas. After a two-race break, Martin picked it right back up with a strong, third-place showing, his fourth top five and fifth top 10 in five starts this season.

RACE RESULTS

NASCAR NEXTEL Cup Series Race No.7 — April 15, 2007
Texas Motor Speedway

SAMSUNG 500

Fin. Pos.	Start Pos.	Car No.	Driver	Team	Laps	Laps Led	Status
1	2	31	Jeff Burton	Prilosec OTC Chevrolet	334	1	Running
2	4	17	Matt Kenseth	DEWALT Ford	334	16	Running
3	6	01	Mark Martin	U.S. Army Chevrolet	334		Running
4	1	24	Jeff Gordon	DuPont Chevrolet	334	173	Running
5	13	26	Jamie McMurray	Crown Royal Ford	334		Running
6	21	16	Greg Biffle	3M/Ameriquest Ford	334		Running
7	24	1	Martin Truex Jr.	Bass Pro Shops/Tracker Chevrolet	334		Running
8	16	42 #	Juan Pablo Montoya	Texaco/Havoline Dodge	334		Running
9	7	11	Denny Hamlin	FedEx Ground Chevrolet	334		Running
10	14	40	David Stremme	Coors Light Dodge	334		Running
11	17	2	Kurt Busch	Miller Lite Dodge	334	42	Running
12	10	99	Carl Edwards	Office Depot Ford	334		Running
13	27	96	Tony Raines	DLP HDTV Chevrolet	334		Running
14	36	83	Brian Vickers	Red Bull Toyota	334	2	Running
15	42	15 #	Paul Menard	Menards/Energizer Chevrolet	333		Running
16	8	07	Clint Bowyer	Jack Daniels Chevrolet	333		Running
17	15	19	Elliott Sadler	Dodge Dealers/UAW Dodge	333	1	Running
18	25	13	Joe Nemechek	CertainTeed/Ginn Resorts Chevrolet	333		Running
19	30	38	David Gilliland	M&M's Ford	332		Running
20	34	9	Kasey Kahne	Dodge Dealers/UAW Dodge	332		Running
21	40	22	Dave Blaney	Caterpillar Toyota	332		Running
22	35	70	Johnny Sauter	Yellow Transportation Chevrolet	332		Running
23	33	25	Casey Mears	National Guard/GMAC Chevrolet	332		Running
24	23	7	Robby Gordon	Jim Beam Ford	332	1	Running
25	9	20	Tony Stewart	Home Depot Chevrolet	332		Running
26	31	66	Jeff Green	Best Buy Chevrolet	332		Running
27	39	10	Scott Riggs	Valvoline/Stanley Tools Dodge	331		Running
28	22	43	Bobby Labonte	Cheerios/Betty Crocker Dodge	331		Running
29	11	29	Kevin Harvick	Shell/Pennzoil Chevrolet	331		Running
30	37	44	Dale Jarrett	UPS Toyota	331		Running
31	38	21	Ken Schrader	Motorcraft Ford	331		Running
32	20	12	Ryan Newman	Alltel Dodge	330		Running
33	29	88	Ricky Rudd	Snickers Ford	321		Running
34	28	14	Sterling Marlin	Panasonic Chevrolet	304		Running
35	32	45	Kyle Petty	Marathon American Spirit Dodge	291		Running
36	12	8	Dale Earnhardt Jr.	Budweiser Chevrolet	288	96	Engine
37	5	5	Kyle Busch	Cheez-It/Carquest Chevrolet	262		Running
38	3	48	Jimmie Johnson	Lowe's Chevrolet	260		Accident
39	19	6 #	David Ragan	AAA Insurance Ford	239		Running
40	26	41	Reed Sorenson	Tums Dodge	197	2	Engine
41	41	49	Mike Bliss	Paralyzed Veterans of America Dodge	42		Accident
42	43	78	Kenny Wallace	Furniture Row Chevrolet	38		Engine
43	18	18	J.J. Yeley	Interstate Batteries Chevrolet	1		Accident

Raybestos Rookie of the Year Contender.

NASCAR NEXTEL CUP SERIES TOP 12

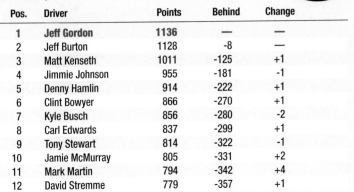

(After 7 Races)

Pos.	Driver	Points	Behind	Change
1	**Jeff Gordon**	1136	—	—
2	Jeff Burton	1128	-8	—
3	Matt Kenseth	1011	-125	+1
4	Jimmie Johnson	955	-181	-1
5	Denny Hamlin	914	-222	+1
6	Clint Bowyer	866	-270	+1
7	Kyle Busch	856	-280	-2
8	Carl Edwards	837	-299	+1
9	Tony Stewart	814	-322	-1
10	Jamie McMurray	805	-331	+2
11	Mark Martin	794	-342	+4
12	David Stremme	779	-357	+1

The day's fifth caution appeared on Lap 240 when Juan Pablo Montoya and Tony Stewart (apparently already perturbed at Montoya for a move he made during a previous restart) both claimed the same piece of Turn-2 real estate, resulting in Stewart spinning across the track. Johnson, who had recently fallen off the leaders' pace with a souring engine, had nowhere to go and broadsided Stewart's Chevrolet, effectively ending his day with a 38th-place finish.

Only a handful of laps passed under green before Stewart felt a tire going down and reported to pit road, losing a lap during a quick stop for new rubber. When Stewart returned to action, he immediately encountered new leader Kurt Busch in Turn 4 and drove deep into the corner trying to regain his lap but lost control and spun.

Earnhardt Jr., second at the time and blinded by Stewart's smoke, climbed on the binders but was slammed from behind by Kyle Busch, who was engulfed in the cloud of smoke as well. Busch took his car to the garage, while Earnhardt's crew managed to keep their driver on the lead lap while making repairs over several stops. Later, engine problems ended Earnhardt's day for good — or so he thought.

Kurt Busch continued to hold the point until he was forced to pit for fuel under green. Unfortunately for Busch, the seventh and final caution flag flew immediately, which dropped the No. 2 Dodge a lap down and ended his bid for the win.

With Busch out of the way, Gordon assumed the lead once again, where he remained until Kenseth got past with 17 laps to go. Four laps later, Burton moved around Gordon as well and zeroed in on Kenseth.

The final 12 laps turned into a classic duel, as Burton searched for an opening around the No. 17 Ford. Three times Burton darted to the inside but was unable to complete the pass. Finally, Burton made one last attempt on the inside as the pair took the white flag.

Burton drove deep into the first corner, able to get underneath Kenseth just enough to hold the inside, and took his first lead of the day as he rolled off Turn 2 and onto the backstretch — a lead he held for barely one mile on his way to the win.

In an ironic twist, Earnhardt drove the last 10 laps of the race in place of Kyle Busch, who left the track unaware that his crew was about to complete repairs on the No. 5 Chevrolet. Earnhardt's laps in the Hendrick car were enough to gain one position, displacing Johnson in 37th place, one spot behind Earnhardt's No. 8. 🏁

SUBWAY FRESH FIT 500

PHOENIX INTERNATIONAL RACEWAY

TOP 10 QUALIFIERS

O ther than the top two positions, the Texas results caused a bit of a shake-up in the point standings as 10 of the top 12 drivers moved either up or down. Jeff Burton remained in second place, but his win combined with Jeff Gordon's fourth-place finish took him to the leader's doorstep, where he was now just eight points away from Gordon with a cushion of 100-plus points over third-place Matt Kenseth.

From there back to ninth-place Tony Stewart, each driver shuffled a spot or two. With a recent run of two straight top 10s followed by a fifth-place finish at Texas, Jamie McMurray rocketed all the way from 18th to 10th in the points, while Mark Martin's return to action resulted in yet another top five (third place) and a jump from 15th to 11th in the points, one spot ahead of David Stremme.

The Phoenix event marked the third appearance of the Car of Tomorrow, and this would be a far greater test for the new configuration that had yet to compete on a track greater than a half mile. In the first two COT events, a pattern had developed. Stewart and his Gibbs Racing teammate, Denny Hamlin, showed great strength by leading a ton of laps and appeared to have a solid handle on the new car, only to be beaten by Hendrick drivers Kyle Busch and Jimmie Johnson.

As the Phoenix weekend got underway, it appeared that trend might continue. Jeff Gordon blistered the one-mile oval with a lap in excess of 133 mph to grab his third Budweiser Pole Award of the young season, barely beating the surging McMurray, who had yet to qualify out of the top five for a COT event. Hamlin confirmed his strength with the third-fastest run, while Hendrick drivers Johnson and Busch, along with Stewart, were all listed among the top 10 starters.

1. JEFF GORDON
27.040 SEC. 133.136 MPH

2. JAMIE MCMURRAY
27.154 SEC. 132.577 MPH

3. DENNY HAMLIN
27.156 SEC. 132.567 MPH

4. SCOTT RIGGS
27.203 SEC. 132.338 MPH

5. JIMMIE JOHNSON
27.216 SEC. 132.275 MPH

6. KURT BUSCH
27.286 SEC. 131.936 MPH

7. MARTIN TRUEX JR.
27.341 SEC. 131.670 MPH

8. KEVIN HARVICK
27.343 SEC. 131.661 MPH

9. TONY STEWART
27.348 SEC. 131.637 MPH

10. KASEY KAHNE
27.363 SEC. 131.565 MPH

(Left) Race winner Jeff Gordon holds a flag to honor the late Dale Earnhardt, who Gordon had just tied on the all-time list with 76 victories.

For the third time in three COT events, a Gibbs Racing Chevrolet, this time Tony Stewart (20), dominated in the laps-led department, and for the third time was beaten by a Hendrick driver.

(Left) Jamie McMurray's smile is an indication of the season he was having. As he prepared to race at Phoenix, he was riding a string of four top 10s in the previous five events and had qualified fifth, second and second in three COT starts.

(Right) This charming little fan makes no secret about who she's pulling for. Her driver, Kurt Busch, pulled away sixth, finished 18th and climbed to the doorstep of the top 12 in points (13th), his highest position in the standings this season.

(Below) Hard-charging Jimmie Johnson jumps on the brakes, lighting up the rotors and sending sparks flying from the car's front splitter. Although he did not lead, his aggressiveness earned him another top-five finish.

Gordon pulled away immediately as the 43 cars rumbled under the green flag to begin 312 laps of competition and held the top spot for the first 28 trips around the one-mile oval. Then Hamlin took over, leading all but one lap until the day's second caution flew on Lap 98. But as Hamlin brought the field down pit road under yellow, he got ticketed for speeding and was sent to the back of the line in 30th place.

While Hamlin began the arduous climb back through the field, teammate Stewart was holding sway with a dominating display of power and handling. Once out front, Stewart led all but one of the next 132 consecutive laps and looked well on the way to gaining his first victory of the season. With 30 miles to go, only a final round of green-flag stops stood between the Indiana native and Victory Lane.

Jeff Gordon's Steve Letarte-led crew prepares their driver for his first win of the year. When Gordon found himself alone on pit road with the yellow flag waving, Letarte seized the moment and put Gordon in position to win.

Gordon was one of the first to come in for fuel, but as he rolled slowly toward his pit box, the caution flew for the sixth time for a Turn-4 tangle involving J.J. Yeley, Dave Blaney and Kenny Wallace. Gordon's instincts told him to forget the stop and return to the track, but crew chief Steve Letarte made an extremely heads-up call, telling Gordon to make his stop for four tires and fuel.

(Below) Jeff Green (66) takes a position from Jeff Burton (31) on the way to a sixth-place finish. That matched Green's previous best this season, both while driving the Car of Tomorrow.

RACE RESULTS

NASCAR NEXTEL Cup Series Race No.8 — April 21, 2007
Phoenix International Raceway

SUBWAY FRESH FIT 500

Fin. Pos.	Start Pos.	Car No.	Driver	Team	Laps	Laps Led	Status
1	1	24	Jeff Gordon	DuPont Chevrolet	312	53	Running
2	9	20	Tony Stewart	Home Depot Chevrolet	312	132	Running
3	3	11	Denny Hamlin	FedEx Kinko's Chevrolet	312	70	Running
4	5	48	Jimmie Johnson	Lowe's Chevrolet	312		Running
5	17	17	Matt Kenseth	DEWALT Ford	312		Running
6	14	66	Jeff Green	Best Buy Chevrolet	312		Running
7	24	5	Kyle Busch	Carquest/Kellogg's Chevrolet	312		Running
8	26	43	Bobby Labonte	Cheerios/Betty Crocker Dodge	312		Running
9	42	70	Johnny Sauter	Haas CNC Machine Tools Chevrolet	312		Running
10	8	29	Kevin Harvick	Shell/Pennzoil Chevrolet	312	54	Running
11	28	99	Carl Edwards	Office Depot Ford	312		Running
12	20	01	Mark Martin	U.S. Army Chevrolet	312		Running
13	31	31	Jeff Burton	Cingular Chevrolet	312		Running
14	23	96	Tony Raines	DLP HDTV Chevrolet	312		Running
15	27	41	Reed Sorenson	Target Dodge	312		Running
16	16	13	Joe Nemechek	Pinnacle Las Vegas Chevrolet	312	1	Running
17	18	16	Greg Biffle	Ameriquest Ford	312		Running
18	6	2	Kurt Busch	Miller Lite Dodge	312		Running
19	15	8	Dale Earnhardt Jr.	Budweiser Chevrolet	312		Running
20	7	1	Martin Truex Jr.	Bass Pro Shops/Tracker Boats Chev.	311		Running
21	22	18	J.J. Yeley	Interstate Batteries Chevrolet	311		Running
22	12	07	Clint Bowyer	DIRECTV Chevrolet	311		Running
23	2	26	Jamie McMurray	Crown Royal Ford	310		Running
24	38	7	Robby Gordon	Jim Beam Ford	310		Running
25	33	15 #	Paul Menard	Menards/Johns Manville Chevrolet	310		Running
26	39	88	Ricky Rudd	Snickers Ford	310		Running
27	37	14	Sterling Marlin	Waste Management Chevrolet	309	1	Running
28	34	21	Ken Schrader	Motorcraft Ford	309		Running
29	43	44	Dale Jarrett	UPS Toyota	309		Running
30	40	45	Kyle Petty	Wells Fargo Dodge	309	1	Running
31	10	9	Kasey Kahne	Dodge Dealers/UAW Dodge	309		Running
32	25	00 #	David Reutimann	Domino's Toyota	309		Running
33	36	42 #	Juan Pablo Montoya	Texaco/Havoline Dodge	309		Running
34	21	19	Elliott Sadler	Dodge Dealers/UAW Dodge	308		Running
35	30	38	David Gilliland	M&M's Ford	308		Running
36	35	4	Ward Burton	State Water Heaters Chevrolet	305		Running
37	13	25	Casey Mears	National Guard/GMAC Chevrolet	303		Running
38	19	12	Ryan Newman	Alltel Dodge	301		Running
39	11	22	Dave Blaney	Caterpillar Toyota	281		Accident
40	29	78	Kenny Wallace	Furniture Row Chevrolet	279		Accident
41	32	6 #	David Ragan	AAA/Show Your Card and Save Ford	264		Running
42	4	10	Scott Riggs	Valvoline/Stanley Tools Dodge	250		Running
43	41	40	David Stremme	Coors Light Dodge	248		Running

\# Raybestos Rookie of the Year Contender.

NASCAR NEXTEL CUP SERIES TOP 12

(After 8 Races)

Pos.	Driver	Points	Behind	Change
1	**Jeff Gordon**	**1,326**	—	—
2	Jeff Burton	1,252	-74	—
3	Matt Kenseth	1,166	-160	—
4	Jimmie Johnson	1,115	-211	—
5	Denny Hamlin	1,084	-242	—
6	Kyle Busch	1,002	-324	+1
7	Tony Stewart	994	-332	+2
8	Carl Edwards	967	-359	—
9	Clint Bowyer	963	-363	-3
10	Mark Martin	921	-405	+1
11	Kevin Harvick	902	-424	+3
12	Jamie McMurray	899	-427	-2

"I was going to drive right though the pit," Gordon said, "but Steve made the call. He knew exactly what to do."

Gordon's crew ripped through a near-perfect stop and sent their driver back onto the track before leader Stewart brought the field around under yellow, leaving Gordon at the end of the lead lap. But when the leaders rolled onto pit road one lap later, Gordon drove straight to the front and inherited his second lead of the day.

Stewart lined up second for the restart, and Gordon knew he needed to get away quickly. That effort was thwarted, however, by Martin Truex Jr., who desperately fought with Gordon to keep from going a lap down.

With Gordon and Truex dicing ahead of him, Stewart zeroed in on the pair, and with 14 laps to go made a spectacular move, splitting the two and taking the lead on Gordon's outside.

But Gordon, already frustrated with Truex and remembering the bitter disappointment of not being able to take the win at Martinsville, would not go down easily. Gordon charged back, dropped to the inside on the very next lap and muscled his Chevrolet into the lead for the last time.

"I was a little bit angry because the team gave me the car and the position [to win], and here I was going to lose it on the race track," Gordon explained. "Luckily, I didn't give up on it and drove into the next corner. … I was able to get close enough to Tony to loosen him up."

Over the remaining dozen laps, Gordon stretched his margin to nearly seven-tenths of a second to gain the victory over Stewart. Hamlin managed to rally all the way back to third place and finished ahead of Johnson and Kenseth.

Jeff Green matched his season high in sixth place to give his team two top 10s in three COT events, while Green's Haas Racing teammate, Johnny Sauter, managed a career-best ninth-place finish.

The victory was No. 76 for Gordon, tying him with Dale Earnhardt for sixth on the all-time list and prompting him to take a victory lap while carrying a black flag emblazoned with the famous "3" to honor his former friend and competitor.

As Gordon arrived in Victory Lane, Dale Earnhardt Jr. was among the very first to greet him with an emotional show of gratitude and congratulations.

"We just wanted to honor him (Earnhardt)," Gordon said. "It was a special moment. It was a special night. It means the world to me." ▰▰▰

AARON'S 499

TALLADEGA SUPERSPEEDWAY

J eff Gordon's win at Phoenix created quite a stir. It wasn't so much that he won, it was that Gordon won for the 76th time in his career, thereby tying Dale Earnhardt for seventh place on the all-time winners' list. And when crew member Aaron Kuehn met him on the frontstretch to deliver a black flag bearing a large No. 3 for a victory lap, emotions — both favorable and unfavorable — spilled over.

The "tribute" had been planned for quite some time, the flag having been hidden on the No. 24 team transporter for the last 24 events dating back to Gordon's most recent win, at Chicagoland in July 2006. No matter how it was perceived by fans, it was, to be sure, meant to honor the late seven-time champion.

For those who took offense, nothing Gordon said — or could have said — would have been satisfactory. But everyone sat up and listened when Dale Earnhardt Jr. weighed in on the subject.

"I don't know how in the world you could take that the wrong way," Earnhardt Jr. remarked. "When I pulled in the garage and saw Jeff doing that on the big screen, I just wanted to make sure that on this side of the fence and with me, that it was really cool and appreciated.

"I thought that was really classy."

At any other time, those words of appeasement from the "Intimidator's" namesake may have been enough to diffuse the situation sufficiently. This, however, was not any other time. In fact, it's hard to imagine a more poignant time for circumstances to come to a head.

This week was all about Talladega, the very track where the driver of the black No. 3 enjoyed tremendous success and built perhaps his most loyal following. Moreover, this weekend marked what would have been the senior Earnhardt's 56th birthday, and one could almost feel those steel-blue eyes penetrating the sky from above.

Could there be a better — or worse — time or place for Gordon to return to Victory Lane and step ahead of Earnhardt on the all-time list?

From Gordon's perspective, none of that mattered. The period between wins No. 75 and 76 had been far too great, and getting No. 77 out of the way right now, this weekend, on a track where he enjoyed so much success in his career (four wins and 11 top fives) was very much on his mind.

So Gordon set the tone immediately by posting his fourth Budweiser Pole Award of the season, beating Daytona 500 pole-winner David Gilliland in a tie-breaker by virtue of his higher ranking in the point standings.

The first three-quarters of the race was typical Talladega, with three-wide packs screaming around the huge tri-oval, swapping the lead 39 times among 19 different drivers. Still, Gordon asserted himself as the strongest of the bunch, taking the lead nine times to rack up a total of 63 laps led, far more than his closest competitor in that category, Sterling Marlin, who managed to front the field on five occasions for 16 total laps.

Jimmie Johnson showed great speed as well, leading six different times for 12 laps, as did Tony Stewart, who led once for seven consecutive laps — the longest stretch other than Gordon — until his car stalled on pit road and dropped him deep into the field.

The complexion of the race changed with the day's fourth caution for a multi-car accident before the 140-lap mark. Johnson and Gordon both had trouble and fell to mid-pack, which gave Denny Hamlin a chance to lead the way.

1. JEFF GORDON	*49.857 SEC. 192.069 MPH*
2. DAVID GILLILAND	*49.857 SEC. 192.069 MPH*
3. DENNY HAMLIN	*49.992 SEC. 191.551 MPH*
4. STERLING MARLIN	*50.130 SEC. 191.023 MPH*
5. RICKY RUDD	*50.156 SEC. 190.924 MPH*
6. KENNY WALLACE	*50.160 SEC. 190.909 MPH*
7. CASEY MEARS	*50.192 SEC. 190.787 MPH*
8. JIMMIE JOHNSON	*50.200 SEC. 190.757 MPH*
9. SCOTT RIGGS	*50.277 SEC. 190.465 MPH*
10. BORIS SAID	*50.296 SEC. 190.393 MPH*

Tony Stewart's race-day crew gathers before the action begins at Talladega. Their driver ran well in the race and was poised for a top-five finish but was involved in a last-lap accident that dropped him to 28th place.

With Gordon, Johnson and Stewart buried in the field, Hamlin took over and led a single-car line around the track for 44 laps. And by the time the day's sixth yellow flag flew for debris, Gordon had managed to climb only to 14th for the restart with less than 10 laps remaining.

(Above) Professional photographers line the fence to capture the action through the turns. It's a tough job for most of these guys, who show up at every race over a grueling 10-month season.

(Left) Ryan Newman slides to a stop after tangling with Juan Pablo Montoya 30 laps from the finish. Quick repairs by his crew kept Newman on the lead lap, which helped him score his second top-10 finish of the season.

"At that point, I would have settled for fifth or sixth, certainly anything in the top five," Gordon admitted later. "I felt it would take some magic for me to win."

On the other hand, Gordon's experience told him it was by no means over, as he radioed to his crew: "Everything is going to change right here, real quick."

On the restart, Johnson dropped to the inside and began a run toward the front with Stewart and Gordon right behind. Gordon eventually moved into the middle lane, and when Johnson drifted high, Gordon dropped to the bottom.

At the front, Jamie McMurray wrested the lead from Hamlin with just five laps to go in the scheduled distance, but behind him, Gordon was slicing through the field, mounting a late-race charge reminiscent of those staged by the "Man in Black" himself. And on Lap 185, with a push from teammate Johnson, Gordon moved around McMurray to take his 10th lead of the day.

Sterling Marlin (14) leads the huge, three-wide pack in the early laps of the Aaron's 499. Marlin qualified fourth in his best effort of the year and passed pole-winner Jeff Gordon (24) for the lead on Lap 2.

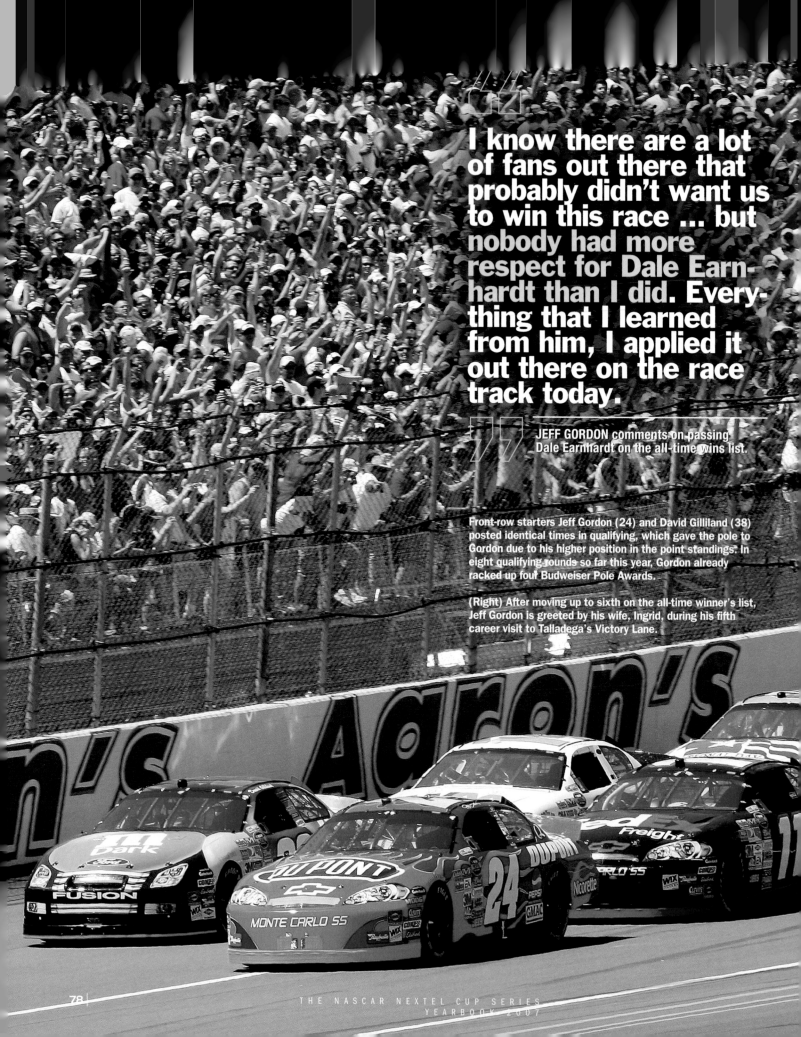

"I know there are a lot of fans out there that probably didn't want us to win this race ... but nobody had more respect for Dale Earnhardt than I did. Everything that I learned from him, I applied it out there on the race track today."

JEFF GORDON comments on passing Dale Earnhardt on the all-time wins list.

Front-row starters Jeff Gordon (24) and David Gilliland (38) posted identical times in qualifying, which gave the pole to Gordon due to his higher position in the point standings. In eight qualifying rounds so far this year, Gordon already racked up four Budweiser Pole Awards.

(Right) After moving up to sixth on the all-time winner's list, Jeff Gordon is greeted by his wife, Ingrid, during his fifth career visit to Talladega's Victory Lane.

RACE RESULTS

NASCAR NEXTEL Cup Series Race No.9 — April 29, 2007
Talladega Superspeedway

AARON'S 499

Fin. Pos.	Start Pos.	Car No.	Driver	Team	Laps	Laps Led	Status
1	1	24	Jeff Gordon	DuPont Chevrolet	192	71	Running
2	8	48	Jimmie Johnson	Lowe's Chevrolet	192	12	Running
3	26	2	Kurt Busch	Miller Lite Dodge	192	7	Running
4	2	38	David Gilliland	M&M's Dark Ford	192		Running
5	25	26	Jamie McMurray	Sharp Vikuiti Ford	192	2	Running
6	41	29	Kevin Harvick	Shell/Pennzoil Chevrolet	192		Running
7	36	8	Dale Earnhardt Jr.	Budweiser Chevrolet	192	2	Running
8	20	40	David Stremme	Wrigley's Winterfresh Dodge	192	1	Running
9	28	12	Ryan Newman	Kodak Dodge	192		Running
10	37	1	Martin Truex Jr.	Bass Pro Shops/Tracker Boats Chev.	192		Running
11	9	10	Scott Riggs	Stanley Tools/Valvoline Dodge	192		Running
12	30	9	Kasey Kahne	Dodge Dealers/UAW Dodge	192	5	Running
13	34	66	Jeff Green	Best Buy Chevrolet	192	3	Running
14	17	17	Matt Kenseth	DEWALT Ford	192	3	Running
15	39	19	Elliott Sadler	Dodge Dealers/UAW Dodge	192	2	Running
16	4	14	Sterling Marlin	Ginn Resorts Chevrolet	192	16	Running
17	10	6 #	David Ragan	AAA Travel Ford	192	1	Running
18	23	45	Kyle Petty	National Tire & Battery Dodge	192		Running
19	31	18	J.J. Yeley	Interstate Batteries Chevrolet	192		Running
20	35	43	Bobby Labonte	Cheerios Racing/Spiderman 3 Dodge	192		Running
21	3	11	Denny Hamlin	FedEx Freight Chevrolet	192	48	Running
22	27	96	Tony Raines	DLP HDTV Chevrolet	192		Running
23	18	36	Jeremy Mayfield	360 OTC Toyota	192		Running
24	22	01	Regan Smith	U.S. Army Chevrolet	192	1	Running
25	29	41	Reed Sorenson	Target Dodge	192		Running
26	6	78	Kenny Wallace	National Day of Prayer/Furn. Row Chev.	192	2	Running
27	11	60	Boris Said	SOBE No Fear Energy Drink Ford	191	1	Running
28	32	20	Tony Stewart	Home Depot Chevrolet	190	7	Accident
29	12	16	Greg Biffle	3M Ford	190	1	Accident
30	21	70	Johnny Sauter	Yellow Fleet Pride Chevrolet	190		Accident
31	24	42 #	Juan Pablo Montoya	Texaco/Havoline Dodge	187		Running
32	14	00 #	David Reutimann	Domino's Toyota	184		Engine
33	5	88	Ricky Rudd	Snickers Ford	155		Running
34	42	31	Jeff Burton	Cingular Wireless Chevrolet	151	2	Running
35	40	07	Clint Bowyer	Jack Daniel's Chevrolet	147		Running
36	15	4	Ward Burton	State Water Heaters Chevrolet	144		Engine
37	13	5	Kyle Busch	Carquest/Kellogg's Chevrolet	130		Accident
38	33	13	Joe Nemechek	CertainTeed/Ginn Resorts Chevrolet	130		Accident
39	7	25	Casey Mears	National Guard/GMAC Chevrolet	124	5	Accident
40	43	44	Dale Jarrett	UPS Toyota	38		Engine
41	38	7	Robby Gordon	Menards/MAPEI Ford	33		Engine
42	16	99	Carl Edwards	Office Depot Ford	27		Engine
43	19	15 #	Paul Menard	Menards Chevrolet	22		Engine

Raybestos Rookie of the Year Contender.

NASCAR NEXTEL CUP SERIES TOP 12
(After 9 Races)

Pos.	Driver	Points	Behind	Change
1	**Jeff Gordon**	1,521	—	—
2	Jeff Burton	1,318	-203	—
3	Matt Kenseth	1,292	-229	—
4	Jimmie Johnson	1,290	-231	—
5	Denny Hamlin	1,189	-332	—
6	Tony Stewart	1,078	-443	+1
7	Jamie McMurray	1,059	-462	+5
8	Kyle Busch	1,054	-467	-2
9	Kevin Harvick	1,052	-469	+2
10	Kurt Busch	1,038	-483	+3
11	Clint Bowyer	1,021	-500	-2
12	Carl Edwards	1,004	-517	-4

Almost immediately, David Reutimann's engine erupted, dropping oil on the track to bring out the caution and assure a green-white-checkered dash to the finish. As the field lined up for the final green flag, the running order showed Gordon out front, ahead of McMurray, Johnson, Kurt Busch and Gilliland.

Moments after the final restart, havoc erupted in Turns 1 & 2 in two separate incidents, one involving Stewart, Gilliland and McMurray, the other a tangle between Greg Biffle and Elliott Sadler. The resulting caution froze the field with Gordon barely edging Johnson's last challenge as they headed onto the backstretch.

"[Johnson] was coming," Gordon recounted. "The last caution saved us. I hate to win like that, but sometimes it works in your favor."

With that, Gordon moved into sole possession of sixth place on the all-time winner's list amidst an obvious display of displeasure from the highly partisan crowd, some of who began pelting the orange-and-blue Chevrolet with debris as he celebrated with a burnout along the frontstretch.

"I know there are a lot of fans out there that probably didn't want us to win this race," Gordon understated, "but nobody had more respect for Dale Earnhardt than I did. Everything that I learned from him, I applied it out there on the race track today." ▰

CROWN ROYAL PRESENTS
THE JIM STEWART 400

RICHMOND INTERNATIONAL RACEWAY

T he 400-lapper at Richmond International Raceway marked the fourth contest using the Car of Tomorrow, and everyone in the Richmond garage had to be looking at the powerhouse teams from Hendrick Motorsports and scratching their heads.

After all, despite some promising performances in the COT by drivers such as Denny Hamlin, Tony Stewart and Kevin Harvick, the Hendrick triumvirate consisting of Kyle Busch, Jimmie Johnson and Jeff Gordon had mopped up all three COT wins.

Taking a closer look, it wasn't just COT events that the Hendrick crew was ruling. In the season's first nine races, winner's trophies had been delivered to Hendrick Motorsports following six of those, with only Richard Childress drivers Harvick and Jeff Burton, along with Roush Fenway Racing's Matt Kenseth, able to put a chink in the Hendrick armor.

Johnson had already grabbed three wins to lead all drivers, followed by Gordon with two and Busch with one. Moreover, Hendrick had placed two or more drivers in the top five in six of the season's nine events.

Gordon was simply red hot. Already having won half of the Budweiser Pole Awards contested this season, he was coming off two straight wins, at Phoenix (a COT event) and at Talladega, both from the pole. So one could almost hear a collective groan throughout the garage area when the four-time champ grabbed his third in a row during Richmond qualifying.

With all that said, if ever there was an opportunity to upset the Hendrick applecart, it was beginning to pan out at Richmond. Rain set in hours before the scheduled Saturday-night start and forced the event to be postponed. NASCAR impounded the entire field, leaving crew chiefs guessing as to their setups when cars were rolled onto the starting grid on a sunny Sunday afternoon.

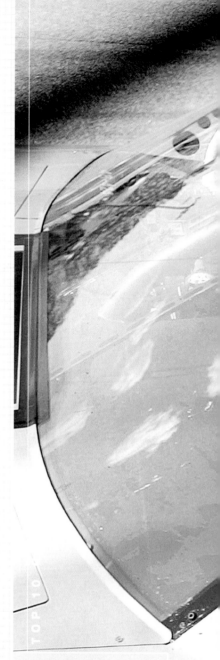

TOP 10

1. **JEFF GORDON**
   21.386 SEC. 126.251 MPH

2. **CARL EDWARDS**
   21.487 SEC. 125.657 MPH

3. **SCOTT RIGGS**
   21.497 SEC. 125.599 MPH

4. **JIMMIE JOHNSON**
   21.502 SEC. 125.570 MPH

5. **KASEY KAHNE**
   21.506 SEC. 125.546 MPH

6. **DENNY HAMLIN**
   21.516 SEC. 125.488 MPH

7. **DALE EARNHARDT JR.**
   21.525 SEC. 125.436 MPH

8. **MARTIN TRUEX JR.**
   21.543 SEC. 125.331 MPH

9. **MARK MARTIN**
   21.570 SEC. 125.174 MPH

10. **DAVE BLANEY**
    21.600 SEC. 125.000 MPH

(Far Left) Engine Specialist Doug Impsen studies his notes during car preparation for driver Carl Edwards. Unfortunately, the engine in the No. 99 Ford let go early in the race, resulting in Edwards' first DNF of the season.

Jimmie Johnson grabs his fourth checkered flag of the season, his second in four COT events. With the win, the reigning champ moved up to second in the standings, his highest ranking of the season.

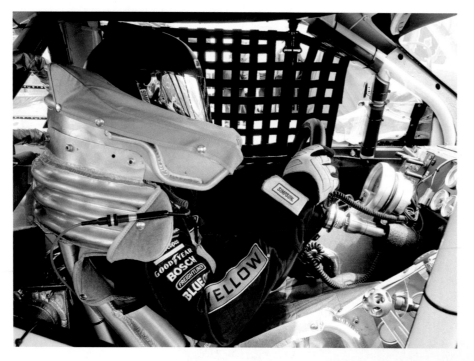

(Left) Johnny Sauter is strapped in and ready to go racing. Running well of late, Sauter's luck ran dry this week when he was caught up in an accident not of his making while running among the top 10.

(Right) Kevin Harvick (29) is fast on the low side of Joe Nemechek (13) as he masters Richmond's three-quarter-mile oval. Harvick was the man to beat in the second half of the race until contact on pit road sidelined his effort.

(Below) The rain showers that cancelled Saturday's scheduled start moved away overnight, and fans were presented with a pleasant Sunday afternoon for racing in Central Virginia.

History was also on the side of those wishing to stop the Hendrick juggernaut. In Gordon's last four Richmond starts, he had not finished better than 30th, and Johnson had just one top 10 in his last 10 starts on the three-quarter-mile oval. Of the three, only Busch had a solid record with top-five finishes in all four of his Richmond starts, but the driver of the No. 5 Chevrolet would have to begin this one all the way back in 34th place after a poor qualifying effort.

As it turned out, others did in fact have their chance to break the Hendrick streak. Gordon was strong early on and paced the field for 114 laps, most of any driver. But by the midpoint of the race, Harvick had stormed to the front after starting 27th and took over, leading 105 laps and looking very stout. That effort came to an excruciating end, however, with a mistake on pit road. Pitting under caution while leading on Lap 253, Harvick, anxious to beat Kurt Busch back onto the track, ran into David Ragan as he was entering his pit. With a damaged front end, Harvick was never again a factor.

It's a good thing we crashed, because it would have been no contest ... Our car was pretty much the class of the field, and we screwed it up.

KEVIN HARVICK comments on the strength of the No. 29 car before a pit road mishap.

Kyle Busch (5), Jimmie Johnson (48) and Elliott Sadler (19) choose different lines as they enter Richmond's 14-degree banks. Hendrick-driving Busch and Johnson swapped the lead over the final 120 laps before Johnson posted his first Richmond victory.

RACE RESULTS

NASCAR NEXTEL Cup Series Race No.10 — May 6, 2007

CROWN ROYAL PRESENTS
THE JIM STEWART 400

Richmond International Raceway

Fin. Pos.	Start Pos.	Car No.	Driver	Team	Laps	Laps Led	Status
1	4	48	Jimmie Johnson	Lowe's Chevrolet	400	105	Running
2	34	5	Kyle Busch	Kellogg's/Carquest Chevrolet	400	27	Running
3	6	11	Denny Hamlin	FedEx Express Chevrolet	400	12	Running
4	1	24	Jeff Gordon	DuPont Chevrolet	400	114	Running
5	33	2	Kurt Busch	Miller Lite Dodge	400	27	Running
6	30	12	Ryan Newman	Alltel Dodge	400	1	Running
7	27	29	Kevin Harvick	Reese's Chevrolet	400	105	Running
8	22	20	Tony Stewart	Home Depot Chevrolet	400	1	Running
9	20	07	Clint Bowyer	DIRECTV Chevrolet	400		Running
10	28	17	Matt Kenseth	DEWALT Ford	400	3	Running
11	10	22	Dave Blaney	Caterpillar Toyota	400	2	Running
12	2	99	Carl Edwards	Office Depot Ford	400		Running
13	7	8	Dale Earnhardt Jr.	Budweiser Chevrolet	400		Running
14	23	18	J.J. Yeley	Interstate Batteries Chevrolet	400		Running
15	18	43	Bobby Labonte	Cheerios/Betty Crocker Dodge	400		Running
16	43	15 #	Paul Menard	Menards/Moen Chevrolet	400		Running
17	9	01	Mark Martin	U.S. Army Chevrolet	400	2	Running
18	15	25	Casey Mears	National Guard/GMAC Chevrolet	400		Running
19	32	16	Greg Biffle	3M Ford	400		Running
20	29	6 #	David Ragan	AAA Travel Ford	400		Running
21	37	41	Reed Sorenson	Target Dodge	400		Running
22	19	96	Tony Raines	DLP HDTV/Shrek the Third Chevrolet	399	1	Running
23	36	14	Sterling Marlin	Waste Management Chevrolet	399		Running
24	12	66	Jeff Green	Haas Automation Chevrolet	399		Running
25	35	45	Kyle Petty	Merchants Tire Dodge	399		Running
26	16	42 #	Juan Pablo Montoya	Texaco/Havoline Dodge	399		Running
27	40	19	Elliott Sadler	Dodge Dealers/UAW Dodge	398		Running
28	8	1	Martin Truex Jr.	Bass Pro Shops/Tracker Chevrolet	398		Running
29	14	00 #	David Reutimann	Domino's Toyota	398		Running
30	3	10	Scott Riggs	Valvoline/Stanley Tools Dodge	397		Running
31	31	46	Johnny Benson	Wyler.com/TRD Toyota	397		Running
32	13	84 #	AJ Allmendinger	Red Bull Toyota	396		Running
33	38	13	Joe Nemechek	CertainTeed Chevrolet	393		Running
34	42	7	Robby Gordon	Menards/MAPEI Ford	378		Running
35	24	4	Ward Burton	State Water Heaters Chevrolet	370		Accident
36	17	70	Johnny Sauter	Yellow Transportation Chevrolet	370		Running
37	11	88	Ricky Rudd	Pedigree Ford	369		Accident
38	21	40	David Stremme	Coors Light Dodge	362		Accident
39	26	78	Kenny Wallace	Furniture Row Chevrolet	331		Running
40	5	9	Kasey Kahne	Dodge Dealers/UAW Dodge	314		Accident
41	25	26	Jamie McMurray	Crown Royal Ford	301		Running
42	41	38	David Gilliland	M&M's Ford	275		Accident
43	39	31	Jeff Burton	Lenox Chevrolet	139		Engine

Raybestos Rookie of the Year Contender.

NASCAR NEXTEL CUP SERIES TOP 12
(After 10 Races)

Pos.	Driver	Points	Behind	Change
1	**Jeff Gordon**	**1,691**	—	—
2	Jimmie Johnson	1,480	-211	+2
3	Matt Kenseth	1,431	-260	—
4	Denny Hamlin	1,359	-332	+1
5	Jeff Burton	1,352	-339	-3
6	Kyle Busch	1,229	-462	+2
7	Tony Stewart	1,225	-466	-1
8	Kevin Harvick	1,203	-488	+1
9	Kurt Busch	1,198	-493	+1
10	Clint Bowyer	1,159	-532	+1
11	Carl Edwards	1,131	-560	+1
12	Dale Earnhardt Jr.	1,118	-573	+1

Penske-driving Kurt Busch took advantage of that mishap and seized the lead, clearly with a car capable of winning. On the next caution and with 121 laps to go, interim crew chief Troy Raker called the former champion into the pits and, as the race leader, when Busch rolled onto pit road, the rest of the field elected to drive past. Busch returned in ninth place and managed to climb back to fifth by the end of the race.

When Busch pitted, Johnson was right there to take over the point, and behind him sat teammate Kyle Busch, who reached the top 10 by the halfway point and had continued to improve from there. Johnson and Busch combined to lead the final 121 laps, swapping the point between them three times until the day's 14th caution for a multi-car accident set up the final restart with just 20 laps to go.

With Busch in front, Johnson got a jump at the drop of the green flag and quickly moved around his teammate, taking the lead he managed to hold over the remaining laps and stretch to a 0.723-second margin over Busch when the checkered flag waved.

With another strong run, Hamlin finished third but admitted his chance of winning was diminished by having to fight his way back to the front after falling behind during the middle portion of the race.

Gordon did not return to the lead after relinquishing it to Harvick, but stayed in touch with the leaders and finished fourth, giving Hendrick Motorsports a 1-2-4 finish and stretching his lead in the standings to a whopping 211 points over teammate Johnson.

And what of putting an end to Hendrick dominance?

"It's a good thing we crashed, because it would have been no contest," Harvick lamented. "Our car was pretty much the class of the field, and we screwed it up."

"We should have a feather in our caps today to know we ran with [the Hendrick cars]," Kurt Busch said. "We definitely had a shot to beat them if we'd had the right pit strategy."

Maybe Hamlin hit the nail on the head by saying, "They've got all the wins because they haven't made any mistakes. I've made mistakes. My pit crew has made mistakes."

Winning crew chief Chad Knaus expanded on that notion. "The level of competition right now is very, very close," Knaus stated. "Where that makes a difference now, you've got to make sure that you have the best team around you possible. ... The teams with the best drivers, the best pit crews, the best strategists, are going to be the teams that win races."

At the moment, it was hard to argue where the best teams resided.

DODGE AVENGER 500

DARLINGTON RACEWAY

*T*he results from Richmond, where Jimmie Johnson posted his third win of the season followed by teammates Kyle Busch in second and Jeff Gordon in fourth, further solidified Hendrick Motorsports' firm grip on the season. With a winning percentage of .700 over the first 10 races, including a perfect four-for-four using the Car of Tomorrow, NASCAR NEXTEL Cup Series teams were well aware that they needed to stretch themselves to the limit just to stay up with such formidable competition.

Now they headed to Darlington — a tough challenge all on its own — with yet another opportunity to sort out the COT and challenge Hendrick's perfect record.

Those storylines — and all others for that matter — faded far into the background on Thursday, May 10, when all of NASCAR zeroed in on Mooresville, N.C., where Dale Earnhardt Jr. held a press conference at his JR Motorsports facility. After months of speculation, Earnhardt announced he was leaving DEI at the end of the 2007 season and would begin to drive for another team that he hoped could propel him to a NASCAR NEXTEL Cup Series championship.

"I can honestly say that we weren't really close with what we both had in mind," Earnhardt said regarding the points being negotiated between him and DEI executives.

The announcement touched off a firestorm of conjecture about where the series' Most Popular Driver would end up in 2008 and beyond, and that got the rumor mill churning at an overwhelming rate.

Earnhardt and his No. 8 team nearly topped their own headlines after arriving at Darlington Raceway, when their Chevrolet Impala SS failed to pass inspection due to modified rear-wing mounting brackets. Ultimately, the team was penalized $100,000 and fined 100 points, and crew chief Tony Eury Jr. was suspended from NASCAR competition until early July.

TOP 10 QUALIFIERS

1. **CLINT BOWYER**
   29.806 SEC. 164.987 MPH

2. **GREG BIFFLE**
   29.826 SEC. 164.876 MPH

3. **JAMIE MCMURRAY**
   29.907 SEC. 164.430 MPH

4. **CARL EDWARDS**
   29.928 SEC. 164.314 MPH

5. **KASEY KAHNE**
   29.972 SEC. 164.073 MPH

6. **KENNY WALLACE**
   30.008 SEC. 163.876 MPH

7. **DENNY HAMLIN**
   30.015 SEC. 163.838 MPH

8. **KEN SCHRADER**
   30.036 SEC. 163.724 MPH

9. **KEVIN HARVICK**
   30.038 SEC. 163.713 MPH

10. **JEFF GORDON**
    30.044 SEC. 163.680 MPH

(Left) Crew chief Steve Letarte fields questions for the media in Darlington's Victory Lane. His call on a late-race caution to leave driver Jeff Gordon on the track led to the team's third win in their last four starts.

Several drivers earned a "Darlington stripe" during the Dodge Avenger 500, including Dale Earnhardt Jr. Undeterred, he finished eighth in the race to end an emotional week during which he announced his decision to leave DEI at the end of the season.

(Above) Denny Hamlin gets the "go" sign after a pit stop under caution. Unfortunately, 15 drivers had already left pit road, which dropped Hamlin from the lead to mid-pack and thwarted yet another opportunity to post a win.

(Left) Clint Bowyer is one happy man at Darlington after winning his first career Budweiser Pole Award. With it, Bowyer qualified for the 2008 Budweiser Shootout, accomplishing one of the team's big goals for the season.

(Right) Mark Martin prepares to go racing on one of the toughest tracks there is. Yet to get a good handle on the COT, Martin struggled to a 14th-place finish but was still listed 15th in the point standings despite missing three of the season's first 11 races.

Thunderstorms postponed the start of the Dodge Avenger 500 from late Saturday afternoon until midday Sunday, when the field of 43 lined up behind Clint Bowyer, who captured his first career Budweiser Pole Award. Next to Bowyer sat Greg Biffle, followed directly by his Roush Fenway teammates Jamie McMurray and Carl Edwards, all hoping to replace a Hendrick Chevrolet in Victory Lane with one of their Fords.

Denny Hamlin started seventh in the pack and immediately went to work, reaching the front of the field and taking the lead on Lap 35, all under green-flag conditions. From there, it was all Hamlin, able to lead in large chunks between caution flags and pit stops for fuel and tires. In all, Hamlin led five times for 179 of the next 265 laps and clearly looked like the car that would stop Hendrick's Victory Express.

(Above) Race leader Denny Hamlin (11) gets a good jump on a restart headed into Turn 1. Hamlin led five times for 179 of the first 300 laps and was clearly the top contender until his crew's gaffe on pit road. Still, he rallied to a second-place finish.

(Left) With his car still blowing steam, Jeff Gordon lights up the tires after his 78th career win, his seventh at Darlington. Gordon was as hot as his engine this season with nine top-four finishes in the first 11 events.

RACE RESULTS

NASCAR NEXTEL Cup Series Race No.11 — May 13, 2007

DODGE AVENGER 500

Darlington Raceway

Fin. Pos.	Start Pos.	Car No.	Driver	Team	Laps	Laps Led	Status
1	10	24	Jeff Gordon	DuPont Chevrolet	367	22	Running
2	7	11	Denny Hamlin	FedEx Express Chevrolet	367	179	Running
3	12	48	Jimmie Johnson	Lowe's Chevrolet	367	44	Running
4	29	12	Ryan Newman	Alltel Dodge	367	39	Running
5	4	99	Carl Edwards	Office Depot Ford	367	33	Running
6	26	20	Tony Stewart	Home Depot Chevrolet	367		Running
7	31	17	Matt Kenseth	DEWALT Ford	367	29	Running
8	21	8	Dale Earnhardt Jr.	Budweiser Chevrolet	367		Running
9	1	07	Clint Bowyer	Jack Daniel's Chevrolet	367	16	Running
10	34	31	Jeff Burton	Cingular Wireless Chevrolet	367		Running
11	25	1	Martin Truex Jr.	Bass Pro Shops/Tracker Chevrolet	367		Running
12	18	2	Kurt Busch	Miller Lite Dodge	367		Running
13	28	14	Sterling Marlin	Ginn Resorts Chevrolet	367		Running
14	37	01	Mark Martin	U.S. Army Chevrolet	367		Running
15	2	16	Greg Biffle	Ameriquest Ford	367		Running
16	3	26	Jamie McMurray	Crown Royal Ford	367		Running
17	9	29	Kevin Harvick	Shell/Pennzoil Chevrolet	367		Running
18	22	18	J.J. Yeley	Interstate Batteries Chevrolet	367		Running
19	13	43	Bobby Labonte	Cheerios/Betty Crocker Dodge	367		Running
20	5	9	Kasey Kahne	Dodge Dealers/UAW Dodge	367		Running
21	17	19	Elliott Sadler	Dodge Dealers/UAW Dodge	367	1	Running
22	39	66	Jeff Green	Best Buy Chevrolet	365		Running
23	41	42 #	Juan Pablo Montoya	Texaco/Havoline Dodge	365		Running
24	6	78	Kenny Wallace	Furniture Row Chevrolet	365		Running
25	42	45	Kyle Petty	Marathon Amer. Spirit Motor Oil Dodge	364		Running
26	40	88	Ricky Rudd	Snickers Ford	364		Running
27	24	6 #	David Ragan	AAA Ford	363		Running
28	35	13	Joe Nemechek	Haier Chevrolet	363		Running
29	19	70	Johnny Sauter	Haas/Yellow Transportation Chevrolet	361		Running
30	38	38	David Gilliland	M&M's Ford	361		Engine
31	23	15 #	Paul Menard	Menards/MOEN Chevrolet	358		Running
32	27	22	Dave Blaney	Caterpillar Toyota	355	2	Engine
33	14	00 #	David Reutimann	Domino's Toyota	351		Engine
34	30	40	David Stremme	Coors Light Dodge	349		Engine
35	11	25	Casey Mears	National Guard/GMAC Chevrolet	345		Engine
36	20	84 #	AJ Allmendinger	Red Bull Toyota	344		Running
37	36	5	Kyle Busch	Carquest/Kellogg's Chevrolet	338		Running
38	33	7	Robby Gordon	Menards/MAPEI Ford	317		Running
39	32	96	Tony Raines	DLP HDTV Chevrolet	310		Engine
40	16	41	Reed Sorenson	Target Dodge	310		Running
41	8	21	Ken Schrader	Motorcraft Ford	254	2	Accident
42	43	37	Kevin Lepage	Long John Silvers Dodge	127		Trans.
43	15	83	Brian Vickers	Red Bull Toyota	122		Accident

Raybestos Rookie of the Year Contender.

NASCAR NEXTEL CUP SERIES TOP 12

(After 11 Races)

Pos.	Driver	Points	Behind	Change
1	Jeff Gordon	1,881	—	—
2	Jimmie Johnson	1,650	-231	—
3	Matt Kenseth	1,582	-299	—
4	Denny Hamlin	1,539	-342	—
5	Jeff Burton	1,486	-395	—
6	Tony Stewart	1,375	-506	+1
7	Kurt Busch	1,325	-556	+2
8	Kevin Harvick	1,315	-566	—
9	Clint Bowyer	1,302	-579	+1
10	Carl Edwards	1,291	-590	+1
11	Kyle Busch	1,281	-600	-5
12	Jamie McMurray	1,214	-667	+1

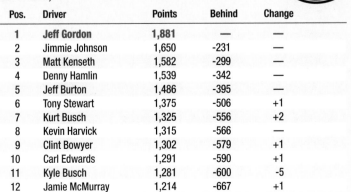

Until Lap 300, that is. That's when Johnson powered past Hamlin to take over the top spot, and the tide began to turn. Five laps later, Kyle Busch got together with A.J. Allmendinger on the backstretch to bring out the day's seventh caution.

Johnson, Hamlin and the rest of the leaders reported to pit road, where a bobble by his crew cost Hamlin dearly. He came to pit road in second place and left in 16th.

Now Johnson, looking for his fifth win of the season, controlled the pace. Teammate Gordon ran second, although the water temperature in his Chevrolet threatened to end his challenge at any moment, his car blowing hot water from the vent tube on the right-front fender.

With 22 laps to go, the caution flew once more, this time for debris, and Johnson, who swept both Darlington events in 2004, knew what he wanted to do.

"New tires always pay off here," Johnson said. So he, along with Matt Kenseth, Bowyer, Hamlin and others peeled onto pit road.

Gordon, on the other hand, still dealing with an overheating Chevrolet, got the call from crew chief Steve Letarte to stay on the track.

"Honestly, had we gotten behind, we probably would have blown up," Gordon said later. "From my standpoint, we didn't have much of a choice, because we thought we were going to blow up. … He (Letarte) said stay out, and I thought it was a great call."

Ryan Newman, Earnhardt, Sterling Marlin, Mark Martin and Martin Truex Jr. stayed on the track as well, leaving Johnson and Hamlin with an uphill battle as the laps wound down.

With lapped cars on the inside and one final caution with 15 laps remaining, Johnson never had the chance to catch Gordon. Hamlin, still with the fastest car, fought gamely through traffic, battled his way around Newman and had Gordon in his sight before running out of laps, leaving him nearly one second behind in the runner-up position.

"I should have more than one or two wins," Hamlin stated flatly after the race. "I gave away Phoenix (speeding penalty), but there are two or three others that we had the best car most of all day and just gave it away on pit road. Today was a prime example of that. I'm pretty mad."

"I think today's performance really showed what kind of race team we've got," Gordon said. "We're going to be on and we're going to be off with the race cars at times, but when we can perform the way we did today with a race car that's not capable of winning, it's got me very, very excited about this entire season."

Sobering words for anyone not sporting the No. 24. ▪▪▪

NASCAR NEXTEL ALL-STAR CHALLENGE

LOWE'S MOTOR SPEEDWAY

A stretch of five straight weekends that took teams west to Texas and Phoenix before returning east to Talladega, Richmond and Darlington led to two weekends at "home" — at least for the vast majority of NASCAR NEXTEL Cup Series team members who live and work in and around Charlotte, N.C.

Locally referred to as "Race Week," festivities begin with the NASCAR NEXTEL All-Star Challenge. In one sense, a weekend without the pressure of competing for championship points is a welcome relief. On the other hand, the $1 million payday awaiting the winner of the all-star event — not to mention garage area bragging rights — is enough to keep everyone hard at work and entirely focused.

In the end, Kevin Harvick demonstrated that he was developing quite a knack for not just winning, but winning big. Last season, Harvick doubled his career total in the win column, jumping from five to 10 — that, while obliterating his competition in capturing his second NASCAR Busch Series championship, the first coming in 2001.

Harvick had won on intermediate super speedways (Atlanta and Chicagoland), short tracks (Bristol and Richmond), one-mile ovals (Phoenix and New Hampshire), on the road course at Watkins Glen and at the prestigious Indianapolis Motor Speedway. Then, to start the 2007 season, he notched his first restrictor-plate victory — and the biggest of his career — by edging Mark Martin to win the Daytona 500.

Now he added yet another jewel to his sparkling resume by placing his name on the winners' list of the sport's annual all-star event. In so doing, Harvick also brought Richard Childress back to the event's Victory Lane after a much-too-long absence. Childress already possessed three all-star trophies as a team owner, those coming with Dale Earnhardt behind the wheel of his Chevrolets. The last of those was earned in 1993, a distant 14 years ago. This win, his fourth, also affirmed the resurgence of his organization — as if anyone doubted it considering all three of his race teams currently were listed among the top 10 in the point standings.

1. **MATT KENSETH**
   121.401 SEC. 133.442 MPH

2. **JIMMIE JOHNSON**
   123.203 SEC. 131.490 MPH

3. **KURT BUSCH**
   123.653 SEC. 131.012 MPH

4. **KEVIN HARVICK**
   123.881 SEC. 130.771 MPH

5. **JEFF BURTON**
   123.891 SEC. 130.760 MPH

6. **KYLE BUSCH**
   123.932 SEC. 130.717 MPH

7. **JEFF GORDON**
   123.950 SEC. 130.698 MPH

8. **RYAN NEWMAN**
   124.443 SEC. 130.180 MPH

9. **DENNY HAMLIN**
   124.515 SEC. 130.105 MPH

10. **DALE EARNHARDT JR.**
    125.009 SEC. 129.591 MPH

11. **KASEY KAHNE**
    125.197 SEC. 129.396 MPH

12. **GREG BIFFLE**
    125.450 SEC. 129.135 MPH

13. **TONY STEWART**
    126.182 SEC. 128.386 MPH

14. **DALE JARRETT**
    126.723 SEC. 127.838 MPH

15. **BRIAN VICKERS**
    126.781 SEC. 127.779 MPH

16. **BOBBY LABONTE**
    127.038 SEC. 127.521 MPH

17. **CASEY MEARS**
    127.406 SEC. 127.153 MPH

18. **MARK MARTIN**
    0.000 SEC. 0.000 MPH

the wrecking Kyle Busch after Kyle and brother Kurt got together in the early laps of the final segment. Burton made it by and finished fourth.

"... Maybe I should have given an inch and maybe he shouldn't have taken that inch. I'm pretty sure we'll discuss this."

KURT BUSCH comments on his tangle with brother Kyle (Busch) during the late stages of the NASCAR NEXTEL All-Star Challenge.

This year's event was divided into four 20-lap segments. Pit stops were optional after the first and second sections, and at least a stop-and-go was required between the third and fourth. Harvick, who finished fourth, third and fourth, respectively, in the first three sprints, wasted no time in the finale. He used the high side to pass Jeff Gordon, teammate Jeff Burton and Kyle Busch almost immediately after the final segment began. He then held off the hard-charging Jimmie Johnson in the closing laps to grab the win with a 0.141-second margin, closest in the event's 23-year history.

It appeared the night would belong to Matt Kenseth. After winning the pole rather handily in the unique, three-laps-and-a-pit-stop format, Kenseth led flag-to-flag in Segment 1, yielded to Kyle Busch (who did not pit between segments) for the next 24 laps, and then reassumed control for the remainder of the third segment. Clearly the class of the field, Kenseth was tagged for speeding while leaving pit road and sent to the back of the line for the restart before the final 20 laps got underway. One last rally took him only as high as seventh place.

"It was a dumb mistake on my part that cost us the win," Kenseth admitted. "Yes, I was speeding; it was my fault."

As usual, there were fireworks both following and during the race. Bobby Labonte, Denny Hamlin and Casey Mears were all eliminated in single-car incidents, while the Busch brothers — Kurt and Kyle — staged the evening's highlight reel.

Gamely putting pressure on Harvick in the

RACE RESULTS

NASCAR NEXTEL Cup Series Non-Points Event — May 19, 2007
Lowe's Motor Speedway

NEXTEL OPEN

Fin. Pos.	Start Pos.	Car No.	Driver	Team	Laps	Laps Led	Status
1	11	1	Martin Truex Jr.	Bass Pro Shops/Tracker Boats Chevrolet	40	3	Running
2	20	70	Johnny Sauter	Yellow Transportation/HAAS Chevrolet	40		Running
3	1	99	Carl Edwards	Office Depot Ford	40	37	Running
4	3	22	Dave Blaney	Caterpillar Toyota	40		Running
5	9	88	Ricky Rudd	Snickers Dark Ford	40		Running
6	22	07	Clint Bowyer	Jack Daniel's Chevrolet	40		Running
7	13	14	Sterling Marlin	PEPBOYS Auto Chevrolet	40		Running
8	26	36	Jeremy Mayfield	360 OTC Toyota	40		Running
9	17	96	Tony Raines	DLP HDTV Chevrolet	40		Running
10	6	26	Jamie McMurray	Crown Royal Ford	40		Running
11	31	40	David Stremme	Coors Light Dodge	40		Running
12	15	66	Jeff Green	Best Buy Chevrolet	40		Running
13	24	18	J.J. Yeley	Interstate Batteries Chevrolet	40		Running
14	27	45	Kyle Petty	Coke Zero Dodge	40		Running
15	8	84	AJ Allmendinger	Red Bull Toyota	40		Running
16	25	7	Robby Gordon	Jim Beam Black Ford	40		Running
17	19	4	Ward Burton	State Water Heaters Chevrolet	40		Running
18	21	78	Kenny Wallace	Furniture Row Chevrolet	40		Running
19	29	34	Kevin Lepage	Front Row Motorsports Dodge	40		Running
20	32	55	Michael Waltrip	NAPA Auto Parts Toyota	38		Running
21	28	00	David Reutimann	Domino's/Burger King Toyota	33		Electrical
22	2	6	David Ragan	AAA Ford	20		Accident
23	7	41	Reed Sorenson	Target Dodge	20		Accident
24	23	19	Elliott Sadler	Dodge Dealers/UAW Dodge	20		Accident
25	16	49	Mike Bliss	Paralyzed Veterans of America Dodge	9		Accident
26	30	37	Boris Said	Huddle House Dodge	9		Accident
27	12	10	Scott Riggs	Valvoline/Stanley Tools Dodge	1		Accident
28	4	38	David Gilliland	M & M's Ford	0		Accident
29	5	42	Juan Pablo Montoya	Texaco/Havoline Dodge	0		Accident
30	10	15	Paul Menard	Menards/Johns Manville Chevrolet	0		Accident
31	14	13	Joe Nemechek	Haier Chevrolet	0		Accident
32	18	21	Jon Wood	Motorcraft Ford	0		Accident

RACE RESULTS

NASCAR NEXTEL Cup Series Non-Points Event — May 19, 2007
Lowe's Motor Speedway

NASCAR NEXTEL ALL-STAR CHALLENGE

Fin. Pos.	Start Pos.	Car No.	Driver	Team	Laps	Laps Led	Status
1	4	29	Kevin Harvick	Pennzoil Platinum/Shell Chevrolet	80	20	Running
2	2	48	Jimmie Johnson	Lowe's/Power of Pride Chevrolet	80		Running
3	18	01	Mark Martin	U.S. Army Chevrolet	80		Running
4	5	31	Jeff Burton	AT&T Mobility Chevrolet	80		Running
5	17	20	Tony Stewart	Home Depot Chevrolet	80		Running
6	20	70	Johnny Sauter	Yellow Transportation/HAAS Chevrolet	80		Running
7	1	17	Matt Kenseth	DeWalt Ford	80	36	Running
8	8	12	Ryan Newman	alltel Dodge	80		Running
9	10	8	Dale Earnhardt Jr.	Budweiser Chevrolet	80		Running
10	19	1	Martin Truex Jr.	Bass Pro Shops/Tracker Boats Chevrolet	80		Running
11	7	24	Jeff Gordon	DuPont Performance Alliance Chevrolet	80		Running
12	13	44	Dale Jarrett	UPS Toyota	80		Running
13	14	83	Brian Vickers	Red Bull Toyota	80		Running
14	11	9	Kasey Kahne	Dodge Dealers/UAW Dodge	80		Running
15	12	16	Greg Biffle	Ameriquest Ford	80		Running
16	21	78	Kenny Wallace	Furniture Row Chevrolet	80		Running
17	9	11	Denny Hamlin	FedEx Freight Chevrolet	63		Accident
18	16	25	Casey Mears	National Guard/GMAC Chevrolet	63		Accident
19	3	2	Kurt Busch	Miller Lite Dodge	62		Accident
20	6	5	Kyle Busch	Kellogg's/Carquest Chevrolet	62	24	Accident
21	15	43	Bobby Labonte	Cheerios/Betty Crocker Dodge	41		Accident

SEGMENT 1

1	Matt Kenseth
2	Jeff Gordon
3	Jimmie Johnson
4	Kevin Harvick
5	Jeff Burton
6	Ryan Newman
7	Kyle Busch
8	Dale Earnhardt Jr.
9	Kasey Kahne
10	Denny Hamlin
11	Johnny Sauter
12	Casey Mears
13	Mark Martin
14	Martin Truex Jr.
15	Bobby Labonte
16	Kurt Busch
17	Brian Vickers
18	Dale Jarrett
19	Greg Biffle
20	Tony Stewart
21	Kenny Wallace

SEGMENT 2

1	Kyle Busch
2	Jeff Gordon
3	Kevin Harvick
4	Matt Kenseth
5	Jeff Burton
6	Mark Martin
7	Johnny Sauter
8	Jimmie Johnson
9	Kurt Busch
10	Ryan Newman
11	Casey Mears
12	Bobby Labonte
13	Tony Stewart
14	Martin Truex Jr.
15	Kasey Kahne
16	Denny Hamlin
17	Dale Jarrett
18	Dale Earnhardt Jr.
19	Greg Biffle
20	Kenny Wallace
21	Brian Vickers

SEGMENT 3

1	Matt Kenseth
2	Jeff Gordon
3	Kyle Busch
4	Kevin Harvick
5	Jeff Burton
6	Mark Martin
7	Ryan Newman
8	Jimmie Johnson
9	Johnny Sauter
10	Kurt Busch
11	Tony Stewart
12	Martin Truex Jr.
13	Denny Hamlin
14	Casey Mears
15	Kasey Kahne
16	Dale Jarrett
17	Brian Vickers
18	Dale Earnhardt Jr.
19	Kenny Wallace
20	Greg Biffle
21	Bobby Labonte

(Left) Martin Truex Jr. (1) and Johnny Sauter (70) finished first and second, respectively, in the NASCAR NEXTEL Open after getting past Carl Edwards in the final laps of the race. As the top two finishers, both advanced to the main event, where Sauter mounted a strong run to sixth place while Truex finished in 10th.

(Right) Kevin Harvick celebrates another huge win and a $1 million payout after leading all 20 laps in the final segment of the NASCAR NEXTEL All-Star Challenge.

opening laps of Segment 4, Kurt, having already charged from sixth to second, stormed into Turn 1, while Kyle, with his own designs on second place, mounted an attack on the inside. Kurt dropped low to block and the two touched, broke traction and spun up the track and into the wall. Both drivers were finished for the evening.

"I knew I had a car on the inside," Kurt explained. "I really didn't know it was him (Kyle), but I knew it was a pretty aggressive move underneath me. … Maybe I should have given an inch and maybe he shouldn't have taken that inch. I'm pretty sure we'll discuss this."

Carl Edwards led the first 37 laps of the 40-lap NASCAR NEXTEL Open but was fighting a car that got tighter and tighter as the race wore on. Finally, with three laps to go, Edwards could no longer fend off the charging Martin Truex Jr., who drove past Edwards followed by Johnny Sauter. Finishing first and second, respectively, Truex and Sauter transferred to the NASCAR NEXTEL All-Star Challenge, along with Kenny Wallace, boosted into the main event by a fan vote.

In Victory Lane, Childress could barely alter the huge grin cemented on his face, saying, "This is a huge win for us. Kevin did a great job, one of the best I've ever seen."

Coming from Childress, that's some high praise, indeed. ◆◆◆

COCA-COLA 600

LOWE'S MOTOR SPEEDWAY

H ere's one for all the Quantitative Analysis buffs: What's the probability of Casey Mears, J.J. Yeley, Kyle Petty, Reed Sorenson and Brian Vickers all finishing in the top five at Lowe's Motor Speedway? And yes, all in the same race.

Before you fry your calculators, we'll just tell you that is exactly what happened in the 2007 Coca-Cola 600.

Casey Mears carried the Hendrick Motorsports banner this time, driving to his first NASCAR NEXTEL Cup Series victory in his 156th career start and thereby extending the Hendrick winning streak to five. For the history buffs, that is the eighth time in NASCAR history a car owner posted five or more consecutive wins, but the first time it has happened since Petty Enterprises did it in 1971, 36 years ago.

Over time, Rick Hendrick's No. 25 produced some very strong performances at the track just a mile or two up the road from the team's headquarters near Concord, N.C. Drivers such as Ricky Craven, Jerry Nadeau, Joe Nemechek and Vickers all flirted with victory there, only to have their efforts dashed by bad luck in one form or another. And while Hendrick's No. 24 and No. 48 teams with drivers Jeff Gordon and Jimmie Johnson combined for 10 wins at the track in a little more than decade, one had to look all the way back to 1989 before finding the No. 25 in the winner's circle, then with driver Ken Schrader.

Fuel mileage undoubtedly played a role in this one, but that does not mean Mears backed into Victory Lane. After starting 16th, he climbed steadily up the running order. At the 100-lap mark Mears was listed 12th. By Lap 200 he was in eighth place. In seventh at Lap 300, he continued to advance into the top five and was second behind Tony Stewart on the final restart with 90 miles left to run.

Mears held his position behind Stewart for the next 40 laps or so before Dale Earnhardt Jr., Johnson and Denny Hamlin all worked past. But as Johnson, then Stewart, then Earnhardt and finally Hamlin dropped onto pit road for a quick splash-and-go, Mears continued with enough speed in his Chevrolet to nurse it to victory with a whopping 9.561 seconds to spare over second-place Yeley.

"We made a lot of changes today to keep up with the track," Mears explained. "We had a really good car at the end, and then started conserving fuel, not knowing how it was going to play out. … We gambled, saved a bunch of fuel and won."

Yeley ran in and around the top 10 from the outset before posting the first top-five finish of his NASCAR NEXTEL Cup Series career.

After starting from the 36th position, Kyle Petty climbed steadily through the field, reaching the top 10 by Lap 300, where he remained before scoring a third-place finish. It was Petty's first top five since finishing fifth at Dover in June 1997 and his best finish since winning at Dover two years earlier.

"I think for me to come out here tonight, I showed a few people I didn't forget how to drive a race car," Petty said, smiling amidst a sea of reporters. "But we've got a great team. That's what it's all about. I'm just one piece in the cog here."

Like Yeley, Sorenson posted a career best and his second-ever top five in fourth place.

Brian Vickers, who started 26th, rocketed to the front over the first 112 laps and literally took over, leading four times for 76 of the next 111 trips around the 1.5-mile super speedway. Unfortunately, his car developed a steering problem that took him off the leaders' pace, but Vickers managed to muscle his Camry to fifth place and score Toyota's first-ever top-five finish.

Stewart dropped from first to sixth place with his stop for fuel in the closing laps, while Ricky Rudd stayed out to finish seventh in his best effort of the season. Earnhardt Jr., Hamlin and Johnson rounded out the top 10.

Casey Mears (right) gets a congratulatory hug from Hendrick teammate Jimmie Johnson at Lowe's Motor Speedway. In his 156th career start, Mears scored his first NASCAR NEXTEL Cup Series victory and extended Hendrick Motorsports' winning streak to five.

TOP 10 QUALIFIERS

1. **RYAN NEWMAN**
   29.140 SEC. 185.312 MPH

2. **KURT BUSCH**
   29.179 SEC. 185.065 MPH

3. **ELLIOTT SADLER**
   29.189 SEC. 185.001 MPH

4. **DALE EARNHARDT JR.**
   29.247 SEC. 184.634 MPH

5. **MATT KENSETH**
   29.311 SEC. 184.231 MPH

6. **DENNY HAMLIN**
   29.312 SEC. 184.225 MPH

7. **RICKY RUDD**
   29.355 SEC. 183.955 MPH

8. **DAVE BLANEY**
   29.370 SEC. 183.861 MPH

9. **BOBBY LABONTE**
   29.422 SEC. 183.536 MPH

10. **DAVID STREMME**
    29.423 SEC. 183.530 MPH

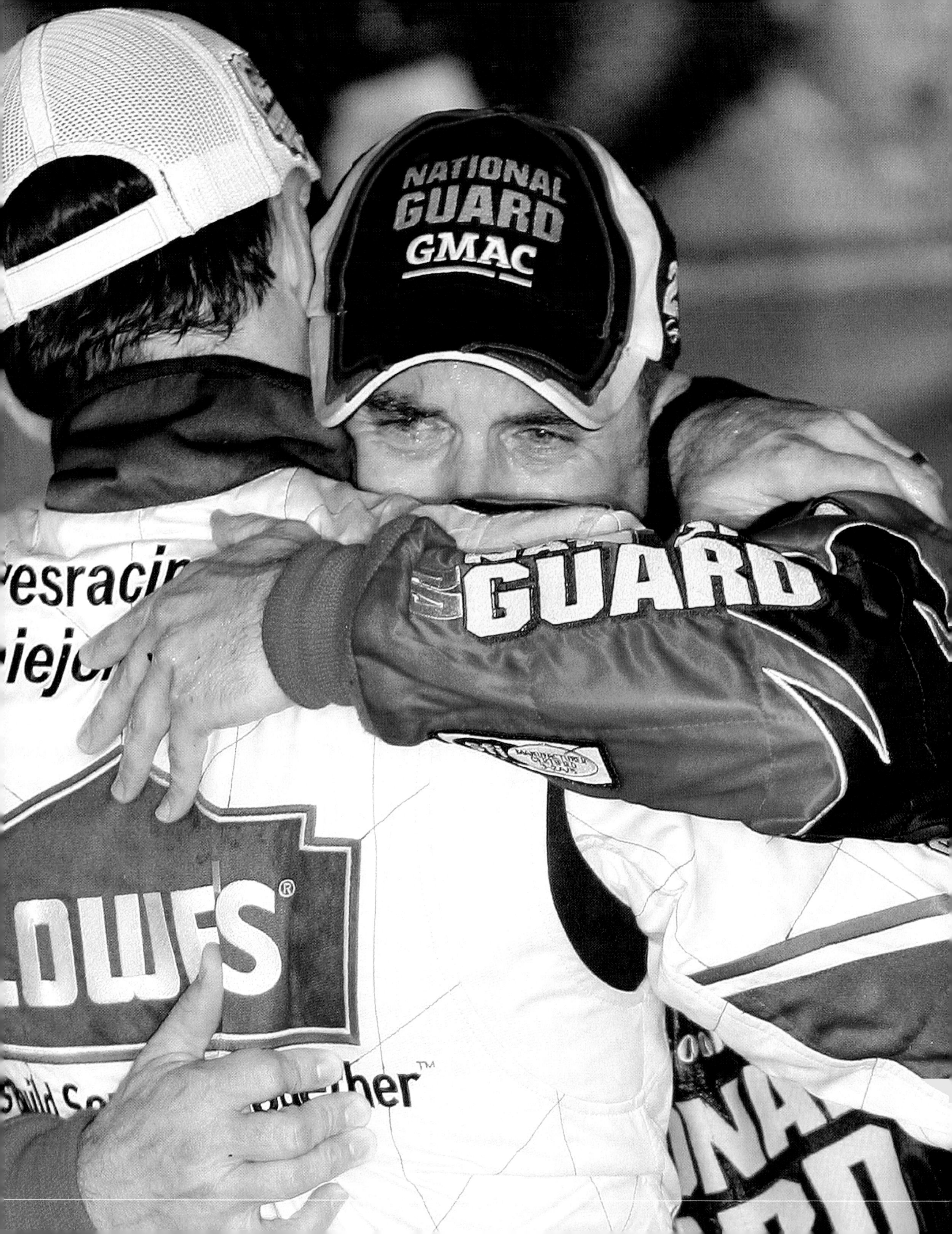
NATIONAL
GUARD
GMAC
GUARD
LOWES

(Left) Team owner Jack Roush studies spark plugs from one of his five Fords, presumably looking for answers. Although his driver Matt Kenseth scored a win earlier in the season, it was the only victory for a non-Chevrolet team in the first 12 events.

(Right) The Coca-Cola 600, held on Memorial Day weekend, is always a grand celebration of patriotism and gratitude for our men and women in uniform.

(Below) Kurt Busch's crew provides service on a car that looked like a winner. Busch led 102 straight laps after passing teammate and pole-winner Ryan Newman early in the race. Unfortunately, an accident before the 200-lap mark sidelined his effort and cost him two positions in the point standings.

The night was not without its share of sparks and bent sheet metal. The caution flag flew 13 times, 10 of those for accidents, with drivers expressing concern over the particularly hard tire compound and its unforgiving nature on Lowe's Motor Speedway's recently repaved surface.

(Above) Brian Vickers (83) and J.J. Yeley (18) race for position in the early evening. Vickers was very strong near the halfway point before problems with his steering proved costly. He still fought back to a fifth-place finish, a milestone for Toyota, while Yeley notched a career-best finish in second place.

(Left) Kyle Petty gets a pat from The King after driving to a third-place finish, the best for the Pettys in a long, long time. Petty hit the top 10 with 100 laps to go and got better as the race drew to its conclusion.

(Right) Casey Mears claims victory in his first big-time win. "This is very, very exciting, and I'm very, very relieved," Mears said. "It's been a long time."

RACE RESULTS

NASCAR NEXTEL Cup Series Race No.12 — May 27, 2007

Lowe's Motor Speedway

COCA-COLA 600

Fin. Pos.	Start Pos.	Car No.	Driver	Team	Laps	Laps Led	Status
1	16	25	Casey Mears	National Guard/American Heroes Chev.	400	6	Running
2	12	18	J.J. Yeley	Interstate Batteries Chevrolet	400	1	Running
3	36	45	Kyle Petty	Coke Zero Dodge	400		Running
4	34	41	Reed Sorenson	Target Dodge	400		Running
5	26	83	Brian Vickers	Red Bull Toyota	400	76	Running
6	14	20	Tony Stewart	Home Depot Chevrolet	400	55	Running
7	7	88	Ricky Rudd	Snickers Dark Ford	400	1	Running
8	4	8	Dale Earnhardt Jr.	Budweiser Chevrolet	400	1	Running
9	6	11	Denny Hamlin	FedEx Freight/Marines Chevrolet	400	1	Running
10	21	48	Jimmie Johnson	Lowe's/Power of Pride Chevrolet	400	83	Running
11	11	01	Mark Martin	U.S. Army Chevrolet	400		Running
12	5	17	Matt Kenseth	R&L Carriers/DEWALT Ford	400	50	Running
13	9	43	Bobby Labonte	Cheerios/Chocolate Chex Dodge	399		Running
14	37	96	Tony Raines	DLP HDTV Chevrolet	399		Running
15	39	99	Carl Edwards	Office Depot Ford	399	1	Running
16	31	1	Martin Truex Jr.	Bass Pro Shops/Tracker Boats Chev.	399		Running
17	10	40	David Stremme	Coors Light Dodge	397		Running
18	8	22	Dave Blaney	Caterpillar Toyota	397		Running
19	28	26	Jamie McMurray	IRWIN Industrial Tools Ford	395		Running
20	15	10	Scott Riggs	Valvoline/Stanley Tools Dodge	394		Running
21	27	29	Kevin Harvick	Shell/Pennzoil Chevrolet	394		Running
22	35	7	Robby Gordon	Jim Beam Black Ford	393		Running
23	18	9	Kasey Kahne	Dodge Dealers/UAW Dodge	390		Running
24	25	31	Jeff Burton	AT&T Mobility Chevrolet	385		Running
25	24	36	Jeremy Mayfield	360 OTC Toyota	382	3	Engine
26	33	13	Joe Nemechek	Haier Chevrolet	377		Running
27	40	70	Johnny Sauter	Radio Active Energy Drink Chevrolet	376		Running
28	20	42 #	Juan Pablo Montoya	Texaco/Havoline Dodge	369		Running
29	41	07	Clint Bowyer	Jack Daniel's Chevrolet	367		Running
30	17	5	Kyle Busch	Carquest/Kellogg's Chevrolet	357	4	Running
31	29	84 #	AJ Allmendinger	Red Bull Toyota	310		Running
32	2	2	Kurt Busch	Miller Lite Dodge	296	107	Accident
33	30	14	Sterling Marlin	PEPBOYS Auto Chevrolet	293		Running
34	43	78	Kenny Wallace	Furniture Row Chevrolet	289		Engine
35	19	38	David Gilliland	M&M's Ford	265		Running
36	3	19	Elliott Sadler	Dodge Dealers/UAW Dodge	261		Running
37	13	6 #	David Ragan	AAA Ford	219		Accident
38	22	21	Bill Elliott	U.S. Air Force Ford	218	1	Accident
39	1	12	Ryan Newman	Alltel Dodge	172	10	Engine
40	23	44	Dale Jarrett	UPS Toyota	82		Engine
41	32	24	Jeff Gordon	DuPont/Department of Defense Chev.	61		Accident
42	42	66	Jeff Green	Best Buy Chevrolet	52		Accident
43	38	16	Greg Biffle	Dish Network Ford	45		Accident

Raybestos Rookie of the Year Contender.

NASCAR NEXTEL CUP SERIES TOP 12

(After 12 Races)

Pos.	Driver	Points	Behind	Change
1	**Jeff Gordon**	1,921	—	—
2	Jimmie Johnson	1,789	-132	—
3	Matt Kenseth	1,714	-207	—
4	Denny Hamlin	1,682	-239	—
5	Jeff Burton	1,577	-344	—
6	Tony Stewart	1,530	-391	—
7	Kevin Harvick	1,415	-506	+1
8	Carl Edwards	1,414	-507	+2
9	Kurt Busch	1,402	-519	-2
10	Clint Bowyer	1,378	-543	-1
11	Kyle Busch	1,359	-562	—
12	Jamie McMurray	1,320	-601	—

The biggest incident of the race occurred along the frontstretch immediately following the first restart on Lap 52. Apparently triggered by a tire tread that flew from Johnson's Chevrolet after he made contact with another car, a total of 13 drivers were involved.

Just a handful of laps later, a five-car incident collected Gordon. That ended a string of nine top-four finishes in the last 10 races, including three wins in his previous four starts. Gordon was listed 41st in the final results but left the track still holding a 132-point advantage over Johnson at the top of the point standings. ▰▰▰

AUTISM SPEAKS 400 PRESENTED BY VISA

DOVER INTERNATIONAL SPEEDWAY

So far this season there were plenty of reasons for Dale Earnhardt, Inc. to be in the news. As far as Martin Truex Jr. was concerned, none of them were the right ones.

So much had been made of Dale Earnhardt Jr.'s contract status, his decision to leave the company at season's end, and now, endless speculation surrounding where he would wind up next year and beyond, everything else that was going on at DEI was well under the media's radar.

Meanwhile, Truex and his team were hard at work. What they hoped would be a strong start to the season, building upon momentum gained toward the end of 2006, suffered an early setback with a blown motor at California in the second race of the year. That early DNF combined with a mediocre 29th-place finish in the Daytona 500 dropped Truex into an early-season hole, 38th in the point standings.

Since then, driver and team had scratched and clawed their way back, gaining consistency while picking up three top 10s. A win in the NASCAR Nextel Open only added fuel to their fire, and the two-time NASCAR Busch Series champion could feel that his first NASCAR NEXTEL Cup Series victory was close at hand.

By the time Truex arrived at Dover International Speedway for the 13th race of 2007, he had advanced to 16th in the standings. He also remembered that his last visit to Dover, in September 2006, resulted in a sixth-place finish, a career best at the time, and began a late-season surge of strong and promising performances.

Another driver relatively unnoticed so far was Ryan Newman. After a rough start to the season, three straight top 10s — at Talladega, Richmond and Darlington — vaulted Newman from 24th in the standings to 13th. He followed that at Lowe's Motor Speedway with his second Budweiser Pole Award of the year but could not capitalize on it due to engine failure in the Coca-Cola 600.

1. RYAN NEWMAN
23.541 SEC. 152.925 MPH

2. DALE EARNHARDT JR.
23.624 SEC. 152.387 MPH

3. BOBBY LABONTE
23.637 SEC. 152.304 MPH

4. KASEY KAHNE
23.678 SEC. 152.040 MPH

5. CARL EDWARDS
23.710 SEC. 151.835 MPH

6. JEFF GORDON
23.754 SEC. 151.553 MPH

7. ELLIOTT SADLER
23.767 SEC. 151.471 MPH

8. JAMIE MCMURRAY
23.793 SEC. 151.305 MPH

9. JEFF BURTON
23.809 SEC. 151.203 MPH

10. SCOTT RIGGS
23.821 SEC. 151.127 MPH

(Left) Owner/driver Michael Waltrip (left) wears a huge smile after successfully qualifying his Toyota for the second time this season. Teammate Dale Jarrett (right), looking rather proud of his boss, made the race as well, but suffered his third straight engine failure in as many starts.

Head to head on pit road, the crews of Clint Bowyer (07), Greg Biffle (16) and Kurt Busch (2) battle for track position under caution. Bowyer grabbed his sixth top-10 finish of the season in sixth place and jumped two positions to eighth place in the point standings.

(Above) Tony Stewart (20) and Kurt Busch (2) wage a heated, side-by-side battle for position that lasted a number of laps. It finally boiled over with both cars spinning down the frontstretch and continued on pit road. Stewart was able to log a few more laps before having to retire from the race, while Busch's team loaded his car on the transporter (left) at the behest of NASCAR. Busch was later penalized 100 points and fell from 11th to 17th in the standings.

(Right) Ryan Newman (12) leads the field down pit road during one of two competition cautions thrown early in the race for teams to check tire wear. Newman won the pole, his second straight and third of the year, and stayed in the hunt all day before finishing second.

Itching to use the Autism Speaks 400 as redemption, Newman grabbed his second consecutive pole and couldn't wait to get the race underway on the track where his record boasted three wins and seven top-10 finishes in 10 career starts.

He would have to wait, however, as heavy rain forced the event to be postponed until Monday afternoon.

AUTISM SPEAKS
400
PRESENTED BY VISA

In his 58th career start, Martin Truex Jr. (1) takes his first checkered flag in a NASCAR NEXTEL Cup Series points race. Second-place finisher Ryan Newman isn't even in the picture, as Truex opened a whopping 7.355-second margin of victory over the final 38 laps.

RACE RESULTS

NASCAR NEXTEL Cup Series Race No.13 — June 4, 2007
Dover International Speedway

AUTISM SPEAKS 400
PRESENTED BY VISA

Fin. Pos.	Start Pos.	Car No.	Driver	Team	Laps	Laps Led	Status
1	26	1	Martin Truex Jr.	Bass Pro Shops/Tracker Chevrolet	400	216	Running
2	1	12	Ryan Newman	Alltel Dodge	400	135	Running
3	5	99	Carl Edwards	Office Depot Ford	400	18	Running
4	29	11	Denny Hamlin	FedEx Kinko's Chevrolet	400		Running
5	17	17	Matt Kenseth	DEWALT Ford	400		Running
6	10	16	Greg Biffle	3M Ford	400		Running
7	21	01	Mark Martin	U.S. Army Chevrolet	400		Running
8	15	07	Clint Bowyer	Jack Daniel's Chevrolet	400	2	Running
9	6	24	Jeff Gordon	DuPont Chevrolet	400		Running
10	33	7	Robby Gordon	Menards/MAPEI Ford	400		Running
11	4	9	Kasey Kahne	Dodge Dealers/UAW Dodge	400	28	Running
12	9	31	Jeff Burton	AT&T Mobility Chevrolet	400		Running
13	41	25	Casey Mears	National Guard/GMAC Chevrolet	400		Running
14	31	6 #	David Ragan	AAA Insurance Ford	399		Running
15	27	48	Jimmie Johnson	Lowe's Chevrolet	399		Running
16	37	14	Sterling Marlin	Waste Management Chevrolet	399		Running
17	19	5	Kyle Busch	Kellogg's/CARQUEST Chevrolet	398		Running
18	3	43	Bobby Labonte	Cheerios/Betty Crocker Dodge	398		Running
19	24	83	Brian Vickers	Red Bull Toyota	398		Running
20	18	29	Kevin Harvick	Shell/Pennzoil Chevrolet	398		Running
21	25	96	Tony Raines	DLP HDTV Chevrolet	398		Running
22	2	8	Dale Earnhardt Jr.	Budweiser Chevrolet	398		Running
23	11	10	Scott Riggs	Stanley Tools/Valvoline Dodge	398		Running
24	8	26	Jamie McMurray	Crown Royal Ford	398		Running
25	35	13	Joe Nemechek	Haier Chevrolet	397		Running
26	7	19	Elliott Sadler	Dodge Dealers/UAW Dodge	397		Running
27	28	41	Reed Sorenson	Target Dodge	397		Running
28	23	55	Michael Waltrip	NAPA Auto Parts Toyota	395		Running
29	36	38	David Gilliland	M&M's Ford	395		Running
30	38	66	Jeff Green	Haas CNC Machine Tools Chevrolet	395		Running
31	16	42 #	Juan Pablo Montoya	Texaco/Havoline Dodge	395		Running
32	42	70	Johnny Sauter	Yellow Transportation Chevrolet	394	1	Running
33	43	84 #	AJ Allmendinger	Red Bull Toyota	394		Running
34	39	45	Kyle Petty	Wells Fargo Dodge	393		Running
35	14	21	Bill Elliott	Little Debbie Ford	393		Running
36	34	40	David Stremme	Coors Light Dodge	390		Running
37	32	18	J.J. Yeley	Interstate Batteries Chevrolet	370		Running
38	20	36	Jeremy Mayfield	360 OTC Toyota	361		Running
39	40	88	Ricky Rudd	Snickers Ford	352		Accident
40	30	20	Tony Stewart	Home Depot Chevrolet	327		Accident
41	13	4	Ward Burton	State Water Heaters Chevrolet	324		Accident
42	12	2	Kurt Busch	Miller Lite Dodge	271		Parked
43	22	44	Dale Jarrett	UPS Toyota	241		Engine

Raybestos Rookie of the Year Contender.

NASCAR NEXTEL CUP SERIES TOP 12

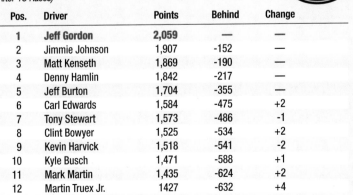

(After 13 Races)

Pos.	Driver	Points	Behind	Change
1	**Jeff Gordon**	2,059	—	—
2	Jimmie Johnson	1,907	-152	—
3	Matt Kenseth	1,869	-190	—
4	Denny Hamlin	1,842	-217	—
5	Jeff Burton	1,704	-355	—
6	Carl Edwards	1,584	-475	+2
7	Tony Stewart	1,573	-486	-1
8	Clint Bowyer	1,525	-534	+2
9	Kevin Harvick	1,518	-541	-2
10	Kyle Busch	1,471	-588	+1
11	Mark Martin	1,435	-624	+2
12	Martin Truex Jr.	1427	-632	+4

Newman bolted straight off the pole and led all but 29 of the first 108 laps, making it clear he had the goods to contend for the win. Truex Jr., meanwhile, picked his way through traffic after starting 26th and arrived at the front to take his first lead of the day on Lap 125.

From that point on, Truex and Newman simply took over. Between them, the pair led all but four of the remaining 276 laps. Newman had the advantage following pit stops with a setup that was quicker on fresh tires, while Truex assumed control on longer runs. With only seven yellow flags, two of those being early-race "competition" cautions to check tire wear, the race played into the hands of Truex with extended runs under green-flag conditions.

Newman led seven times for a total of 135 laps, while Truex led six times for 216 laps, including the final 54.

"I was sitting there with 70 or 80 laps to go thinking, 'What's going to happen?'" Truex said. "We've been in position before where we had a shot. It seemed like when we do run good ... something happens to give us some trouble.

"I was hoping it would stay green because that's when our car was best."

Truex got his wish, as he led on the final restart with 39 laps to go and was able to stretch his advantage over Newman to 7.355 seconds in taking his first NASCAR NEXTEL Cup Series win in his 58th career start.

Among the first to greet Truex in Victory Lane was Earnhardt Jr. "He said, 'I told you you could do it, man,'" said Truex. "It means a lot. He's been a great friend."

Carl Edwards led three times for 18 total laps on the way to his best finish of the season in third, while Denny Hamlin and Matt Kenseth rounded out the top five.

The day's most colorful action came courtesy of Tony Stewart and Kurt Busch in a Lap-271 altercation that began on the frontstretch and continued on pit road. After waging a rather fierce battle for position that lasted some 15 laps, Busch attempted to gain the spot for good while coming off of Turn 4. As he moved up the track, Stewart's left-front fender came in contact with Busch's right-rear quarter panel, and both cars went spinning across the track and into the wall.

Stewart made it to pit road first, followed by Busch, who drove into the side of Stewart's parked car, causing jack man, Jason Lee, to leap over the Chevrolet's hood to avoid being hit. After a brief exchange Busch continued to the garage, where NASCAR officials summarily parked him for the remainder of the event.

Ultimately, Busch was fined $100,000, docked 100 points and put on probation for the rest of the year as a result of his actions. ▰▰▰

POCONO 500

Word came during Monday's rain-delayed race at Dover that the sport had lost one of its great pioneers and visionaries. Bill France Jr. passed away at his home in the early afternoon that day, leaving a tremendous void in the hearts of so many who worked with and benefited from the man responsible for bringing NASCAR to national, if not worldwide, prominence.

In the days between then and the start of activities at Pocono Raceway, services were held in Daytona Beach, Fla., to honor and bid farewell to France. The list of names of those who attended included virtually everyone who was, or had been, closely associated with the sport during France's 31 years at the helm. Stories of the many lives he touched were both plentiful and moving.

At Pocono, there were various tributes throughout the weekend, including a pre-race moment of silence, Air Force Color Guard and a video shown on Nextel Vision featuring highlights from France's life. And on each car that competed during the weekend, a decal was added with the initials "WCF" followed simply by the words, "Pioneer, Innovator, Friend." France was 74.

It seemed almost fitting then, that on a day forecasted to be bright and sunny, dark clouds shrouded the 2.5-mile triangular raceway nestled in Pennsylvania's Pocono Mountains. Persistent showers finally gave way, if only temporarily, to allow enough of a weather window to get the scheduled 200-lapper underway.

Riding momentum gained in recent weeks, Ryan Neman led the field under green from the pole, his third in as many weeks and fourth of the season. Before the first lap was complete, Denny Hamlin, winner of both Pocono events in 2006, moved ahead of Newman to lead the first of a 25-lap stretch.

The series' latest first-time winners, Martin Truex Jr. and Casey Mears, took turns at the front as the field cycled through the first round of fuel stops, after which Hamlin and his Joe Gibbs Racing teammate, Tony Stewart, assumed command of the race.

Three quick cautions appeared in a 15-lap stretch beginning on Lap 50, the first and third of which were for debris, the second for Greg Biffle and Dave Blaney, who got together in Turn 3. It was, however, the third of those yellow flags, on Lap 65, that proved crucial in determining the race's eventual outcome.

With an eye toward the darkening sky, each crew chief was thrust into a chess game, trying to craft a strategy that pitted fuel mileage against the increasing chance the event would be truncated by approaching rain. With 35 laps to go before reaching halfway, the point where the race becomes "official," the caution seemed timely enough for pit stops to top off with fuel and take fresh tires.

While driver after driver peeled onto pit road, Jeff Gordon, running in the bottom half of the top 10 and already experiencing brake problems, got the call from crew chief Steve Letarte: "We're going to stay out. This is going to work."

"Steve didn't think anybody could get to halfway [on fuel], and he wanted to see our car out front in clean air," Gordon explained later.

Letarte's strategy moved Gordon to the top of the running order when the race resumed under green on Lap 67.

"We weren't getting any farther up than ninth with the brake issues," Gordon said, "so it was a risk worth taking."

And it paid off as Gordon used the undisturbed air to keep his Chevrolet in front for the next 15 laps. With 20 to go before reaching the magical midpoint, Gordon handed the lead back to Newman when he dropped to pit road for fuel.

At the front, Newman, Truex Jr., Hamlin and Carl Edwards were hoping for one more caution and a chance to take on fuel, while the threat of rain looked more imminent with each additional lap. A glimmer of hope appeared for them when Jimmie Johnson lost a left-front tire on Lap 91, but Johnson was able to pull his Chevrolet off the track without forcing a break in the action, and each of the front-runners reluctantly headed for their pits for a final gas-and-go.

1.	RYAN NEWMAN	52.922 SEC. 170.062 MPH
2.	DENNY HAMLIN	53.167 SEC. 169.278 MPH
3.	MARTIN TRUEX, JR.	53.346 SEC. 168.710 MPH
4.	KYLE BUSCH	53.527 SEC. 168.139 MPH
5.	CLINT BOWYER	53.553 SEC. 168.058 MPH
6.	TONY STEWART	53.572 SEC. 167.998 MPH
7.	JIMMIE JOHNSON	53.590 SEC. 167.942 MPH
8.	KASEY KAHNE	53.750 SEC. 167.442 MPH
9.	BRIAN VICKERS	53.784 SEC. 167.336 MPH
10.	JEFF BURTON	53.804 SEC. 167.274 MPH

Jeff Gordon signs autographs for the fans at Pocono Raceway. For the second time in four races, a great call by Gordon's crew chief, Steve Letarte, lifted an ailing No. 24 Chevrolet to the top of the running order and ultimately to Victory Lane.

Robby Gordon's crew gives it everything they have to get their driver back into action. After starting 37th, Gordon had a strong run and was headed toward the top 10 when a flat tire derailed his effort.

(Above) Denny Hamlin (11), who started on the front row next to pole-winner Ryan Newman (12), leads in the early laps. With a dominant car, Hamlin led five times for 49 of the 106 laps run but had to settle for a sixth-place finish when rain and pit strategy did not go his way.

(Left) All race cars at Pocono Raceway donned a special decal in honor of former NASCAR Chairman Bill France Jr., who passed away several days before the Pocono weekend began.

(Right) Winner of the ARCA race held the day before the Pocono 500, Chad McCumbee filled in for Kyle Petty, who traded his steering wheel for a TNT microphone over the weekend. McCumbee started 35th and advanced 10 positions before rain stopped the race in his NASCAR NEXTEL Cup Series debut.

With his car sniffing fumes, Edwards was the last to pit and passed the lead back to Gordon two laps before Lap 100. Riding on heavily worn tires from his charge back to the front and still suffering brake troubles, Gordon held on while he watched Newman's Dodge close the gap from behind.

RACE RESULTS

NASCAR NEXTEL Cup Series Race No.14 — June 10, 2007
Pocono Raceway

POCONO 500

Fin. Pos.	Start Pos.	Car No.	Driver	Team	Laps	Laps Led	Status
1	18	24	Jeff Gordon	DuPont Chevrolet	106	26	Running
2	1	12	Ryan Newman	Alltel Dodge	106	20	Running
3	3	1	Martin Truex Jr.	Bass Pro Shops/Tracker Boats Chev.	106	1	Running
4	12	25	Casey Mears	National Guard/GMAC Chevrolet	106	2	Running
5	6	20	Tony Stewart	The Home Depot Chevrolet	106	3	Running
6	2	11	Denny Hamlin	FedEx Ground Chevrolet	106	49	Running
7	34	01	Mark Martin	U.S. Army Chevrolet	106	1	Running
8	4	5	Kyle Busch	Kellogg's/CARQUEST Chevrolet	106		Running
9	24	17	Matt Kenseth	DEWALT Ford	106		Running
10	5	07	Clint Bowyer	Jack Daniel's Chevrolet	106		Running
11	19	29	Kevin Harvick	Shell/Pennzoil Chevrolet	106		Running
12	13	8	Dale Earnhardt Jr.	Budweiser Chevrolet	106		Running
13	10	31	Jeff Burton	AT&T Mobility Chevrolet	106		Running
14	32	99	Carl Edwards	Office Depot Ford	106	4	Running
15	33	13	Joe Nemechek	Haier Chevrolet	106		Running
16	27	2	Kurt Busch	Miller Lite Dodge	106		Running
17	11	18	J.J. Yeley	Interstate Batteries Chevrolet	106		Running
18	31	10	Scott Riggs	Valvoline/Stanley Tools Dodge	106		Running
19	26	43	Bobby Labonte	Cheerios/Betty Crocker Dodge	106		Running
20	38	42 #	Juan Pablo Montoya	Texaco/Havoline Dodge	106		Running
21	15	19	Elliott Sadler	Dodge Dealers/UAW Dodge	106		Running
22	8	9	Kasey Kahne	Dodge Dealers/UAW Dodge	106		Running
23	29	40	David Stremme	Coors Light Dodge	106		Running
24	22	41	Reed Sorenson	Target Dodge	106		Running
25	35	45	Chad McCumbee	Goody's Cool Orange Dodge	106		Running
26	36	6 #	David Ragan	AAA Ford	106		Running
27	30	88	Ricky Rudd	Snickers Ford	106		Running
28	21	15 #	Paul Menard	Pittsburgh Paints/Menards Chevrolet	106		Running
29	25	26	Jamie McMurray	IRWIN Industrial Tools Ford	106		Running
30	41	16	Greg Biffle	Dish Network Ford	106		Running
31	42	14	Sterling Marlin	PEPBOYS Auto Chevrolet	106		Running
32	39	66	Jeff Green	Best Buy Chevrolet	106		Running
33	20	4	Ward Burton	State Water Heaters Chevrolet	106		Running
34	16	38	David Gilliland	M&M's Ford	106		Running
35	9	83	Brian Vickers	Red Bull Toyota	106		Running
36	17	96	Tony Raines	DLP HDTV Chevrolet	106		Running
37	43	21	Bill Elliott	Little Debbie Snack Cakes Ford	105		Running
38	23	00 #	David Reutimann	Burger King Toyota	105		Running
39	28	84 #	AJ Allmendinger	Red Bull Toyota	104		Running
40	40	70	Johnny Sauter	Yellow Transportation Chevrolet	103		Running
41	37	7	Robby Gordon	Jim Beam Ford	103		Running
42	7	48	Jimmie Johnson	Lowe's Chevrolet	97		Running
43	14	22	Dave Blaney	Caterpillar Toyota	55		Accident

Raybestos Rookie of the Year Contender.

NASCAR NEXTEL CUP SERIES TOP 12

(After 14 Races)

Pos.	Driver	Points	Behind	Change
1	Jeff Gordon	2,249	—	—
2	Matt Kenseth	2,007	-242	+1
3	Denny Hamlin	2,002	-247	+1
4	Jimmie Johnson	1,944	-305	-2
5	Jeff Burton	1,828	-421	—
6	Tony Stewart	1,733	-516	+1
7	Carl Edwards	1,710	-539	-1
8	Clint Bowyer	1,659	-590	—
9	Kevin Harvick	1,648	-601	—
10	Kyle Busch	1,613	-636	—
11	Martin Truex Jr.	1,597	-652	+1
12	Mark Martin	1,586	-663	-1

By Lap 105, Newman had zeroed in on the leader and, as he pulled alongside to attempt a pass through the Tunnel Turn, the clouds let go. The caution lights came on immediately, freezing the running as of that instant. Replays confirmed that Gordon was barely ahead.

Already past 7:00 pm and with darkness beginning to set in, the race was declared official some 30 minutes later, giving Gordon his fourth victory of the year and Hendrick Motorsports its 10th win in the season's 14th race.

"We were fortunate or lucky or whatever," Gordon said from a makeshift Victory Lane inside the Pocono garage, "but Steve (Letarte) made a great, gutsy call.

"He is the one who won this race today, not me." 🏁

CITIZENS BANK 400

MICHIGAN INTERNATIONAL SPEEDWAY

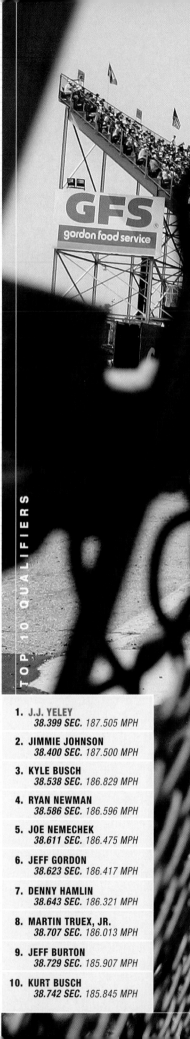

TOP 10 QUALIFIERS

T he rich get richer and the strong get stronger. That certainly seemed true in the days between races at Pocono and Michigan, when a winner was announced in the sweepstakes to land Dale Earnhardt Jr. On June 13, a press conference was held to reveal that NASCAR's most popular driver would be moving to none other than Hendrick Motorsports to drive in 2008 and beyond.

The announcement was a surprise to many in light of the fact that Hendrick already had four teams, the maximum number allowed. But that situation changed suddenly and seemingly without notice.

"I didn't think I had a chance," Earnhardt Jr. said of the opportunity to join the Hendrick organization. "I thought I basically had to look elsewhere because of him (Hendrick) having four teams."

What people failed to realize was that negotiations to extend the contract of Hendrick driver Kyle Busch had recently stalled. Timing being what it was, Rick Hendrick and Earnhardt Jr. seized the opportunity and reached an agreement expeditiously and with relative ease.

"At the root of it, this negotiation was done between Rick and Dale," said Marshall Carlson, Hendrick Motorsports' general manager. "When they looked at each other and shook hands, it was a done deal."

Now it was reality, although details such as sponsorship and car number had yet to be worked out. Busch was out at the end of the season, and Earnhardt was in, joining the company that holds six NASCAR NEXTEL Cup Series championships and was clearly the series' dominant team with 10 wins in the season's first 14 events.

1. J.J. YELEY
38.399 SEC. 187.505 MPH

2. JIMMIE JOHNSON
38.400 SEC. 187.500 MPH

3. KYLE BUSCH
38.538 SEC. 186.829 MPH

4. RYAN NEWMAN
38.586 SEC. 186.596 MPH

5. JOE NEMECHEK
38.611 SEC. 186.475 MPH

6. JEFF GORDON
38.623 SEC. 186.417 MPH

7. DENNY HAMLIN
38.643 SEC. 186.321 MPH

8. MARTIN TRUEX, JR.
38.707 SEC. 186.013 MPH

9. JEFF BURTON
38.729 SEC. 185.907 MPH

10. KURT BUSCH
38.742 SEC. 185.845 MPH

(Left) Matt Kenseth's crew gets busy on repairs to their Ford after Kenseth was caught up in an early-race accident. Unable to continue, Kenseth posted a rare DNF (his first in the last 45 races) and fell two spots in the point standings to fourth place.

Carl Edwards (99) blasts through the frontstretch tri-oval ahead of Denny Hamlin (11). After recovering from a penalty for speeding on pit road, Edwards led all but eight of the last 70 laps including the final 35 en route to the win.

Only two years earlier, a different multi-car outfit towered over the competition. Roush Racing was collecting wins and top fives in bunches on the way to placing all five of its teams in the Chase for the NASCAR NEXTEL Cup. Kurt Busch was the reigning champion, having followed teammate Matt Kenseth in giving team owner Jack Roush back-to-back titles. And the organization's newest young star, Carl Edwards, was making headlines everywhere he went.

Edwards posted four wins and 13 top fives in 2005 and was listed third in the final point standings, but only after losing a tie-breaker to teammate Greg Biffle for second place. Between his engaging personality and hard-charging driving style, everyone expected Edwards to be a popular contender for the 2006 crown.

J.J. Yeley is strapped in and ready to lead the field under green at Michigan. Yeley scored the first Budweiser Pole Award of his career by a scant one one-thousandth of a second over Jimmie Johnson.

(Left) Denny Hamlin gets a quiet moment alone to contemplate the day's events before 300 laps at New Hampshire. Already having an outstanding sophomore season, Hamlin needed a win to fill the one stat column that remained empty.

Dave Blaney rolls through the garage area on his way to log some practice laps. Blaney's Camry was plenty fast at New Hampshire, and he proved it by posting his first career Budweiser Pole Award, which was also the first for Toyota.

Oh yes, the pressure was building, and although the likeable, mild-mannered Virginian kept his easy-going image intact, he needed to release some steam.

So Hamlin pulled into New Hampshire International Speedway for the eighth COT race of the season and qualified 11th for the LENOX Industrial Tools 300, a good starting spot, but not a great one. He needed to figure out a way to get to the front.

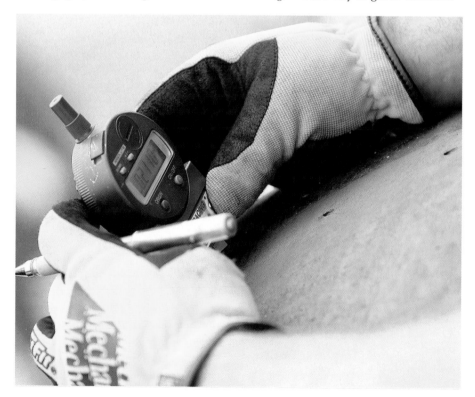

(Above) Reed Sorenson (41) tackles New Hampshire's relatively flat turns ahead of Dale Earnhardt Jr. Sorenson scored a career best in qualifying with the third-fastest lap but fought an ill-handling car in the race. Earnhardt Jr. ran among the top five for the entire day and finished a season-best fourth for his third top five of the year.

(Left) A crewman checks tire wear, a critical piece of information in plotting race strategy. As it turned out, crew chief Mike Ford's decision to stay with used tires late in the race paved the way for Denny Hamlin's win.

(Right) Riding the pit boxes at New Hampshire were Jeff Meendering (left) and Ron Malec (right), who were filling in for crew chiefs Steve Letarte and Chad Knaus as they began serving six-race suspensions. Both teams had good days, with Johnson fifth for the Lowe's team and Gordon second after nearly taking the win.

(Below) Martin Truex Jr. (1) takes the outside line ahead of Tony Stewart (20) in his charge toward the front of the field. Truex was extremely fast and looked poised for the win until a late-race caution disrupted his effort.

Dave Blaney got the race underway after grabbing his first career Budweiser Pole Award and, in the process, posting the first ever No. 1 starting position for Toyota. Blaney backed that up by leading the first 30 laps before yielding to Gordon.

Jimmie Johnson, Dale Earnhardt Jr., Gordon and brothers Kurt and Kyle Busch swapped the lead amongst themselves for the next 170 laps or so until the fourth caution of the race flew on Lap 203, when Joe Nemechek had a tire go down and hit the third-turn wall.

Earnhardt Jr. took the field under green on the Lap-209 restart, but within two laps his DEI teammate, Martin Truex Jr., sailed past to take his first lead of the day. Truex, with three top fives in his last four starts including his win at Dover, had been trailing Earnhardt before the caution after running in the top 10 throughout the race.

"YOU SEE JEFF COMING, and you're trying your best not to be that guy who chokes under pressure.

DENNY HAMLIN comments after holding off Jeff Gordon by less than a car length for his first NASCAR NEXTEL Cup Series victory of the season.

Denny Hamlin celebrates in a cloud of smoke after taking his first win of the season, the third of his career. It was anything but easy, however, as Hamlin had to fend off one of the very best in Jeff Gordon as they crossed the finish line together.

RACE RESULTS

NASCAR NEXTEL Cup Series Race No.17 — July 1, 2007
New Hampshire International Speedway

LENOX INDUSTRIAL TOOLS 300

Fin. Pos.	Start Pos.	Car No.	Driver	Team	Laps	Laps Led	Status
1	11	11	Denny Hamlin	FedEx Ground Chevrolet	300	46	Running
2	8	24	Jeff Gordon	DuPont Chevrolet	300	37	Running
3	9	1	Martin Truex Jr.	Bass Pro Shops/Tracker Boats Chev.	300	46	Running
4	6	8	Dale Earnhardt Jr.	Budweiser Chevrolet	300	64	Running
5	10	48	Jimmie Johnson	Lowe's Chevrolet	300	12	Running
6	15	66	Jeff Green	HAAS CNC/Best Buy Chevrolet	300		Running
7	26	31	Jeff Burton	LENOX Industrial Tools Chevrolet	300		Running
8	7	29	Kevin Harvick	Shell/Pennzoil Chevrolet	300		Running
9	30	17	Matt Kenseth	Carhartt/DEWALT Ford	300	2	Running
10	12	12	Ryan Newman	Alltel Dodge	300	3	Running
11	18	5	Kyle Busch	Kellogg's/CARQUEST Chevrolet	300	48	Running
12	14	20	Tony Stewart	The Home Depot Chevrolet	300		Running
13	22	99	Carl Edwards	Lumber Liquidators/Red Sox Ford	300	2	Running
14	4	70	Johnny Sauter	HAAS CNC /Yellow Chevrolet	300		Running
15	32	6 #	David Ragan	AAA Ford	300		Running
16	38	26	Jamie McMurray	IRWIN Industrial Tools Ford	300		Running
17	16	7	Robby Gordon	Menards/MAPEI Ford	300		Running
18	31	43	Bobby Labonte	Cheerios/Betty Crocker Dodge	300		Running
19	5	42 #	Juan Pablo Montoya	Texaco/Havoline Dodge	300		Running
20	39	96	Tony Raines	DLP HDTV Chevrolet	300		Running
21	2	2	Kurt Busch	Miller Lite Dodge	300	10	Running
22	19	18	J.J. Yeley	Interstate Batteries Chevrolet	300		Running
23	21	25	Casey Mears	National Guard/GMAC Chevrolet	300		Running
24	41	14	Sterling Marlin	Ginn Racing Chevrolet	300		Running
25	28	9	Kasey Kahne	Dodge Dealers/UAW Dodge	300		Running
26	3	41	Reed Sorenson	Target Dodge	300		Running
27	24	40	David Stremme	Coors Light Dodge	300		Running
28	27	38	David Gilliland	M&M's Ford	299		Running
29	1	22	Dave Blaney	Caterpillar Toyota	299	30	Running
30	42	88	Ricky Rudd	Snickers Ford	299		Running
31	34	16	Greg Biffle	Aflac Ford	298		Running
32	13	01	Regan Smith	U.S. Army Chevrolet	298		Running
33	23	19	Elliott Sadler	Dodge Dealers/UAW Dodge	297		Running
34	36	21	Bill Elliott	Little Debbie Snack Cakes Ford	297		Running
35	37	37	Kevin Lepage	Front Row Motorsports Dodge	294		Running
36	43	49	Chad Chaffin	Paralyzed Veterans Dodge	293		Running
37	20	07	Clint Bowyer	Camping World/Jack Daniel's Chev.	293		Running
38	17	00 #	David Reutimann	Burger King Toyota	293		Running
39	35	15 #	Paul Menard	Menards/Sylvania Chevrolet	286		Running
40	29	36	Jeremy Mayfield	360 OTC Toyota	259		Running
41	33	13	Joe Nemechek	Haier Chevrolet	197		Accident
42	40	45	John Andretti	Wells Fargo Dodge	109		Engine
43	25	4	Ward Burton	State Water Heaters Chevrolet	4		Engine

Raybestos Rookie of the Year Contender.

NASCAR NEXTEL CUP SERIES TOP 12

(After 17 Races)

Pos.	Driver	Points	Behind	Change
1	**Jeff Gordon**	2,613	—	—
2	Denny Hamlin	2,457	-156	—
3	Matt Kenseth	2,248	-365	—
4	Jimmie Johnson	2,232	-381	+1
5	Jeff Burton	2,230	-383	-1
6	Tony Stewart	2,185	-428	—
7	Carl Edwards	2,148	-465	—
8	Kevin Harvick	2,106	-507	—
9	Martin Truex Jr.	2,033	-580	+2
10	Kyle Busch	2,015	-598	—
11	Clint Bowyer	1,986	-627	-2
12	Dale Earnhardt Jr.	1,985	-628	—

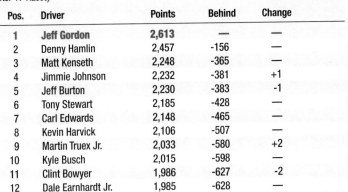

Once in front, Truex pointed his Chevrolet into clean air and took off, able to open a healthy three-second lead while Earnhardt and Gordon fought over second place. Truex led 46 consecutive laps and clearly looked as though he might notch his second win of the year when caution No. 5 flew for debris with 45 laps to go.

This was the break Hamlin was looking for. He and crew chief Mike Ford, after being foiled several times already this year with strong efforts that fell short, devised a strategy before the race to put the No. 11 car out front in the closing laps. Ford's feeling that track position (read: clean air) at New Hampshire was so valuable, it was worth getting it by staying on older tires, which he thought would not wear that quickly on the COT anyway.

So when the field rolled down pit road, Hamlin, who entered in fourth place, took two tires and left, winning the race off pit road ahead of Truex, Gordon, Jeff Green and Earnhardt, all riding on four fresh Goodyears.

"We had thought about it pre-race and had made that commitment," Ford said. "We didn't have anything to lose and everything to gain. That's the opportunity we were looking for."

Now it was time to make the most of it. With no one in his way, Hamlin drove off, able to open a 0.7-second lead as the laps dwindled down. With 10 to go, Gordon pulled alongside Truex and the two drivers began scrapping for second place. Gordon finally came out ahead with six laps left in which to track down Hamlin.

Remember the pressure cooker? Hamlin could see Gordon coming in his rearview mirror and knew his challenger was riding on fresher tires. He could only wonder if he would, once again, finish second to a Hendrick driver in a COT event.

"You see Jeff coming, and you're trying your best not to be that guy who chokes under pressure," Hamlin said, admitting his right foot was shaking so badly he could barely keep it on the accelerator.

Gordon continued to close the gap until, with two laps to go, he pulled up on Hamlin.

"He started watching his mirror a little bit with about one or two to go," Gordon said. "When he did that, he started running the inside lane ... and it allowed me to get right up to him."

As the pair rolled off the fourth turn with the checkered flag ready to wave, both cars began to slide and Gordon darted to the inside where he was able to pull even with Hamlin's rear quarter panel. But that's as far as he got as Hamlin held on, taking his third career victory and his first of the season by a scant 0.068-second margin — less than a car-length.

The smoke that poured off his tires during a well-deserved victory burnout enveloped the outside of his car, but for Hamlin, that was nothing compared to the steam escaping from the pressure cooker inside. ◄▪▪

PEPSI 400

DAYTONA INTERNATIONAL SPEEDWAY

(Left) The U.S. Armed Forces presented this huge flag during pre-race ceremonies at Daytona, part of the annual recognition of Independence Day that surrounds the Pepsi 400.

Saturday night at the races takes on a whole new meaning when it's held under the lights at Daytona International Speedway. A crowd estimated at 150,000 was on hand this year as the Race to the Chase heated up.

The checkered flag at New Hampshire officially kicked off the Race to the Chase, the 10-race stretch ending at Richmond International Raceway in early September, where the field of drivers for the 2007 Chase for the NASCAR NEXTEL Cup would be decided.

If the New Hampshire results were any indication, the battle for the top 12 positions was going to be a dogfight from here on out. Twelve of the top 13 finishers held positions in the top 13 in the point standings, with only Jeff Green crashing the contenders' party with yet another strong COT finish in sixth place.

Jeff Gordon remained nearly invincible atop the standings, having held that position at the end of the last 13 races. In the first 17 events, Gordon finished out of the top 10 only twice — a 12th place at Atlanta and a 41st-place finish at Charlotte due to an accident, his only DNF of the season.

Hamlin's New Hampshire win put him 156 behind Gordon as the only driver with a realistic shot to catch the red-hot Hendrick driver over the next nine races. More than 200 points behind Hamlin, Matt Kenseth, Jimmie Johnson and Jeff Burton were bunched together in the third through fifth positions. They were followed by Tony Stewart, Carl Edwards and Kevin Harvick, who were regularly swapping the sixth, seventh and eighth spots among them.

The real fight began with ninth place. Martin Truex Jr. held the position after Kyle Busch was hit with a 25-point penalty for failing post-race inspection at New Hampshire and dropped to 10th, 18 points behind Truex. Clint Bowyer was 11th after falling two positions with a poor finish at New Hampshire (37th). He was 29 points behind Busch, while Dale Earnhardt Jr. held the 12th position in the standings, just a single point behind Bowyer.

Earnhardt Jr. had a tenuous 127-point cushion over Ryan Newman, who had been inching his way up in the standings, and it appeared at this point that he, Jamie McMurray and Kurt Busch would be the ones who would challenge Earnhardt and Bowyer for the final slots in the field of championship contenders over the next nine weeks.

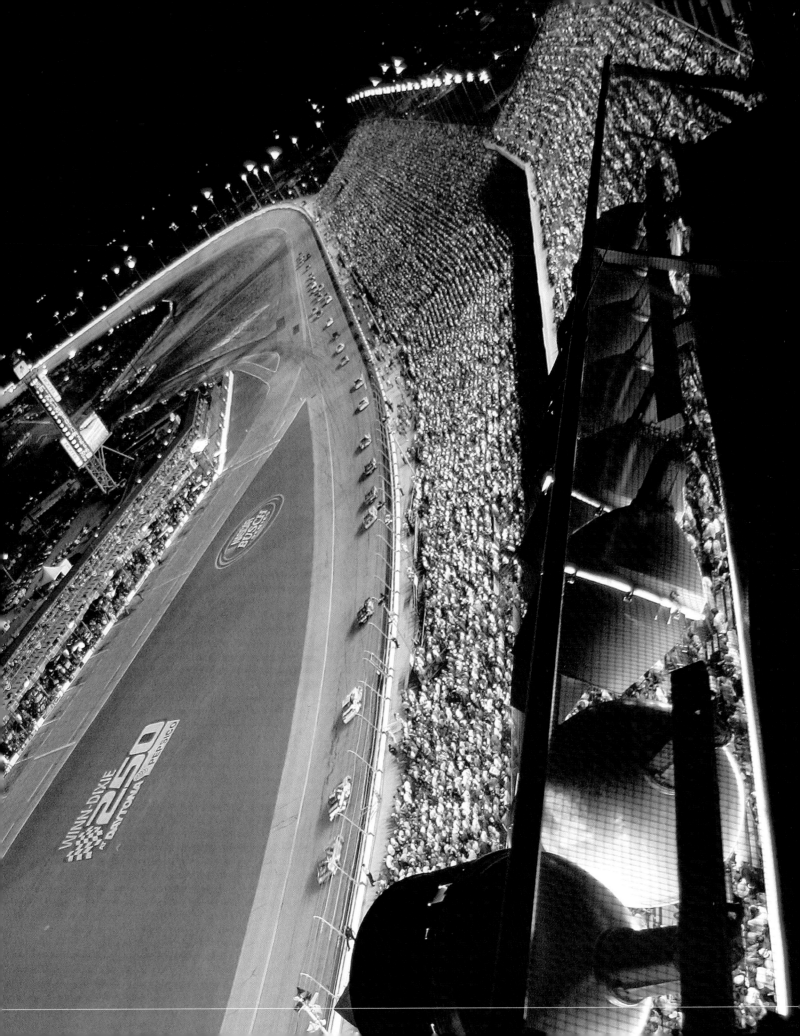

Jamie McMurray (26) literally edges out the win over Kyle Busch (5) in the second-closest finish on record. In a race where drafting partners are key, McMurray had teammates Carl Edwards (99) and Greg Biffle (16) behind him, while Busch got help from his brother, Kurt (2), and teammate Jeff Gordon (24).

All of the drivers at the top of the standings got a bit of a break at Daytona International Speedway courtesy of the weather. Qualifying was well under way for the Pepsi 400 with Boris Said at the top of the speed chart when rain clouds rolled in, dumping enough moisture on the track to abruptly end the session. All attempts were negated and the starting field was set according to car owner points, placing Gordon and Hamlin together on the front row.

Hamlin, hoping to gather more momentum after his New Hampshire win — the first for Joe Gibbs Racing this season — took an early lead. In a strange twist, however, he was hit from behind by teammate Stewart, which triggered the first major accident of the race on Lap 14. Both cars were heavily damaged, as were those of Reed Sorenson and Earnhardt Jr., ending hope for any of them to contend for a win.

Gordon, Bowyer, Casey Mears, Kurt Busch and Kyle Busch split time leading the pack for a combined 140 laps, with Bowyer out front for 55 to take the lap-leader bonus for the race. There were eight cautions in all, the last of which set up a seven-lap sprint to the finish.

It became a race of making decisions and picking partners, with the leaders circling the track in a tightly-bunched, two- and three-wide pack while drivers darted in and out, trying to find the fastest row or a friendly draft. In the tussle for position, Bowyer fell from the lead to seventh. Mears went from first to 19th, while Gordon got shuffled off the point to an eventual fifth-place finish.

While those drivers fell back, Kurt Busch drove from ninth to third and Kyle Busch advanced from seventh to the front, where he found McMurray leading with five laps

(Above) In a rather bizarre twist during the early laps, race leader Denny Hamlin (11) got tagged from behind by team-mate Tony Stewart (20), trig-gering this accident that also collected Reed Sorenson (41) and Dale Earnhardt Jr. (8).

(Far Right) Jamie McMurray emerges from his race-winning car in Victory Lane to a shower of water and sports drinks, courtesy of his crew. McMurray's second career vic-tory was long awaited, break-ing a 166-race winless string.

RACE RESULTS

NASCAR NEXTEL Cup Series Race No.18 — July 7, 2007
Daytona International Speedway

PEPSI 400

Fin. Pos.	Start Pos.	Car No.	Driver	Team	Laps	Laps Led	Status
1	15	26	Jamie McMurray	Irwin Marathon Tool Ford	160	3	Running
2	11	5	Kyle Busch	Kellogg's/CARQUEST Chevrolet	160	20	Running
3	16	2	Kurt Busch	Miller Lite Dodge	160	45	Running
4	7	99	Carl Edwards	Office Depot Ford	160		Running
5	1	24	Jeff Gordon	DuPont/Pepsi Chevrolet	160	9	Running
6	18	16	Greg Biffle	Dish Network Ford	160		Running
7	12	07	Clint Bowyer	Jack Daniels Chevrolet	160	55	Running
8	3	17	Matt Kenseth	R&L Carriers/DEWALT Ford	160		Running
9	27	9	Kasey Kahne	Chuck & Larry Dodge	160		Running
10	4	48	Jimmie Johnson	Lowe's Chevrolet	160		Running
11	32	38	David Gilliland	M&M's Ford	160		Running
12	24	6 #	David Ragan	AAA Travel Ford	160		Running
13	10	1	Martin Truex Jr.	Bass Pro Shops/NWTF Chevrolet	160		Running
14	14	12	Ryan Newman	Alltel Dodge	160		Running
15	25	7	Robby Gordon	Camping World Ford	160		Running
16	5	31	Jeff Burton	AT&T Mobility Chevrolet	160		Running
17	9	01	Mark Martin	Principal Financial Chevrolet	160		Running
18	35	70	Johnny Sauter	Haas Automation Chevrolet	160		Running
19	21	25	Casey Mears	National Guard/GMAC Chevrolet	160	11	Running
20	17	18	J.J. Yeley	Interstate Batteries Chevrolet	160		Running
21	41	15 #	Paul Menard	Menards/Pittsburgh Paints Chevrolet	160		Running
22	26	40	David Stremme	Coors Light Dodge	160		Running
23	40	22	Dave Blaney	Caterpillar Toyota	160		Running
24	38	21	Bill Elliott	U.S. Air Force Ford	160	2	Running
25	43	78	Kenny Wallace	Furniture Row Chevrolet	160	1	Running
26	42	00 #	David Reutimann	Burger King Toyota	160		Running
27	37	44	Dale Jarrett	UPS Toyota	160		Running
28	34	45	John Andretti	Tire Kingdom Dodge	160		Running
29	36	83	Brian Vickers	Red Bull Toyota	160		Running
30	33	13	Joe Nemechek	Charleston, SC Fire Dept. Chevrolet	160		Running
31	31	88	Ricky Rudd	M&M's Ford	158		Running
32	20	42 #	Juan Pablo Montoya	Texaco/Havoline Dodge	157		Running
33	22	19	Elliott Sadler	Dodge Dealers/UAW Dodge	153		Running
34	8	29	Kevin Harvick	Shell/Pennzoil Chevrolet	147	3	Running
35	19	43	Bobby Labonte	Cheerios/Pillsbury Cinnabon Dodge	137	1	Running
36	13	8	Dale Earnhardt Jr.	Budweiser Chevrolet	134		Running
37	30	66	Jeff Green	Haas Automation Chevrolet	131		Running
38	6	20	Tony Stewart	Home Depot Chevrolet	125		Running
39	23	96	Tony Raines	DLP HDTV Chevrolet	120		Running
40	29	14	Sterling Marlin	Waste Management Chevrolet	114		Accident
41	39	10	Scott Riggs	Valvoline/Stanley Tools Dodge	105		Engine
42	28	41	Reed Sorenson	Target Dodge	103		Running
43	2	11	Denny Hamlin	FedEx Kinko's Chevrolet	99	10	Running

Raybestos Rookie of the Year Contender.

NASCAR NEXTEL CUP SERIES TOP 12

(After 18 Races)

Pos.	Driver	Points	Behind	Change
1	**Jeff Gordon**	2,773	—	—
2	Denny Hamlin	2,496	-277	—
3	Matt Kenseth	2,390	-383	—
4	Jimmie Johnson	2,366	-407	—
5	Jeff Burton	2,345	-428	—
6	Carl Edwards	2,308	-465	+1
7	Tony Stewart	2,234	-539	-1
8	Kyle Busch	2,190	-583	+2
9	Kevin Harvick	2,172	-601	-1
10	Martin Truex Jr.	2,157	-616	-1
11	Clint Bowyer	2,142	-631	—
12	Dale Earnhardt Jr.	2,040	-733	—

to go. Kyle Busch surged ahead to lead the next two, with McMurray able to inch ahead at the stripe with two laps to go.

They took the white flag running side by side, with Busch taking a slight edge heading into the final lap. Behind Busch as they crossed the line, Edwards found a hole between teammates McMurray and Greg Biffle on the outside and jumped in it.

"I was pushing Kyle under the white flag, and I'm like, 'Man, I'm pushing the wrong guy,'" Edwards said. "I saw a gap open on the outside, so I filled it and pushed Jamie."

Edwards' move allowed Kurt Busch to pull up to his younger brother, and the two leaders surged back and forth while swapping the point seven times over the last two-and-a-half miles.

McMurray and Busch were still side by side coming off the fourth turn with the checkered flag in sight and crossed the line together, so close that neither driver knew who had won until they saw the No. 26 flash atop the scoring pylon. The winning margin of 0.005 second is the second closest in NASCAR history.

"I wasn't sure I won," an emotional McMurray said after breaking a 166-race winless streak to gain his second career victory. "There was so much screaming on the radio and I couldn't tell.

"It's emotional because you worked so hard for something, and you finally get it." ◆◆◆

USG SHEETROCK 400

CHICAGOLAND SPEEDWAY

Jamie McMurray had not yet finished celebrating his thrilling victory over Kyle Busch at Daytona before stories began to appear in various newspapers and on Web sites about the early-race run-in between teammates Tony Stewart and Denny Hamlin. The incident occurred on Lap 14 of the Pepsi 400 when Stewart, running second, ran into the back of Hamlin, who was leading at the time. Both cars were heavily damaged, along with those of Dale Earnhardt Jr., Reed Sorenson and Bobby Labonte, dropping all of them to the bottom fourth of the finishing order, with Hamlin listed in last place.

Hamlin and Stewart took any opportunity to continue their "he-said/he-said" dispute during the week that followed, and while both drivers were doing plenty of talking, none of it was with each other. That prompted team owner Joe Gibbs to make a trip to Chicagoland Speedway where he and co-owner J.D. Gibbs invited the two drivers to sit down behind closed doors and "discuss" the issue. Everyone was smiling when they emerged from the team transporter, although the tension was still palpable.

Apparently, it was just what Stewart needed.

Never lacking an opinion or a chance to express it, Stewart always does his best (as in most effective) talking on the race track. Welcome to Chicagoland.

Stewart rolled off the line in 19th place and immediately went to work, muscling his way through traffic in pursuit of the leaders. By the first caution at Lap 60 he was running among the top five, while Jimmie Johnson and Kevin Harvick split time at the front of the field. When the second caution appeared on Lap 155, Stewart reported to his pit for tires, fuel and a fine tune on his chassis and returned to the track with the lead. From there, he simply took over.

Stewart led all but seven of the remaining 112 laps, including the final 36, on the way to his first victory of the season, breaking a 20-race winless string that began in November 2006 at Phoenix.

TOP 10 QUALIFIERS

1. **CASEY MEARS**
   29.580 SEC. 182.556 MPH

2. **MARTIN TRUEX JR.**
   29.593 SEC. 182.476 MPH

3. **RYAN NEWMAN**
   29.595 SEC. 182.463 MPH

4. **MARK MARTIN**
   29.622 SEC. 182.297 MPH

5. **DALE EARNHARDT JR.**
   29.626 SEC. 182.272 MPH

6. **KYLE BUSCH**
   29.689 SEC. 181.886 MPH

7. **CLINT BOWYER**
   29.727 SEC. 181.653 MPH

8. **JIMMIE JOHNSON**
   29.739 SEC. 181.580 MPH

9. **JOHN ANDRETTI**
   29.764 SEC. 181.427 MPH

10. **MATT KENSETH**
    29.767 SEC. 181.409 MPH

(Left) Casey Mears grabs the spotlight after taking the Budweiser Pole Award at Chicagoland, his first of the season and the third of his career. Mears led the first five laps of the race before settling in for a fifth-place finish, his fourth top five in the last eight events.

(Below) Kevin Harvick's crew goes into action on a green-flag pit stop. Harvick reached the leaders quickly after starting 14th, led four times for 54 laps and finished fourth for his fourth finish of eighth or better in the last five races.

(Above) Carl Edwards (99), David Reutimann (00) and Johnny Sauter (70) race three wide through Chicagoland's wide turns banked at 18 degrees. Edwards, who started 25th, overcame traffic and a few sub-par pit stops to post a hard-fought, third-place finish and moved up to fifth in the point standings.

(Right) Dale Earnhardt Jr. takes time to sign autographs for a few lucky fans. In the race, Earnhardt was running a strong third when his power steering failed, causing him to steadily drop back to an eventual 19th-place finish.

Tony Stewart (20) sets sail after fending off a challenge from Matt Kenseth (17) late in the race. Stewart was simply superb over the second half and drove away to his 30th career victory.

RACE RESULTS

NASCAR NEXTEL Cup Series Race No.19 — July 15, 2007
Chicagoland Speedway

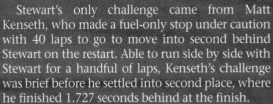

USG SHEETROCK 400

Fin. Pos.	Start Pos.	Car No.	Driver	Team	Laps	Laps Led	Status
1	19	20	Tony Stewart	Home Depot Chevrolet	267	108	Running
2	10	17	Matt Kenseth	USG Sheetrock/DEWALT Ford	267	1	Running
3	25	99	Carl Edwards	Office Depot Ford	267		Running
4	14	29	Kevin Harvick	Shell/Pennzoil Chevrolet	267	54	Running
5	1	25	Casey Mears	National Guard/GMAC Chevrolet	267	5	Running
6	35	2	Kurt Busch	Miller Lite Dodge	267	2	Running
7	23	31	Jeff Burton	AT&T Mobility Chevrolet	267		Running
8	3	12	Ryan Newman	Mobil 1/Alltel Dodge	267		Running
9	11	24	Jeff Gordon	DuPont/Nicorette Chevrolet	267		Running
10	7	07	Clint Bowyer	Jack Daniel's Chevrolet	267	1	Running
11	33	16	Greg Biffle	Aflac Ford	267		Running
12	22	41	Reed Sorenson	Target/Maxwell House Dodge	267		Running
13	6	5	Kyle Busch	Kellogg's/CARQUEST Chevrolet	267		Running
14	4	01	Mark Martin	U.S. Army Chevrolet	267		Running
15	30	42 #	Juan Pablo Montoya	Wrigley's Big Red Dodge	267		Running
16	42	38	David Gilliland	M&M's Ford	267		Running
17	13	11	Denny Hamlin	FedEx Express Chevrolet	267		Running
18	9	45	John Andretti	National Tire & Battery Dodge	267		Running
19	5	8	Dale Earnhardt Jr.	Budweiser Chevrolet	267	2	Running
20	12	43	Bobby Labonte	Cheerios/Betty Crocker Dodge	266		Running
21	41	88	Ricky Rudd	Pedigree/Snickers Ford	266		Running
22	18	70	Johnny Sauter	Yellow Transportation Chevrolet	266		Running
23	37	14	Sterling Marlin	Waste Management Chevrolet	266		Running
24	40	96	Tony Raines	DLP HDTV Chevrolet	265		Running
25	32	6 #	David Ragan	AAA Insurance Ford	265		Running
26	20	36	Jeremy Mayfield	360 OTC Toyota	265		Running
27	29	66	Jeff Green	Comcast/Best Buy Chevrolet	265		Running
28	17	21	Bill Elliott	Little Debbie Snack Cakes Ford	265		Running
29	27	13	Joe Nemechek	CertainTeed Chevrolet	264		Running
30	28	55	Michael Waltrip	NAPA Auto Parts Toyota	264		Running
31	26	49	Chad Chaffin	Paralyzed Veterans Dodge	263		Running
32	24	9	Kasey Kahne	Dodge Dealers/UAW Dodge	262		Running
33	31	19	Elliott Sadler	Dodge Dealers/UAW Dodge	260		Running
34	38	40	David Stremme	TUMS/Coors Light Dodge	257		Engine
35	36	18	J.J. Yeley	Interstate Batteries Chevrolet	243		Accident
36	39	7	Robby Gordon	Jim Beam Ford	225		Running
37	8	48	Jimmie Johnson	Lowe's Chevrolet	222	82	Accident
38	34	26	Jamie McMurray	Crown Royal Ford	214		Running
39	2	1	Martin Truex Jr.	Bass Pro Shops/Tracker Boats Chev.	211	12	Engine
40	15	22	Dave Blaney	Caterpillar Toyota	199		Accident
41	14	4	Ward Burton	State Water Heaters Chevrolet	197		Accident
42	16	15 #	Paul Menard	Menards/Turtle Wax Ice Chevrolet	132		Running
43	21	00 #	David Reutimann	Burger King Toyota	43		Engine

Raybestos Rookie of the Year Contender.

NASCAR NEXTEL CUP SERIES TOP 12

(After 19 Races)

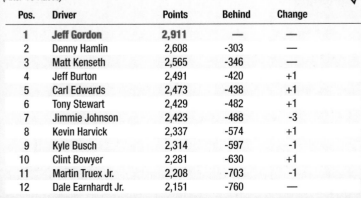

Pos.	Driver	Points	Behind	Change
1	**Jeff Gordon**	2,911	—	—
2	Denny Hamlin	2,608	-303	—
3	Matt Kenseth	2,565	-346	—
4	Jeff Burton	2,491	-420	+1
5	Carl Edwards	2,473	-438	+1
6	Tony Stewart	2,429	-482	+1
7	Jimmie Johnson	2,423	-488	-3
8	Kevin Harvick	2,337	-574	+1
9	Kyle Busch	2,314	-597	-1
10	Clint Bowyer	2,281	-630	+1
11	Martin Truex Jr.	2,208	-703	-1
12	Dale Earnhardt Jr.	2,151	-760	—

Stewart's only challenge came from Matt Kenseth, who made a fuel-only stop under caution with 40 laps to go to move into second behind Stewart on the restart. Able to run side by side with Stewart for a handful of laps, Kenseth's challenge was brief before he settled into second place, where he finished 1.727 seconds behind at the finish.

"I stayed under him (Stewart) for about two laps," Kenseth explained, "and finally I went off into [Turn 3]. We went up in there side by side, and I got so loose I was afraid I was going to wipe us both out, so I had to get back behind him."

Stewart's strongest competition might have come from Johnson, but his effort was sidelined when a left-rear tire went down and sent the No. 48 Chevrolet into the Turn 4 wall on Lap 222. Johnson was done for the day in 37th place and fell three positions in the point standings to seventh.

Carl Edwards grabbed his second consecutive top-five finish in third place, one spot ahead of Harvick in fourth and Budweiser Pole Award winner Casey Mears in fifth.

Nine of the top 10 finishers in the USG SHEETROCK 400 were involved in the Chase for the NASCAR NEXTEL Cup point battle. Still sitting on the so-called bubble in 12th place, Dale Earnhardt Jr. was listed 19th in the finishing order. Combined with his 36th-place finish in the Pepsi 400, a somewhat comfortable cushion in the points had now been reduced to a narrow 30-point margin over surging Ryan Newman.

Newman, who finished eighth at Chicago, and Kurt Busch, who added a sixth-place finish to the top five he scored at Daytona, moved up one position each in the standings to 13th and 14th, respectively. That came at the expense of Daytona winner McMurray, who struggled at Chicago and finally slapped the wall, finishing 38th and falling two places to 15th in points.

Jeff Gordon tightened his grip on first place in the standings with yet another top-10 finish (9th), his seventh straight finish of ninth or better and his 17th top 10 in the season's first 19 events. Gordon's margin increased to more than 300 points over second-place Hamlin, whose 17th-place finish did little to make up for his disastrous outing at Daytona.

Hamlin nonetheless seemed pleased with the overall results at Chicago, offering a cheery outlook for his race-winning JGR teammates. "I'm really happy for them," said Hamlin. "To finally get a win and do it in the dominating fashion that he did was really good for that team. … Whenever there is adversity, it always seems like they're able to pull together and come back and get a win. We got ours a couple weeks ago and they get theirs this week."

Everyone, in fact, seemed somewhat jovial as the weekend's activities concluded. A weekend off lay ahead, and the next event, at Indianapolis, would begin a stretch of 16 straight weeks that would ultimately decide the NASCAR NEXTEL Cup Series championship. ◢◢◢

ALLSTATE 400 AT THE BRICKYARD

INDIANAPOLIS MOTOR SPEEDWAY

Tony Stewart characterized his 2005 win at Indianapolis Motor Speedway as the biggest of his career. It also was the springboard that vaulted the Indiana native to his second NASCAR NEXTEL Cup Series championship. Who could blame him for wanting to do it all again?

Stewart and his No. 20 Joe Gibbs Racing team have developed a habit of mid-summer rallies over the years, to the point where Stewart and crew chief Greg Zipadelli have even questioned why.

"This time of year, it seems like we get hot," explained Stewart. "We've even tried to sit down and figure out what we miss in the spring."

Maybe it just takes half the season to brew up enough turmoil to light a fire under the orange-and-white-clad team. "It seems like things have to stack up against us in order for us to bust out," Zipadelli guessed. "But thank God we've been able to continue to bust out."

In the final analysis, the reason why matters little. Of consequence is that once again Stewart and Company conjured up a head of steam leading to the Allstate 400 at the Brickyard, and once again they came away with a win, their second straight.

Maybe it's just the heat of summer. "I prayed for a day like today," continued Stewart. "I wanted it to be hot. I wanted it to be sunny to where the track would get a little slippery.

"It seems like when it starts getting slick, that's when we really excel at this place."

Excel he did. After starting 14th, Stewart headed directly to the front, aided by a series of early-race cautions — six in the first 62 laps, all for accidents that involved a total of 16 cars.

With each interruption, Stewart regrouped and thundered his way back to the front. "It just seems like our cars were never really good at the front of a run," Stewart said, "but it seems like 15 laps into a run, here we come."

And so the see-saw began. Stewart led seven different times (five more than anyone else) for a total of 65 laps (more than twice as many as anyone else). When things finally settled down — seven of nine cautions flew before the halfway point — Stewart settled in, able to keep his Chevrolet in clean air for longer stretches between stops for tires and fuel.

The final restart came with 20 laps to go, which allowed Kevin Harvick to dart past Stewart immediately after taking the green flag. He didn't get far. Stewart battled right back, not letting Harvick open much of a gap while his Monte Carlo warmed to the task. When it did, the two former winners of the event went at it in no uncertain terms, staging a side-by-side scrap for the lead that lasted several laps and left neither car undamaged.

With 10 laps left, Stewart settled it for good, bruising his way past Harvick for the last time and turning into the undisturbed air that allowed him to sail to victory. Harvick, meanwhile, faded to seventh over the final 10 laps, largely due to fender damage suffered in his clash with Stewart.

Juan Pablo Montoya, who made history by becoming the first driver to race in the Indianapolis 500, a Formula One event and a NASCAR race at the Brickyard, finished second. Although he had thoughts of adding this win to his Indy 500 victory in 2000, they were brief. "No way," Montoya said, "I don't think anybody had anything for Tony today."

"I definitely didn't," agreed Jeff Gordon, who finished third ahead of teammate Kyle Busch.

Reed Sorenson capped off a fine weekend by finishing fifth for his second top five of the season. The 21-year-old driver of Chip Ganassi's Dodge led the first 16 laps of the race after posting his first career Budweiser Pole Award earlier in the weekend.

TOP 10 QUALIFIER

1. **REED SORENSON**
   48.858 SEC. 184.207 MPH

2. **JUAN PABLO MONTOYA**
   49.048 SEC. 183.494 MPH

3. **RYAN NEWMAN**
   49.053 SEC. 183.475 MPH

4. **DALE EARNHARDT JR.**
   49.068 SEC. 183.419 MPH

5. **KASEY KAHNE**
   49.080 SEC. 183.374 MPH

6. **KURT BUSCH**
   49.159 SEC. 183.079 MPH

7. **JEFF BURTON**
   49.167 SEC. 183.050 MPH

8. **GREG BIFFLE**
   49.174 SEC. 183.024 MPH

9. **CASEY MEARS**
   49.177 SEC. 183.012 MPH

10. **DENNY HAMLIN**
    49.233 SEC. 182.804 MPH

Reed Sorenson (41) paces the field in preparation for the 14th running of the Allstate 400 at the Brickyard. Sorenson earned his place by winning the first Budweiser Pole Award of his career, which he turned into his second top-five finish of the season.

(Above) Casey Mears (25) gets sandwiched between Elliott Sadler (19), Johnny Sauter (70) and Kyle Petty (45) coming off Turn 3. The incident, on Lap 55, was the fifth of eight cautions that occurred before the 100-lap mark.

Dale Earnhardt Jr.'s crew dejectedly pushes their driver toward the garage after engine failure, the team's third of the season, ended a very strong outing. The resulting 34th-place finish slashed his margin over 13th place in the standings to a mere 13 points.

(Right) Balloons released in front of the infield pagoda signal the beginning of race-day events at Indianapolis Motor Speedway.

A very happy Tony Stewart does one of his favorite things — climbing the fence at Indianapolis. His second victory at the famous track near his boyhood home was also his second in as many weeks.

(Right) Kevin Harvick streaks down the frontstretch with the late-race lead, one he held until Tony Stewart arrived and took it away with 10 laps to go. In Stewart's wake, Harvick nursed his damaged car to a seventh-place finish.

RACE RESULTS

ALLSTATE 400 AT THE BRICKYARD

Fin. Pos.	Start Pos.	Car No.	Driver	Team	Laps	Laps Led	Status
1	14	20	Tony Stewart	Home Depot Chevrolet	160	65	Running
2	2	42 #	Juan Pablo Montoya	Texaco/Havoline Dodge	160		Running
3	21	24	Jeff Gordon	DuPont Chevrolet	160		Running
4	18	5	Kyle Busch	Kellogg's/CARQUEST Chevrolet	160	17	Running
5	1	41	Reed Sorenson	Target Dodge	160	16	Running
6	13	01	Mark Martin	U.S. Army Chevrolet	160		Running
7	20	29	Kevin Harvick	Reese's Racing Chevrolet	160	18	Running
8	7	31	Jeff Burton	AT&T Mobility Chevrolet	160		Running
9	27	22	Dave Blaney	Caterpillar Toyota	160		Running
10	31	17	Matt Kenseth	DEWALT Ford	160		Running
11	6	2	Kurt Busch	Miller Lite Dodge	160		Running
12	33	1	Martin Truex Jr.	Bass Pro Shops/Tracker Chevrolet	160		Running
13	26	07	Clint Bowyer	Jack Daniel's Chevrolet	160		Running
14	40	4	Ward Burton	State Water Heaters/Lucas Chev.	160		Running
15	8	16	Greg Biffle	Dish Network Ford	160	11	Running
16	30	6 #	David Ragan	AAA Insurance Ford	160		Running
17	38	38	David Gilliland	M&M's Ford	160		Running
18	35	99	Carl Edwards	Office Depot Ford	160		Running
19	29	43	Bobby Labonte	Totino's Pizza Rolls Dodge	160		Running
20	28	15 #	Paul Menard	Menards/Johns Manville Chevrolet	160		Running
21	25	83	Brian Vickers	Red Bull Toyota	160		Running
22	10	11	Denny Hamlin	FedEx Kinko's Chevrolet	159		Running
23	32	21	Bill Elliott	Little Debbie Ford	159		Running
24	37	88	Ricky Rudd	Snickers Ford	159		Running
25	36	49	Ken Schrader	Paralyzed Veterans Dodge	159		Running
26	12	40	David Stremme	Target Dodge	158		Running
27	42	7	Robby Gordon	Johns Manville/Menards Ford	157		Running
28	17	19	Elliott Sadler	Dodge Dealers/UAW Dodge	155		Running
29	16	10	Scott Riggs	Stanley Tools/Valvoline Dodge	154		Running
30	43	55	Terry Labonte	NAPA Auto Parts Toyota	150		Engine
31	22	33	Scott Wimmer	Holiday Inn Chevrolet	145		Running
32	41	45	Kyle Petty	Marathon Motor Oil Dodge	141		Running
33	15	26	Jamie McMurray	Crown Royal Ford	139		Running
34	4	8	Dale Earnhardt Jr.	Budweiser Chevrolet	136	33	Engine
35	9	25	Casey Mears	National Guard/GMAC Chevrolet	132		Running
36	23	18	J.J. Yeley	Interstate Batteries Chevrolet	120		Accident
37	39	70	Johnny Sauter	Radioactive Energy Chevrolet	100		Running
38	34	00 #	David Reutimann	Burger King Toyota	92		Engine
39	19	48	Jimmie Johnson	Lowe's Chevrolet	59		Accident
40	5	9	Kasey Kahne	Dodge Dealers/UAW Dodge	39		Accident
41	11	96	Tony Raines	DLP HDTV Chevrolet	39		Accident
42	3	12	Ryan Newman	Alltel Dodge	20		Accident
43	24	66	Jeff Green	Haas Automation Chevrolet	13		Accident

Raybestos Rookie of the Year Contender.

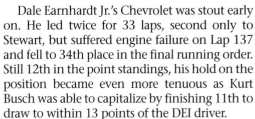

NASCAR NEXTEL CUP SERIES TOP 12

(After 20 Races)

Pos.	Driver	Points	Behind	Change
1	Jeff Gordon	3,076	—	—
2	Denny Hamlin	2,705	-371	—
3	Matt Kenseth	2,699	-377	—
4	Jeff Burton	2,633	-443	—
5	Tony Stewart	2,599	-477	+1
6	Carl Edwards	2,582	-494	-1
7	Kevin Harvick	2,488	-588	+1
8	Kyle Busch	2,479	-597	+1
9	Jimmie Johnson	2,469	-607	-2
10	Clint Bowyer	2,405	-671	—
11	Martin Truex Jr.	2,335	-741	—
12	Dale Earnhardt Jr.	2,217	-859	—

Dale Earnhardt Jr.'s Chevrolet was stout early on. He led twice for 33 laps, second only to Stewart, but suffered engine failure on Lap 137 and fell to 34th place in the final running order. Still 12th in the point standings, his hold on the position became even more tenuous as Kurt Busch was able to capitalize by finishing 11th to draw to within 13 points of the DEI driver.

Others in contention for the final spot to qualify for the Chase for the NASCAR NEXTEL Cup did not fare as well as Busch. Ryan Newman, 13th in the standings with a 30-point deficit to Earnhardt going into the race, completed just 20 laps before he was swept into an accident. He finished 42nd and left the track 59 points behind 12th position.

McMurray started the day 111 points out of the 12th place but, like Newman, was not able to take advantage of Earnhardt's misfortune, finishing 33rd after suffering accident damage and falling to 15th in the standings, 113 points away from a place in the championship-contending field. 🏁

PENNSYLVANIA 500

POCONO RACEWAY

Six races remained in the Race to the Chase as NASCAR NEXTEL Cup Series teams rolled into Pocono Raceway for the 21st event of the 2007 season. For all intents and purposes, the battle in the point standings was clearly focused on the so-called "bubble" — the 12th and final position to qualify for the Chase for the NASCAR NEXTEL Cup.

Dale Earnhardt Jr. currently held 12th place in the standings, as he had following the last six events. Week after week, it seemed, he said his team was worthy of competing for the championship and that he fully expected to be among the field of contenders when all was said and done.

Ahead of him, his DEI teammate, Martin Truex Jr., and RCR driver Clint Bowyer had been swapping the 10th and 11th positions between them for a number of weeks. They had, however, been able to maintain enough of a point cushion over 12th place that neither driver was in immediate danger of falling out of the championship-contending field.

Behind Earnhardt was a completely different story. Penske Racing South teammates Kurt Busch and Ryan Newman, along with Jamie McMurray, had been doing their best each week to displace him in the final spot. Earnhardt had not been able to help himself much, either, finishing 36th at Daytona, 19th at Chicagoland and 34th at Indianapolis due to his third engine failure of the season. His lead had dwindled to a mere 13 points over Kurt Busch, with Newman 59 points back and McMurray 113 behind.

Busch upped the ante as the Pocono weekend got started by posting a blazingly fast lap in qualifying that placed him at the top of the speed chart. After a brief shower interrupted the session, Earnhardt took to the cooler, cleaner track and posted a lap good enough to grab his first Budweiser Pole Award in nearly five years and shove Busch to the outside of the front row.

"We stole that pole ... with the weather and all. ... And we stole it from the Miller car, so that was really cool," Earnhardt said with a smile, referring to the inherent rivalry between the two beer makers. Sponsors aside, both Busch and Earnhardt fully knew what was at stake when it came time to count points.

Despite lining up together on the front row, any notion that the cars driven by Earnhardt Jr. and Busch were well matched was put to rest immediately after the green flag waved to begin the Pennsylvania 500. Busch bolted to the lead on the first lap and all but disappeared.

How good was Busch? He led 175 of the 200-lap distance, setting a record at the 33-year-old raceway. Busch led seven times in all, and although 10 other drivers took turns at the front, none of them led more than one time, six of those led but one lap each, and only Earnhardt Jr. led more than five total laps.

Earnhardt's chance to lead the field was the result of rather odd circumstances. Although able to hang among the top five, he was fighting a race car that was way too tight and getting worse, the result of what the team called an "aggressive shock package."

It finally became too much, and Earnhardt spun in the Tunnel Turn on Lap 123, bringing out the day's fourth caution. It turned out to be to his advantage, as his crew took the opportunity to change the left-front shock absorber without losing a lap, while the field crawled around the giant 2.5-mile super speedway behind the pace car.

Earnhardt lined up 26th for the restart and picked up 12 positions in nine laps before the next yellow flag flew on Lap 138. This time, Earnhardt elected to take two tires and jumped to fifth place for the restart.

TOP 10 QUALIFIERS

1. **DALE EARNHARDT JR.**
   52.949 SEC. 169.975 MPH

2. **KURT BUSCH**
   52.984 SEC. 169.863 MPH

3. **KYLE BUSCH**
   53.009 SEC. 169.782 MPH

4. **RYAN NEWMAN**
   53.023 SEC. 169.738 MPH

5. **KASEY KAHNE**
   53.070 SEC. 169.587 MPH

6. **DENNY HAMLIN**
   53.097 SEC. 169.501 MPH

7. **JIMMIE JOHNSON**
   53.153 SEC. 169.323 MPH

8. **CASEY MEARS**
   53.170 SEC. 169.268 MPH

9. **JUAN PABLO MONTOYA**
   53.281 SEC. 168.916 MPH

10. **REED SORENSON**
    53.367 SEC. 168.644 MPH

Dale Earnhardt Jr. entertains questions for reporters after grabbing his first Budweiser Pole Award in five years. It came at exactly the right time, as Earnhardt was battling to maintain 12th place in the point standings.

(Left) Jamie McMurray (26) gets chased by Michael Waltrip in the early laps at Pocono. McMurray, fighting to remain in contention for a spot in the top 12 in the standings, had a rough day, spinning twice before retiring in 40th place.

(Right) Ryan Newman contemplates the job ahead while waiting for practice to begin. Currently in a dogfight for the 12th position in points with teammate Kurt Busch and Dale Earnhardt Jr., Newman's seventh-place finish at Pocono did not help and left him 14th in the standings.

(Below) Brian Vickers (left) has some fun with Ward Burton while signing autographs for the Pocono faithful.

(Above) Kurt Busch goes it alone in his blue Dodge at Pocono. Busch was so fast, he spent a good portion of the race unchallenged at the front of the field. He led 88 percent of the laps and finished with a gaping 4.131-second margin over second-place Dale Earnhardt Jr.

(Left) When Busch pulled into Victory Lane, he had completed a climb of five positions in the point standings over an eight-week span and had displaced Dale Earnhardt Jr. in 12th place.

(Right) Mark Martin sports a brand new hat carrying the name of his new employer, Dale Earnhardt Inc., after his former team, Ginn Racing, continued to divest by selling the "01" team to DEI.

RACE RESULTS

NASCAR NEXTEL Cup Series Race No. 21 — August 5, 2007
Pocono Raceway

PENNSYLVANIA 500

Fin. Pos.	Start Pos.	Car No.	Driver	Team	Laps	Laps Led	Status
1	2	2	Kurt Busch	Miller Lite Dodge	200	175	Running
2	1	8	Dale Earnhardt Jr.	Budweiser Chevrolet	200	8	Running
3	6	11	Denny Hamlin	FedEx Express Chevrolet	200		Running
4	11	24	Jeff Gordon	DuPont Chevrolet	200		Running
5	7	48	Jimmie Johnson	Lowe's Chevrolet	200		Running
6	24	20	Tony Stewart	Home Depot Chevrolet	200		Running
7	4	12	Ryan Newman	Mobil 1/Alltel Dodge	200	1	Running
8	15	07	Clint Bowyer	Camping World Chevrolet	200	1	Running
9	25	01	Mark Martin	U.S. Army Chevrolet	200		Running
10	8	25	Casey Mears	National Guard/GMAC Chevrolet	200		Running
11	18	31	Jeff Burton	AT&T Mobility Chevrolet	200		Running
12	3	5	Kyle Busch	Kellogg's/CARQUEST Chevrolet	200	2	Running
13	20	88	Ricky Rudd	Combos Ford	200		Running
14	37	17	Matt Kenseth	DEWALT Ford	200	1	Running
15	17	96	Tony Raines	DLP HDTV/Rush Hour 3 Chev.	200		Running
16	9	42 #	Juan Pablo Montoya	Texaco/Havoline Dodge	200		Running
17	23	29	Kevin Harvick	Shell/Pennzoil Chevrolet	200		Running
18	21	21	Bill Elliott	Air Force Ford	200	1	Running
19	32	66	Jeff Green	HAAS Automation/Garmin Chev.	200	4	Running
20	19	22	Dave Blaney	Caterpillar Toyota	200		Running
21	29	99	Carl Edwards	Office Depot Ford	200		Running
22	13	1	Martin Truex Jr.	Bass Pro Shops/Tracker Chev.	200	1	Running
23	12	16	Greg Biffle	Dish Network/DOG Ford	200		Running
24	16	10	Scott Riggs	Stanley Tools/Valvoline Dodge	200		Running
25	34	40	David Stremme	Target Dodge	200		Running
26	35	15 #	Paul Menard	Menards/Energizer Chevrolet	200		Running
27	5	9	Kasey Kahne	Dodge Dealers/UAW Dodge	200		Running
28	10	41	Reed Sorenson	Target Dodge	200	5	Running
29	28	83	Brian Vickers	Red Bull Toyota	200		Running
30	26	43	Bobby Labonte	Cheerios/Betty Crocker Dodge	199	1	Running
31	43	36	Jeremy Mayfield	360 OTC Toyota	199		Running
32	14	19	Elliott Sadler	Dodge Dealers/UAW Dodge	198		Running
33	36	6 #	David Ragan	AAA Insurance Ford	198		Running
34	42	45	Kyle Petty	Marathon Dodge	198		Running
35	27	18	J.J. Yeley	Interstate Batteries Chevrolet	198		Running
36	41	70	Johnny Sauter	HAAS Automation Chevrolet	198		Running
37	30	7	P.J. Jones	Menards/MAPEI Ford	198		Running
38	39	55	Michael Waltrip	NAPA Auto Parts Toyota	194		Fuel Pump
39	33	38	David Gilliland	M&M's Ford	192		Running
40	22	26	Jamie McMurray	Crown Royal Ford	177		Accident
41	31	00 #	David Reutimann	Burger King Toyota	159		Fuel Pump
42	40	44	Dale Jarrett	UPS Toyota	151		Fuel Pump
43	38	4	Ward Burton	State Water Heaters/LUCAS Chev.	109		Engine

Raybestos Rookie of the Year Contender.

Busch pitted with the lead, but his crew encountered a problematic lug nut that ended up dropping him to ninth place when the racing resumed on Lap 143.

No matter. While Earnhardt Jr. drove from fifth to first in the first two laps under green, Busch merely dropped the hammer in his Dodge and began picking off positions with relative ease. Eight laps after Earnhardt pulled out front, here came the blue No. 2. Busch simply drove past and waved goodbye, able to open more than a two-second lead over the next 10 laps. One final stop for fresh tires and fuel with 25 laps to go was all Busch needed to seal one of the most dominating performances in recent memory.

Earnhardt Jr. took "best of the rest" honors in second place, while Denny Hamlin, Jeff Gordon and Jimmie Johnson rounded out the top five.

With the win and a 10-point bonus for leading the most laps, Busch hopped over Earnhardt into 12th place in the point standings with a slim, seven-point margin. Newman finished seventh and fell to 14th in the standings, but was still squarely in the hunt, 83 behind Earnhardt and 90 away from the coveted 12th position. McMurray wasn't as lucky; damage from a pair of early-race spins placed him 40th in the finishing order, dropped him to 17th in the points and, with five races to go, effectively ended his hopes of making the 2007 Chase for the NASCAR NEXTEL Cup. ❖

NASCAR NEXTEL CUP SERIES TOP 12

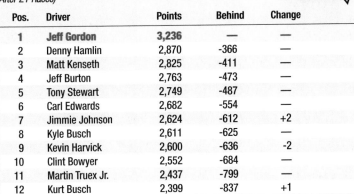

(After 21 Races)

Pos.	Driver	Points	Behind	Change
1	**Jeff Gordon**	3,236	—	—
2	Denny Hamlin	2,870	-366	—
3	Matt Kenseth	2,825	-411	—
4	Jeff Burton	2,763	-473	—
5	Tony Stewart	2,749	-487	—
6	Carl Edwards	2,682	-554	—
7	Jimmie Johnson	2,624	-612	+2
8	Kyle Busch	2,611	-625	—
9	Kevin Harvick	2,600	-636	-2
10	Clint Bowyer	2,552	-684	—
11	Martin Truex Jr.	2,437	-799	—
12	Kurt Busch	2,399	-837	+1

CENTURION BOATS
AT THE GLEN

WATKINS GLEN INTERNATIONAL

Jeff Gordon has won more road-course races than any driver in NASCAR NEX-
TEL Cup Series history — nine in all. Four of those came at Watkins Glen
International, again, more than any other driver. So you couldn't blame him
for being upset when, while holding the lead and with less than two laps to go in the
Centurion Boats at The Glen, he blew it.

Entering Turn 1, Gordon jumped on the brakes a little too hard and immediately
felt the dreaded "wheel hop" as his rear tires stopped spinning, jumped up and
down a couple of times and then lost their grip on the race track. With his steering
wheel already cocked to the right as he set up for the turn, the back end of Gordon's
Chevrolet broke loose, sending the four-time champ spinning off the course.

Popping through the tire smoke was Tony Stewart, who darted to the inside and
drove off toward Turn 2, lead in hand and a wry smile on his face. Stewart could
understand what happened to Gordon; he did the same thing 44 laps earlier, a mistake that dropped him from the lead to 19th place in the running order.

But Stewart had time to recover and was right where he needed to be at exactly
the right instant. He checked his rearview mirror in time to see Gordon's car stop
spinning before he disappeared through the next turn on his way to a 2.46-second
win over teammate Denny Hamlin.

"We were putting a lot of pressure on him," Stewart said of the final laps when he
was chasing Gordon. "We knew our only shot of getting by him was to keep the
pressure on him and hope that he made a mistake. Trust me; I was probably the most
shocked person to see it happen. … He's the last guy you would expect to have a problem like that."

Gordon regrouped and pulled back into traffic to complete the last two laps, taking the checkered flag in ninth place.

(Left) There is never a shortage of Boris Said fans at a road course, such as this lady who found a cardboard likeness of her favorite driver. Bill Elliott asked Said to drive the No. 21 car in his place, and he responded with a 14th-place run, just what the team needed to reach the important 35th position in owner points.

Robby Gordon, the 2003 winner at Watkins Glen, discusses his car's setup with crew members. Gordon started 29th (qualifying was cancelled due to rain) and worked to a season-best fifth-place finish.

QUALIFYING RAINED OUT

Kurt Busch (2) heads toward pit road under caution, vacating his position behind race-leader Jeff Gordon (24). His decision to pit for fuel came shortly after Dale Earnhardt Jr. retired with a failed engine, a strategic move that allowed Busch to solidify his 12th-place position in the points.

"That wasn't bad luck, trust me," Gordon said flatly. "When you drive in the corner too deep, and you step on the brake pedal too hard and you wheel hop, it's not bad luck. It's all my foot. … I just drove too hard.

"I was pushing really hard."

For good reason, too. In less than a month, Gordon's commanding lead in the point standings would be wiped clean and he would be ranked alongside the other championship contenders according to bonus points — 10 per victory — earned during the season. Tied with Jimmie Johnson at four wins each, two more than Stewart, a win at Watkins Glen would have put Gordon 10 points ahead of Johnson and 30 in front of Stewart. Instead, Stewart was now just 10 behind Gordon, whose late-race mistake became, in effect, a 20-point swing.

(Left) Tony Stewart (20) powers out of the Inner Loop ahead of Dale Earnhardt Jr., making up ground after an early-race spin in Turn 1. When Jeff Gordon spun in the same spot as Stewart with two laps to go, he was there to snatch the win.

(Right) Jeff Gordon (24) stretches his lead over Denny Hamlin and Tony Stewart. Gordon led three times for 51 laps and was poised to take the win before a late-race mistake dropped him to a ninth-place finish.

(Below) Patrick Carpentier was on hand at Watkins Glen for his NASCAR NEXTEL Cup Series debut. Carpentier put the No. 10 Dodge in front for the first time this season, leading seven laps before fading to a 22nd-place finish.

Then there's the momentum factor. "I feel like we're in the best position of anybody right now with what's happened three out of the last four weeks," Stewart said, referring to his recent onslaught of wins.

The race also had a significant impact further down the point standings. After dropping out of the 12th position in points at Pocono a week earlier, Dale Earnhardt Jr. took another huge hit at Watkins Glen. While running among the top three in the race, yet another blown engine, his fourth of the season, relegated Earnhardt to the garage after 63 laps and left him with a 42nd-place finish.

Kurt Busch and crew chief Pat Tryson seized the opportunity. Although running second behind Gordon and hoping for a second consecutive win, Busch and Tryson realized that their Dodge was not getting superior fuel mileage. With Earnhardt in the garage, they gutted their plans to go for the win and brought the car down pit road for enough fuel to make sure they could complete the 90-lap distance.

In 11th place at the finish, Busch padded his point cushion by 93 over Earnhardt, who fell to 14th place, 100 points back. Busch's teammate, Ryan Newman, recovered

RACE RESULTS

NASCAR NEXTEL Cup Series Race No. 22 — August 12, 2007
Watkins Glen International

CENTURION BOATS AT THE GLEN

Fin. Pos.	Start Pos.	Car No.	Driver	Team	Laps	Laps Led	Status
1	5	20	Tony Stewart	Home Depot Chevrolet	90	20	Running
2	2	11	Denny Hamlin	FedEx Ground Chevrolet	90		Running
3	7	48	Jimmie Johnson	Lowe's Chevrolet	90		Running
4	26	96	Ron Fellows	DLP HDTV Chevrolet	90		Running
5	29	7	Robby Gordon	Jim Beam Ford	90		Running
6	12	1	Martin Truex Jr.	Bass Pro Shops Chevrolet	90		Running
7	8	5	Kyle Busch	Kellogg's/CARQUEST Chevrolet	90		Running
8	6	99	Carl Edwards	Office Depot Ford	90		Running
9	1	24	Jeff Gordon	DuPont Chevrolet	90	51	Running
10	16	16	Greg Biffle	Nintendo Wii Ford	90		Running
11	13	2	Kurt Busch	Miller Lite Dodge	90		Running
12	3	17	Matt Kenseth	DEWALT Ford	90		Running
13	15	12	Ryan Newman	Kodak Dodge	90		Running
14	39	21	Boris Said	Little Debbie Ford	90		Running
15	19	25	Casey Mears	National Guard/GMAC Chevrolet	90		Running
16	11	07	Clint Bowyer	Jack Daniel's Chevrolet	90		Running
17	23	19	Elliott Sadler	Dodge Dealers/UAW Dodge	90		Running
18	21	18	J.J. Yeley	Interstate Batteries Chevrolet	90		Running
19	31	15 #	Paul Menard	Menards/Quaker State Chevrolet	90		Running
20	32	66	Jeff Green	HAAS Automation Chevrolet	90		Running
21	25	40	David Stremme	Coors Light Dodge	90		Running
22	40	10	Patrick Carpentier	Valvoline/Stanley Tools Dodge	90	7	Running
23	34	70	Johnny Sauter	HAAS Automation Chevrolet	90		Running
24	20	43	Bobby Labonte	Cheerios/Betty Crocker Dodge	90	4	Running
25	41	00	P.J. Jones	Burger King Toyota	90		Running
26	28	9	Kasey Kahne	Dodge Dealers/UAW Dodge	90		Running
27	42	36	Jeremy Mayfield	360 OTC Toyota	90	2	Running
28	24	41	Reed Sorenson	Target Dodge	90		Running
29	37	44	Dale Jarrett	UPS Toyota	90		Running
30	38	55	Terry Labonte	NAPA Auto Parts Toyota	90		Running
31	43	78	Kenny Wallace	Furniture Row Chevrolet	90		Running
32	22	6 #	David Ragan	AAA Insurance Ford	90		Running
33	30	38	David Gilliland	M&M's Ford	90		Running
34	17	26	Jamie McMurray	Crown Royal Ford	89	6	Running
35	35	22	Dave Blaney	Caterpillar Toyota	89		Running
36	9	29	Kevin Harvick	Shell/Pennzoil Chevrolet	84		Running
37	10	01	Regan Smith	U.S. Army Chevrolet	82		Running
38	27	88	Ricky Rudd	Snickers/EA Sports Ford	77		Electrical
39	18	42 #	Juan Pablo Montoya	Wrigley's Big Red Dodge	72		Accident
40	4	31	Jeff Burton	AT&T Mobility Chevrolet	72		Accident
41	36	83	Brian Vickers	Red Bull Toyota	69		Trans.
42	14	8	Dale Earnhardt Jr.	Budweiser Chevrolet	63		Engine
43	33	45	Kyle Petty	Marathon American Spirit Dodge	56		Radiator

Raybestos Rookie of the Year Contender.

NASCAR NEXTEL CUP SERIES TOP 12

(After 22 Races)

Pos.	Driver	Points	Behind	Change
1	**Jeff Gordon**	**3,384**	—	—
2	Denny Hamlin	3,040	-344	—
3	Matt Kenseth	2,952	-432	—
4	Tony Stewart	2,939	-445	+1
5	Carl Edwards	2,824	-560	+1
6	Jeff Burton	2,806	-578	-2
7	Jimmie Johnson	2,789	-595	—
8	Kyle Busch	2,757	-627	—
9	Clint Bowyer	2,667	-717	+1
10	Kevin Harvick	2,655	-729	-1
11	Martin Truex Jr.	2,587	-797	—
12	Kurt Busch	2,529	-855	—

from an early-race excursion through the pea-gravel off of Turn 10 and finished 13th in the race. That moved Newman up to 13th in the standings with a 96-point deficit to Busch.

There were eight cautions in the race, five for various spins and accidents, the most significant of which occurred less than 20 laps from the finish when Juan Pablo Montoya went sliding through Turn 1 immediately following a restart, courtesy of a push from behind by Martin Truex Jr. Montoya collected Kevin Harvick, winner of the NASCAR Busch Series race the day before, and his Richard Childress Racing teammate, Jeff Burton.

Furious, Harvick climbed from his car and went head to head with Montoya, neither one at all happy with the other, before Burton intervened, playing the role of peacekeeper. Montoya and Burton were finished for the day, while Harvick was able to return to the race, where he wound up 36th, six laps down at the finish. ▬▬

3M PERFORMANCE 400

MICHIGAN INTERNATIONAL SPEEDWAY

In the winner's circle at Michigan International Speedway, Kurt Busch bubbled with excitement while celebrating his second victory of the 2007 season. His huge smile and clear, confident tone was evidence that he and his team felt they were doing exactly what they needed to do, and doing it at exactly the right time.

For Busch, though, it had not been the perfect season — anything but that, in fact. For 17 races, the former series champion struggled through an up-and-down stretch devoid of consistency, both competitively and emotionally. A 41st-place finish in the season-opening Daytona 500 started an uphill climb that culminated 10 races later at Darlington, where, after just two top fives plus one other top-10 finish, Busch found himself all the way up to seventh in the point standings and feeling as though things were moving in the right direction.

Then the bottom fell out. After leading the most laps in the Coca-Cola 600, an accident resulted in his first DNF of the season. Things came to a head the following week at Dover, when an on-track incident with Tony Stewart spilled onto pit road. Clearly frustrated, his actions resulted in his second straight DNF when he was parked by NASCAR. Including the 100-point penalty that followed, Busch had fallen from seventh to 17th in the point standings over a two-week stretch.

A handful of mid-pack finishes over the next few events took him no higher than 16th in the standings, and when crew chief Roy McCauley left the team to attend to family matters, the team could have easily folded up their tent.

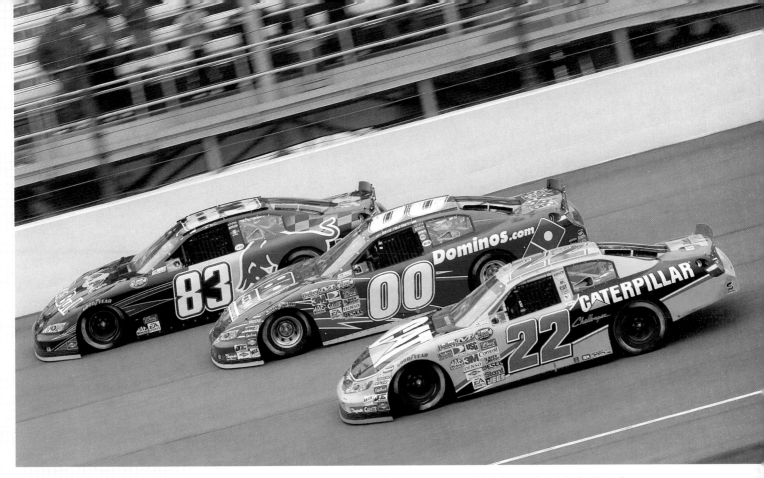

(Above) A trio of Toyotas with Dave Blaney (22), David Reutimann (00) and Brian Vickers (83) spread three-wide on Michigan's roomy frontstretch. Blaney and Vickers scored top-10 finishes for Toyota, in sixth and eighth place, respectively.

(Left) Kasey Kahne's crew exchanges tires on a stop under caution. With the track washed clean by two days of rain, NASCAR brought the teams in for an early-race competition caution to check tire wear.

(Right) Old friends have a laugh during some down time at Michigan. As a driver-crew chief combination, Ray Evernham (left) and Jeff Gordon combined for 47 wins and three championships in just under seven seasons together.

Enter Pat Tryson. Bush and the veteran crew chief, formerly with the Roush organization, clicked almost immediately, and the results were evident. Finishes of third at Daytona, sixth at Chicagoland and 11th at Indianapolis were precursors to a dominating performance at Pocono that broke a 51-race winless streak for Busch and moved him back into the top 12 in points for the first time in nine weeks.

At Watkins Glen, Busch was challenging for the lead when Dale Earnhardt Jr.'s engine expired. Wisely, Busch and Tryson decided to take advantage by playing it safe on fuel mileage and settled for an 11th-place finish. That was good enough to open

"PAT HAS BROUGHT A GREAT DEAL OF EXPERIENCE TO OUR TEAM. ... His ability to make decisions has helped us close the deal."

Kurt Busch celebrates with teammates following his 17th career win, his second at Michigan International Speedway. The victory pushed his lead over Dale Earnhardt Jr. to 163 points with just three races remaining in the Race to the Chase.

RACE RESULTS

NASCAR NEXTEL Cup Series Race No. 23 — August 21, 2007
Michigan International Speedway

3M PERFORMANCE 400

Fin. Pos.	Start Pos.	Car No.	Driver	Team	Laps	Laps Led	Status
1	15	2	Kurt Busch	Miller Lite Dodge	203	92	Running
2	14	1	Martin Truex Jr.	Bass Pro Shops/Tracker Chev.	203		Running
3	7	48	Jimmie Johnson	Lowe's Chevrolet	203	15	Running
4	21	17	Matt Kenseth	DEWALT Ford	203	31	Running
5	8	11	Denny Hamlin	FedEx Kinko's Chevrolet	203		Running
6	17	22	Dave Blaney	Caterpillar Toyota	203		Running
7	13	99	Carl Edwards	Office Depot Ford	203		Running
8	18	83	Brian Vickers	Red Bull Toyota	203	11	Running
9	4	43	Bobby Labonte	Cheerios/Betty Crocker Dodge	203		Running
10	35	20	Tony Stewart	Home Depot Chevrolet	203		Running
11	29	25	Casey Mears	National Guard/GMAC Chevrolet	203		Running
12	39	8	Dale Earnhardt Jr.	Budweiser Chevrolet	203	1	Running
13	6	5	Kyle Busch	Kellogg's/CARQUEST Chevrolet	203		Running
14	19	31	Jeff Burton	AT&T Mobility Chevrolet	203		Running
15	28	29	Kevin Harvick	Shell/Pennzoil Chevrolet	203		Running
16	34	12	Ryan Newman	Alltel Dodge	203	2	Running
17	9	07	Clint Bowyer	Jack Daniel's Chevrolet	203		Running
18	25	6 #	David Ragan	AAA Insurance Ford	203		Running
19	2	16	Greg Biffle	3M Ford	203	20	Running
20	27	4	Ward Burton	State Water Heaters/Lucas Chev.	203	4	Running
21	20	40	David Stremme	Tums Dodge	202		Running
22	40	66	Jeff Green	Best Buy Chevrolet	202		Running
23	12	00 #	David Reutimann	Dominos.com Toyota	202		Running
24	30	7	Robby Gordon	Jim Beam Ford	202	2	Running
25	31	18	J.J. Yeley	Interstate Batteries Chevrolet	202		Running
26	26	42 #	Juan Pablo Montoya	Texaco/Havoline Dodge	202		Running
27	1	24	Jeff Gordon	DuPont Chevrolet	202	25	Running
28	24	38	David Gilliland	M&M's Ford	202		Running
29	41	70	Johnny Sauter	Yellow Transportation Chevrolet	202		Running
30	36	26	Jamie McMurray	Irwin Industrial Tools Ford	202		Running
31	3	9	Kasey Kahne	Dodge Dealers/UAW Dodge	201		Running
32	5	19	Elliott Sadler	Dodge Dealers/UAW Dodge	201		Running
33	22	88	Ricky Rudd	Snickers Ford	201		Running
34	37	96	Tony Raines	DLP HDTV Chevrolet	201		Running
35	23	21	Bill Elliott	Little Debbie Ford	201		Running
36	43	10	Scott Riggs	Valvoline Dodge	201		Running
37	16	49	John Andretti	Paralyzed Veterans Dodge	201		Running
38	33	41	Reed Sorenson	Target Dodge	200		Running
39	38	15 #	Paul Menard	Menards/Sylvania Chevrolet	167		Running
40	11	55	Michael Waltrip	NAPA Auto Parts Toyota	135		Running
41	42	45	Chad McCumbee	Marathon American Dodge	134		Running
42	10	01	Mark Martin	U.S. Army Chevrolet	101		Oil Leak
43	32	08	Joe Nemechek	R & J Racing Dodge	92		Accident

Raybestos Rookie of the Year Contender.

NASCAR NEXTEL Cup Series TOP 12

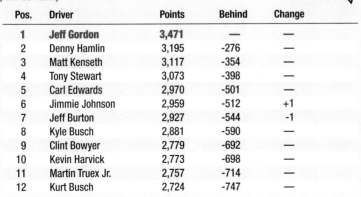

(After 23 Races)

Pos.	Driver	Points	Behind	Change
1	**Jeff Gordon**	3,471	—	—
2	Denny Hamlin	3,195	-276	—
3	Matt Kenseth	3,117	-354	—
4	Tony Stewart	3,073	-398	—
5	Carl Edwards	2,970	-501	—
6	Jimmie Johnson	2,959	-512	+1
7	Jeff Burton	2,927	-544	-1
8	Kyle Busch	2,881	-590	—
9	Clint Bowyer	2,779	-692	—
10	Kevin Harvick	2,773	-698	—
11	Martin Truex Jr.	2,757	-714	—
12	Kurt Busch	2,724	-747	—

an advantage of 96 points over 13th-place Ryan Newman and 100 points over Earnhardt as they arrived at Michigan with just a handful of races left to decide who would make the Chase for the NASCAR NEXTEL Cup.

"Pat has brought a great deal of experience to our team," Busch said. "Our guys have latched on to him and started feeding off that. His ability to make decisions has helped us close the deal."

Two days of rain that forced the race at Michigan to be postponed until Tuesday morning was enough to disrupt anyone's momentum. Not Busch. After starting from the 15th position, he methodically worked his way through the field, patiently testing his car on the freshly-washed racing surface. He reached the top 10 in the first 40 laps, pulled into fifth place on Lap 55 and found himself second behind Matt Kenseth on Lap 77 after completing a round of green-flag pit stops.

In second place for a Lap-100 restart, Busch needed just two laps to move past Kenseth and take his first lead of the day. Kenseth fought back briefly before Busch came roaring back, and then it was all Busch. He led 89 of the remaining 96 laps in stretches of 22, 34 and 33 laps, while relinquishing the top position only during routine pit stops under green.

Busch was not unchallenged, due mainly to late-race cautions. Jeff Gordon, who fought an ill-handling Chevrolet all day, slid in front of Kenseth on Lap 190 and got spun into the frontstretch grass. Busch lined up for the restart ahead of strong-running Martin Truex Jr. and Jimmie Johnson, but their battle for second place allowed Busch to pull away yet again.

Even a green-white-checkered finish, forced by Greg Biffle's spin on Lap 199, could not deter the driver of the blue-and-white No. 2 from completing his second dominating win in his last three starts. Maybe more important to Busch was that he further solidified his position in the point standings with just three races remaining in the Race to the Chase.

"I think he is right at the top of his game," team owner Roger Penske beamed when asked about Busch and his performance of late. "And now with us giving him the tools that he needs, he's going to be fine.

"If he's in [the Chase], he's going to be a car that they're going to have to beat."

Earnhardt finished 12th and moved up to 13th in points, but still lost ground to Busch and now faced a 163-point deficit. Ryan Newman, 13th in the standings heading into Michigan, finished 16th in the race and fell to 14th in points, eight behind Earnhardt and 171 back of Busch.

"They did what they had to do," Earnhardt said when asked about the No. 2 team's performance. "They've got a great feel going right now. They're really quick. When you get beat fair like that, you can't be frustrated. You have to take it like a man. We'll just go on and go next week." ❖

SHARPIE 500

BRISTOL MOTOR SPEEDWAY

When Kasey Kahne checked his rearview mirror just before the green flag fell at Bristol Motor Speedway, he must have seen those same three girls he keeps running into on TV, because he took off like a scalded cat. And he didn't stop.

Either that, or Kahne was so happy to be out front — a place he was once accustomed to running — he was not about to give it up. Or maybe it was that with each passing lap, little bits of frustration that had collected under Kahne's skin throughout the season were slowly being dissolved. Whatever the reason, Kahne used the Sharpie 500 as both an emotional release and a healing process as he rocketed around the freshly-paved half mile in a place called Thunder Valley.

After a true breakout season in 2006 that took him to Victory Lane six times and put him squarely in the Chase for the NASCAR NEXTEL Cup, "frustrating" was about the only way Kahne could describe 2007. A promising start to the season — a seventh-place finish at Daytona — was marred by a 50-point penalty after his car failed inspection. It wasn't until he returned to Daytona, 17 races later, that Kahne collected his second top-10 finish of the season, a ninth place in the Pepsi 400.

When he arrived at Bristol for the 24th race of the year, Kahne, 27th in the point standings with no hope of contending for the title, could only focus on salvaging whatever he could from his disappointing season. Qualifying was a bright spot he could build upon (one pole and eight other top-five starts in 2007), and he did so by posting his second Budweiser Pole Award of the year.

When the race got underway, Kahne simply took off, leaving outside pole-winner Juan Pablo Montoya and the rest of the field in his dust. The only other driver able to keep Kahne in sight was Carl Edwards, who managed to catch the swift-running Dodge when Kahne began lapping traffic 35 laps into the race.

Between Kahne and Edwards, no one else had a winning chance. The two drivers combined to lead all but 13 of the event's 500 laps. Six other drivers led the race, none of them more than once and none for more than three laps, with all six able to lead solely due to the fact that Kahne and Edwards had to stop periodically to refuel.

Kahne was so dominant over the first two-thirds of the race that he stayed in front for 305 of the first 334 laps, including a stretch of 266 consecutive trips around the high-banked oval, from Lap 65 to Lap 330. That's when Kahne encountered Michael Waltrip, and the complexion of his race changed.

Waltrip, already two laps down, battled fiercely against Kahne for a number of laps, which allowed Edwards, running a distant second at the time, to erase the gap between them. While Kahne continued to try to find an answer to Waltrip, Edwards scooted past and into the lead, followed by Dale Earnhardt Jr., while Kahne dropped to third.

A round of green-flag pit stops followed, and when the field finished the cycle, Edwards remained in front with Kahne running second.

There were only nine cautions in the race — a total uncharacteristically low for Bristol — with six of those coming during the last 130 laps. With Kahne unable to build momentum without extended runs under green, the advantage went to Edwards, who led the final 130 laps of the race on the way to his second win of the season.

"This is the biggest win of my career," Edwards said. "Winning here at Bristol is everybody's dream. This is the night race at Bristol, 500 laps, and we won it!"

Kahne finished a strong second, his first top five of the season, ahead of Clint Bowyer and Tony Stewart.

TOP 10 QUALIFIERS

1. **KASEY KAHNE**
   16.016 SEC. 119.805 MPH

2. **JUAN PABLO MONTOYA**
   16.064 SEC. 119.447 MPH

3. **JAMIE MCMURRAY**
   16.103 SEC. 119.158 MPH

4. **DAVID RAGAN**
   16.105 SEC. 119.143 MPH

5. **DAVE BLANEY**
   16.110 SEC. 119.106 MPH

6. **CARL EDWARDS**
   16.122 SEC. 119.017 MPH

7. **RYAN NEWMAN**
   16.122 SEC. 119.017 MPH

8. **RICKY RUDD**
   16.135 SEC. 118.922 MPH

9. **JIMMIE JOHNSON**
   16.159 SEC. 118.745 MPH

10. **JEFF BURTON**
    16.161 SEC. 118.730 MPH

Carl Edwards prepares to go racing at Bristol. After qualifying sixth for the race, Edwards went to school on the new track surface by watching the NASCAR Craftsman Truck Series event and used what he learned to turn the fastest times in the final practice session.

(Above) The scoreboard lists the top 10 starters as Kasey Kahne prepares the field to go green in one of the most anticipated events of the year. Kahne jumped to an early lead and dominated the first two-thirds of the race.

(Left) A lucky fan chats with her favorite driver, Kasey Kahne, who seems relaxed and ready to go as they wait for driver introductions and the traditional lap around the track.

(Right) Fans swarm around the stage for a pre-race television show on SPEED. It is just one of many activities for visitors during a typical NASCAR NEXTEL Cup Series weekend.

(Below) Dale Earnhardt Jr.'s pit is a blur of activity as his Chevrolet is outfitted with fresh tires. Earnhardt drove to a strong fifth-place finish but gained just five points in his quest to reach the top 12 in the point standings, as Kurt Busch, currently 12th, finished one spot behind in sixth.

(Above) Kasey Kahne (9) had smooth sailing for more than 300 laps until he came upon Michael Waltrip (55). Fighting to keep from going three laps down, Waltrip raced him hard, which ultimately erased Kahne's commanding lead.

In only his second career start, Aric Almirola (01) slams into A.J. Allmendinger (84) after being tagged from behind by Jimmie Johnson. The incident produced the third of nine cautions in the race.

(Right) Carl Edwards claims the win after leading the final 130 laps of the race. It marked his sixth career win in 109 starts and his second victory of the season.

RACE RESULTS

NASCAR NEXTEL Cup Series Race No. 24 — August 25, 2007
Bristol Motor Speedway

SHARPIE 500

Fin. Pos.	Start Pos.	Car No.	Driver	Team	Laps	Laps Led	Status
1	6	99	Carl Edwards	Office Depot Ford	500	182	Running
2	1	9	Kasey Kahne	Dodge Dealers/UAW Dodge	500	305	Running
3	15	07	Clint Bowyer	Jack Daniel's Chevrolet	500		Running
4	23	20	Tony Stewart	The Home Depot Chevrolet	500		Running
5	17	8	Dale Earnhardt Jr.	Budweiser Chevrolet	500	1	Running
6	19	2	Kurt Busch	Miller Lite Dodge	500	2	Running
7	7	12	Ryan Newman	Alltel Dodge	500	2	Running
8	22	43	Bobby Labonte	Cheerios/Betty Crocker Dodge	500		Running
9	20	5	Kyle Busch	Kellogg's/CARQUEST Chevrolet	500	3	Running
10	34	16	Greg Biffle	Dish Network Ford	500		Running
11	25	1	Martin Truex Jr.	Bass Pro Shops/Tracker Boats Chev.	500		Running
12	10	31	Jeff Burton	RCR Chevrolet	500		Running
13	40	18	J.J. Yeley	Interstate Batteries Chevrolet	500		Running
14	36	40	David Stremme	Coors Light Dodge	500		Running
15	29	41	Reed Sorenson	Target Dodge	500		Running
16	13	29	Kevin Harvick	Shell/Pennzoil Platinum Chevrolet	500		Running
17	2	42 #	Juan Pablo Montoya	Texaco/Havoline Dodge	500		Running
18	11	10	Scott Riggs	Valvoline/Stanley Tools Dodge	500		Running
19	18	24	Jeff Gordon	DuPont Chevrolet	500	2	Running
20	24	7	Robby Gordon	Camping World Ford	500	3	Running
21	9	48	Jimmie Johnson	Lowe's Chevrolet	499		Running
22	30	25	Casey Mears	National Guard/GMAC Chevrolet	498		Running
23	16	55	Michael Waltrip	NAPA Auto Parts Toyota	498		Running
24	41	15 #	Paul Menard	Menards/Turtle Wax Ice Chevrolet	498		Running
25	26	21	Bill Elliott	U.S. Air Force Ford	498		Running
26	3	26	Jamie McMurray	IRWIN Industrial Tools Ford	498		Running
27	39	66	Jeff Green	HAAS Automation/Best Buy Chev.	498		Running
28	42	96	Tony Raines	DLP HDTV Chevrolet	498		Running
29	21	19	Elliott Sadler	Dodge Dealers/UAW Dodge	497		Running
30	27	38	David Gilliland	M&M's Ford	497		Running
31	5	22	Dave Blaney	Caterpillar Toyota	496		Running
32	32	45	Kenny Wallace	Wells Fargo Dodge	496		Running
33	14	4	Ward Burton	Miccosukee/Food City/State Chev.	494		Running
34	33	44	Dale Jarrett	UPS Toyota	494		Running
35	43	84 #	AJ Allmendinger	Red Bull Toyota	491		Running
36	35	01	Aric Almirola	U.S. Army Chevrolet	485		Running
37	31	36	Jeremy Mayfield	360 OTC Toyota	481		Running
38	8	88	Ricky Rudd	Snickers Ford	478		Accident
39	12	17	Matt Kenseth	DEWALT Ford	452		Accident
40	28	49	John Andretti	Paralyzed Veterans Dodge	416		Electrical
41	4	6 #	David Ragan	AAA Ford	414		Accident
42	38	70	Johnny Sauter	HAAS Automation/Yellow Chevrolet	280		Running
43	37	11	Denny Hamlin	FedEx Freight Chevrolet	209		Engine

Raybestos Rookie of the Year Contender.

NASCAR NEXTEL CUP SERIES TOP 12

(After 24 Races)

Pos.	Driver	Points	Behind	Change
1	**Jeff Gordon**	3,582	—	—
2	Tony Stewart	3,233	-349	+2
3	Denny Hamlin	3,229	-353	-1
4	Matt Kenseth	3,163	-419	-1
5	Carl Edwards	3,160	-422	—
6	Jimmie Johnson	3,059	-523	—
7	Jeff Burton	3,054	-528	—
8	Kyle Busch	3,024	-558	—
9	Clint Bowyer	2,944	-638	—
10	Kevin Harvick	2,888	-694	—
11	Martin Truex Jr.	2,887	-695	—
12	Kurt Busch	2,879	-703	—

Earnhardt bounced back form a blown engine at Watkins Glen and a 12th-place finish at Michigan to post a fifth-place finish at Bristol. That, however, did him little good in his effort to reach the top 12 in the point standings, as Kurt Busch brought his Dodge home right behind Earnhardt, in sixth place. The five-point loss to Earnhardt was of little consequence to Busch, who remained 12th in the standings with a 158-point cushion and just two races remaining in the Race to the Chase.

"I had a good night, a fun night," Earnhardt said. "I just ran 500 laps at Bristol, so I'm pretty stoked about finishing fifth. We didn't get the win we wanted, but I had a good time.

"All we can do is run as good as we can," Earnhardt continued when asked about his chances of reaching the top 12. "I'll be more ticked off at not winning a race than if I don't make the Chase."

With the victory, Edwards clinched a position in the Chase for the NASCAR NEXTEL Cup, joining Jeff Gordon, Stewart, Denny Hamlin and Matt Kenseth as the first five drivers locked in to compete for the 2007 NASCAR NEXTEL Cup Series championship. ◄►◄►

SHARP AQUOS 500

CALIFORNIA SPEEDWAY

C arl Edwards' win at Bristol Motor Speedway was, of course, a huge emotional boost for him and his team, but its significance could be felt in other ways as well. Although Edwards' position in the point standings did not change with the win — he remained in fifth place — it did give him enough points to clinch a place in the Chase for the NASCAR NEXTEL Cup. More importantly (since there was little chance he would not have made it anyway), the win was worth 10 extra points when the totals were adjusted prior to the final 10 races. At that time, the only thing separating one driver from another would be the 10-point bonuses gained for each victory.

Now, with only two races to go in the Race to the Chase, winning, and therefore picking up the precious points that went along with it, was paramount. Jimmie Johnson and Jeff Gordon led all drivers with four wins each, but in case no one had noticed, the early-season onslaught by Hendrick Motorsports had ended. Ten races had passed since a Hendrick driver won, while Tony Stewart scored three wins, Carl Edwards and Kurt Busch posted two wins apiece, and Denny Hamlin won once. The other two victories during that stretch went to Juan Pablo Montoya and Jamie McMurray, who were not in contention to compete for the championship.

The other factor on the minds of teams that would vie for the title was having positive momentum going into the Chase for the NASCAR NEXTEL Cup. Kurt Busch certainly had it, as did Edwards and Stewart. The rest were doing everything they could to make sure their teams were pointed in the right direction as the final 10-race stretch approached, and that included Johnson.

TOP 10 QUALIFIERS

1. **KURT BUSCH**
   39.474 SEC. 182.399 MPH

2. **JIMMIE JOHNSON**
   39.475 SEC. 182.394 MPH

3. **KASEY KAHNE**
   39.556 SEC. 182.020 MPH

4. **RYAN NEWMAN**
   39.688 SEC. 181.415 MPH

5. **KYLE BUSCH**
   39.704 SEC. 181.342 MPH

6. **ELLIOTT SADLER**
   39.706 SEC. 181.333 MPH

7. **DALE EARNHARDT JR.**
   39.750 SEC. 181.132 MPH

8. **MARTIN TRUEX JR.**
   39.819 SEC. 180.818 MPH

9. **DENNY HAMLIN**
   39.822 SEC. 180.805 MPH

10. **GREG BIFFLE**
    39.866 SEC. 180.605 MPH

A summer slump beginning at Dover in early June and lasting through the race at Indianapolis in August yielded but one top-five finish for the defending champion. The team had also taken a 100-point penalty with the rule violation at Infineon Raceway, and in total, Johnson dropped from second in the point standings to ninth over that mid-summer span.

(Above) Race leader Kyle Busch (5) gets pressure from frontrunners Kurt Busch (2), Dale Earnhardt Jr. (8), Elliott Sadler (19) and Jimmie Johnson (48). Kyle Busch took his first lead on Lap 24 and led a race-high 97 laps on the way to a third-place finish.

(Right) Crews for Kurt Busch (2) and Martin Truex Jr. (1) go at it on pit road under caution. Busch, using the first pit stall by virtue of winning his first pole of the year, led early and finished ninth, good enough to advance to 11th in the point standings.

(Left) Music legend Stevie Wonder, one of several celebrities on hand at the track near Los Angeles, gives the command to start engines.

(Above) California Speedway's wide, smooth racing surface gives drivers a chance to spread out across the track, often resulting in three-wide racing. Here, Denny Hamlin (11) pressures David Ragan (6), the top-finishing rookie, on the inside.

(Left) Jimmie Johnson guides his Chevrolet through Turn 4 in the early running. Johnson, who started on the front row, came on strong at the mid-point of the race and sailed to his series-leading fifth win of the season.

RACE RESULTS

NASCAR NEXTEL Cup Series Race No. 25 — September 2, 2007
California Speedway

SHARP AQUOS 500

Fin. Pos.	Start Pos.	Car No.	Driver	Team	Laps	Laps Led	Status
1	2	48	Jimmie Johnson	Lowe's Chevrolet	250	84	Running
2	19	99	Carl Edwards	Office Depot Ford	250		Running
3	5	5	Kyle Busch	Cheez-it/CARQUEST Chevrolet	250	97	Running
4	15	31	Jeff Burton	RCR Chevrolet	250	1	Running
5	7	8	Dale Earnhardt Jr.	Budweiser Chevrolet	250	15	Running
6	8	1	Martin Truex Jr.	Bass Pro Shops/Tracker Boats Chev.	250	4	Running
7	36	17	Matt Kenseth	R&L Carriers/DEWALT Ford	250		Running
8	17	83	Brian Vickers	Red Bull Toyota	250	3	Running
9	1	2	Kurt Busch	Miller Lite Dodge	250	21	Running
10	3	9	Kasey Kahne	Dodge Dealers/UAW Dodge	250		Running
11	11	43	Bobby Labonte	Cheerios/Totino's Pizza Rolls Dodge	250	4	Running
12	33	6 #	David Ragan	AAA Insurance Ford	250		Running
13	22	20	Tony Stewart	Home Depot Chevrolet	250	12	Running
14	12	29	Kevin Harvick	Shell/Pennzoil Chevrolet	250		Running
15	13	25	Casey Mears	National Guard/GMAC Chevrolet	250	1	Running
16	38	26	Jamie McMurray	Sharp AQUOS Ford	250		Running
17	10	16	Greg Biffle	Aflac Ford	250		Running
18	18	84 #	AJ Allmendinger	Red Bull Toyota	249		Running
19	9	11	Denny Hamlin	FedEx Express Chevrolet	249		Running
20	24	07	Clint Bowyer	DirecTV Chevrolet	249		Running
21	31	41	Reed Sorenson	Target/Memorex Dodge	249		Running
22	16	24	Jeff Gordon	DuPont/Cromax Pro Chevrolet	249		Running
23	32	66	Jeff Green	Best Buy Chevrolet	249		Running
24	20	15 #	Paul Menard	Menards/Johns Manville Chev.	249		Running
25	14	38	David Gilliland	M&M's Ford	249		Running
26	26	21	Bill Elliott	Motorcraft Ford	248	1	Running
27	34	96	Tony Raines	DLP HDTV/Best Buy Chevrolet	248		Running
28	39	45	Kyle Petty	Wells Fargo Dodge	248	1	Running
29	23	18	J.J. Yeley	Interstate Batteries Chevrolet	248		Running
30	41	70	Johnny Sauter	HAAS Automation/Yellow Chev.	248	2	Running
31	40	01	Aric Almirola	U.S. Army Chevrolet	248		Running
32	28	00 #	David Reutimann	Burger King Toyota	247	1	Running
33	42	42 #	Juan Pablo Montoya	Wrigley's Big Red Dodge	247		Running
34	21	40	David Stremme	Target Dodge	245		Running
35	6	19	Elliott Sadler	Dodge Dealers/UAW Dodge	245		Running
36	27	36	Jeremy Mayfield	360 OTC Toyota	229		Accident
37	43	49	John Andretti	Paralyzed Veterans Dodge	203	2	Accident
38	30	22	Dave Blaney	Caterpillar Toyota	201		Engine
39	4	12	Ryan Newman	Kodak Dodge	194	1	Engine
40	37	88	Ricky Rudd	Snickers/Generation Max Ford	179		Accident
41	35	7	Robby Gordon	Road House Grill/Jim Beam Ford	159		Running
42	25	55	Michael Waltrip	NAPA Auto Parts Toyota	38		Accident
43	29	78	Joe Nemechek	Furniture Row Chevrolet	9		Engine

Raybestos Rookie of the Year Contender.

NASCAR NEXTEL CUP SERIES TOP 12

(After 25 Races)

Pos.	Driver	Points	Behind	Change
1	**Jeff Gordon**	**3,679**	—	—
2	Tony Stewart	3,362	-317	—
3	Denny Hamlin	3,335	-344	—
4	Carl Edwards	3,330	-349	+1
5	Matt Kenseth	3,309	-370	-1
6	Jimmie Johnson	3,249	-430	—
7	Jeff Burton	3,219	-460	—
8	Kyle Busch	3,199	-480	—
9	Clint Bowyer	3,047	-632	—
10	Martin Truex Jr.	3,042	-637	+1
11	Kurt Busch	3,022	-657	+1
12	Kevin Harvick	3,009	-670	-2

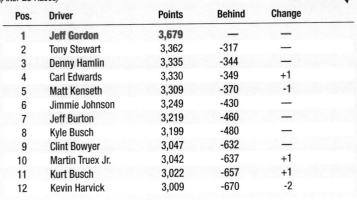

Recent strong performances — three top fives in his last four starts — were a source of encouragement, but there's nothing like a trip to Victory Lane to get the competitive juices flowing in earnest. As far as Johnson was concerned, the Sharp AQUOS 500 at California Speedway, just down the road from his native El Cajon, Calif., was the perfect time and place to do just that.

Johnson got things started by blistering the already hot California asphalt — daily temperatures in Southern California were well above 100 degrees — with a qualifying lap good enough to hike his number to the top of the scoring pylon. It didn't last long. On a hot streak all his own, Kurt Busch stepped up and pushed Johnson to the outside of the front row with his fast lap, while grabbing his first Budweiser Pole Award of the season.

Busch took the early lead on a hot Saturday night in a race that challenged or broke several track records. There were 11 yellow flags over the 250-lap distance, tying the record for cautions. The lead changed hands a record-tying 30 times among a record-breaking 16 different drivers.

After Busch led twice for 21 of the first 23 laps, younger brother Kyle, along with Dale Earnhardt Jr. and Johnson proved to be the top contenders. Kyle Busch led seven times for a race-high 97 laps, while Earnhardt took the point six times for 15 laps and Johnson four times for a total of 84.

Johnson came on strong in the second half of the race, leading 43 consecutive laps before making his final stop for fresh tires and fuel under green with 38 laps to go. By the time the rest of the field cycled through, Johnson was back in front with Kyle Busch in pursuit.

Busch began chipping away at Johnson's lead while running a very high line around the two-mile oval. It was so high in fact, he finally slipped out of the groove and slapped the third-turn wall, pushing the front fender in on his Chevrolet.

Just when Johnson thought he was clear to cruise the rest of the way, Edwards appeared in his mirror. Edwards had been involved in an accident on pit road in the opening laps that dropped him to the back of the field, and he spent the majority of the race fighting his way back. With a handful of laps remaining, he was gunning for his third win of the season and the 10-point bonus that went along with it.

With that, Johnson simply picked up his pace, able to stretch and hold a 1.8-second advantage through the closing laps on the way to his fifth win of the season — and the bonus points that would put him on top of the standings when the Chase for the NASCAR NEXTEL Cup began.

CHEVY ROCK & ROLL 400

RICHMOND INTERNATIONAL RACEWAY

Jimmie Johnson (48) brings the field to the green flag to begin the Chevy Rock & Roll 400. Still riding high after his victory at California, Johnson notched his first pole of the season, the 10th of his career, and went on to post his sixth win of the year.

With the lights on and the sun below the horizon, the crowd estimated at over 112,000 stands in anticipation of 400 laps on the exciting, three-quarter-mile oval in central Virginia.

The Race to the Chase was all but over when the NASCAR NEXTEL Cup Series arrived at Richmond International Raceway for the 26th race of the season, the last before the 2007 Chase for the NASCAR NEXTEL Cup.

Jimmie Johnson's win at California guaranteed the defending champion at least a share of the top position entering the final 10 races. Jeff Gordon, with four wins compared to Johnson's five, would have to win at Richmond just to tie his teammate as the title stretch began.

Gordon, Tony Stewart, Denny Hamlin and Carl Edwards gained guaranteed spots in the championship field after the Bristol race. Matt Kenseth, Jeff Burton, Kyle Busch and Johnson locked up their berths at California, while Clint Bowyer and Martin Truex Jr. needed only to start the race at Richmond to secure their places in the field.

For all of them, the Chevy Rock & Roll 400 was an opportunity to go all out for the win and thereby pick up the important 10 bonus points that would be added to their totals when points were adjusted after the race. In addition, the Richmond event was a chance to build momentum going into the Chase for the NASCAR NEXTEL Cup.

That left three drivers to compete for the two available positions that were not already sewn up. Kurt Busch, 11th in the point standings entering the race, needed to finish 36th or better to nail down a spot, while 12th-place Kevin Harvick needed at least a 32nd-place finish to remain in the top 12.

The odd man out — and the only other driver with a chance to make it — was Dale Earnhardt Jr., 128 points behind Harvick and 141 behind Busch. Earnhardt's mission was clear: He needed the best finish possible — preferably a win while leading the most laps — and hope that either Busch or Harvick met with some sort of disaster that would place them at or near the bottom of the finishing order.

TOP 10 QUALIFIERS

1. **JIMMIE JOHNSON**
   21.378 SEC. 126.298 MPH

2. **JEFF GORDON**
   21.541 SEC. 125.342 MPH

3. **KYLE BUSCH**
   21.543 SEC. 125.331 MPH

4. **RYAN NEWMAN**
   21.557 SEC. 125.249 MPH

5. **DENNY HAMLIN**
   21.585 SEC. 125.087 MPH

6. **CARL EDWARDS**
   21.597 SEC. 125.017 MPH

7. **TONY STEWART**
   21.612 SEC. 124.931 MPH

8. **DAVID RAGAN**
   21.617 SEC. 124.902 MPH

9. **ELLIOTT SADLER**
   21.645 SEC. 124.740 MPH

10. **BOBBY LABONTE**
    21.650 SEC. 124.711 MPH

Johnson, with a ton of momentum after his convincing win at California, made his intentions clear upon arriving at Richmond by grabbing his first Budweiser Pole Award of the year with a lap nearly a full mile per hour faster than his closest competitor, Jeff Gordon. Title contenders Kyle Busch, Hamlin, Edwards and Stewart all qualified in the top 10 as well, indicating that each had designs on adding to their victory total before the evening was over.

Gordon established himself at the drop of the green flag, jumping to the early lead and holding it for most of the first half of the race. Johnson, Stewart and Hamlin ran solidly among the top 10, where Harvick, Kurt Busch and Earnhardt Jr. joined them, all showing strength and speed as the event entered its final 200 laps.

Although Earnhardt Jr. did not lead a lap, his Chevrolet was stout and allowed him to consistently challenge Stewart and Gordon in the top five. And when Ryan Newman spun on Lap 242, a glimmer of hope ignited for the thousands of fans dressed in red.

Carl Edwards (99) challenges Jeff Gordon (24), who led four times for a race-high 191 laps, on the inside. Edwards took Gordon's lead away before the halfway point, but his engine let go 15 laps later, sending him to the garage in 42nd place.

(Above) Dale Earnhardt Jr. (8) is squarely in the middle of the action, dicing with Jeff Gordon on his right and Tony Stewart on his left. Earnhardt put together a stirring charge among the top five for most of the race before his engine failed six laps short of the finish line.

(Right) Johnny Sauter (70) had a great run at Richmond that ended with a career-best fifth-place finish.

Caught in the accident sparked by Newman's spin was Kurt Busch, with damage to the rear of his Dodge, and Harvick, whose evasive maneuvers sent him flying across the frontstretch grass, leaving his Chevrolet with a snout full of mud and an engine spewing hot water and steam.

A red flag to allow cleanup on the track gave the Busch and Harvick crews time to evaluate the damage — and Harvick's car a chance to cool — and by the time the race resumed, both cars were deemed fit to return to action with minimal repairs. While fighting their way back into the top 10, both drivers received word that enough cars had fallen away to lock them into the top 12 in the standings.

Johnson's Impala SS, meanwhile, was receiving the magical touch from the hands of crew chief Chad Knaus — the kind that can take a fifth-place car and make it a hands-down winner. By the time the event reached the three-quarter mark, Johnson was in control, leading 102 of the final 104 laps, including the last 60, on the way to his sixth win of the season and his second in as many weeks.

(Above) Chase for the NASCAR NEXTEL Cup competitors celebrate their accomplishment by spraying photographers and reporters with victory champagne. In 10 short weeks, one of the 12 would be celebrating a championship.

(Left) With all the focus on Jimmie Johnson and the rest of the championship field, David Ragan's brilliant run in the No. 6 Ford almost went unnoticed. Ragan finished third in the event, a career best, and tightened his race with Juan Pablo Montoya for Raybestos Rookie of the Year honors.

RACE RESULTS

CHEVY ROCK & ROLL 400

Fin. Pos.	Start Pos.	Car No.	Driver	Team	Laps	Laps Led	Status
1	1	48	Jimmie Johnson	Lowe's Chevrolet	400	104	Running
2	7	20	Tony Stewart	The Home Depot Chevrolet	400	27	Running
3	8	6 #	David Ragan	AAA Ford	400		Running
4	2	24	Jeff Gordon	DuPont/Nicorette Chevrolet	400	191	Running
5	35	70	Johnny Sauter	Radioactive Energy Drink Chev.	400		Running
6	5	11	Denny Hamlin	FedEx Express Chevrolet	400	17	Running
7	13	29	Kevin Harvick	Shell/Pennzoil Chevrolet	400		Running
8	17	9	Kasey Kahne	Dodge Dealers/UAW Dodge	400		Running
9	14	2	Kurt Busch	Miller Lite Dodge	400		Running
10	36	18	J.J. Yeley	Interstate Batteries Chevrolet	400		Running
11	4	12	Ryan Newman	Alltel Dodge	400	33	Running
12	20	07	Clint Bowyer	Jack Daniel's Chevrolet	400	4	Running
13	24	00 #	David Reutimann	Burger King Toyota	400		Running
14	18	17	Matt Kenseth	DEWALT Ford	400		Running
15	40	1	Martin Truex Jr.	Bass Pro Shops/Tracker Boats Chev.	400		Running
16	10	43	Bobby Labonte	Cheerios/Labonte's 500th Dodge	400		Running
17	23	25	Casey Mears	National Guard/GMAC Chevrolet	400	6	Running
18	11	31	Jeff Burton	AT&T Mobility Chevrolet	400		Running
19	26	40	David Stremme	Energizer Dodge	400		Running
20	3	5	Kyle Busch	Kellogg's/CARQUEST Chevrolet	400		Running
21	19	01	Mark Martin	U.S. Army Chevrolet	400		Running
22	41	38	David Gilliland	M&M's Ford	400		Running
23	27	84 #	AJ Allmendinger	Red Bull Toyota	400		Running
24	28	83	Brian Vickers	Red Bull Toyota	400		Running
25	30	45	Kyle Petty	Marathon Motor Oil Dodge	400	2	Running
26	38	15 #	Paul Menard	Menards/PEAK Chevrolet	399	1	Running
27	9	19	Elliott Sadler	Dodge Dealers/UAW Dodge	399		Running
28	22	88	Kenny Wallace	Snickers Ford	399		Running
29	42	21	Bill Elliott	U.S. Air Force Ford	395		Running
30	21	8	Dale Earnhardt Jr.	Budweiser/Elvis Chevrolet	394		Engine
31	32	44	Dale Jarrett	UPS Toyota	394		Running
32	25	41	Reed Sorenson	Target Dodge	393		Running
33	33	66	Jeff Green	Best Buy Chevrolet	380		Running
34	29	22	Dave Blaney	Caterpillar Toyota	353		Running
35	34	96	Tony Raines	DLP HDTV Chevrolet	345		Running
36	39	7	Robby Gordon	Jim Beam Black Ford	335		Accident
37	43	49	John Andretti	LifeLock Dodge	299		Engine
38	12	26	Jamie McMurray	Crown Royal Ford	292		Accident
39	37	16	Greg Biffle	Dish Network/voomhd.com Ford	261		Trans.
40	16	10	Scott Riggs	Valvoline/Stanley Tools Dodge	251		Running
41	15	42 #	Juan Pablo Montoya	Texaco/Havoline Dodge	241		Accident
42	6	99	Carl Edwards	Office Depot Ford	182	15	Engine
43	31	78	Joe Nemechek	Furniture Row Chevrolet	130		Accident

Raybestos Rookie of the Year Contender.

NASCAR NEXTEL CUP SERIES TOP 12
(After 26 Races)

Pos.	Driver	Points	Behind	Change
1	**Jeff Gordon**	**3849**	—	—
2	Tony Stewart	3537	-312	—
3	Denny Hamlin	3490	-359	—
4	Jimmie Johnson	3439	-410	+2
5	Matt Kenseth	3430	-419	—
6	Carl Edwards	3372	-477	-2
7	Jeff Burton	3328	-521	—
8	Kyle Busch	3302	-547	—
9	Clint Bowyer	3179	-670	—
10	Kurt Busch	3160	-689	+1
11	Martin Truex Jr.	3160	-689	-1
12	Kevin Harvick	3155	-694	—

"I'm upset for my team. ... They deserve better."

Earnhardt fought valiantly with Gordon and Stewart as the trio diced back and forth for second place behind Johnson. With just six laps to go, however, a telltale trail of smoke appeared as Earnhardt pulled to the apron with yet another blown engine, ending his charge in bitter disappointment.

"I'm upset for my team," Earnhardt said, clearly frustrated with his fifth engine failure of the season. "They deserve better."

Edwards suffered a similar fate when his motor gave up while leading in his bid for another win. Bowyer, the only driver without a win going into the title hunt, was disappointed as well. Battling for the lead with hometown favorite Hamlin, the two cars touched, sending Bowyer into a spin. He rallied to finish in 12th place, while Hamlin drove to a sixth-place finish. ▰▰▰

2007 CHASE FOR
THE NASCAR NEXTEL CUP INTRO

With the checkered flag at Richmond, the field for the 2007 Chase for the NASCAR NEXTEL Cup was set. For the first time, 12 drivers were included in the title hunt, up from 10 as was the case in the previous three years since the format's inception in 2004.

The group included five former champions — Jimmie Johnson, Jeff Gordon, Tony Stewart, Kurt Busch and Matt Kenseth — with Johnson and Kenseth joining the field for the fourth time in as many years. Gordon, Stewart and Busch were making their third appearances, while Kyle Busch, Denny Hamlin, Jeff Burton, Kevin Harvick and Carl Edwards became title contenders for the second time. Martin Truex Jr. and Clint Bowyer rounded out the field, making their first attempts to win the NASCAR NEXTEL Cup Series championship.

One thing became evident when looking at how the field shaped up: changes in the point system initiated this season with an increased emphasis on winning had done its job. Of the 26 victories posted to this point, 23 were accounted for in the list of 12 title contenders. The importance of those wins became clear when ranking the field. Each of the drivers had their point totals adjusted to an even 5000. Then, 10 points were added based on the number of victories attained by each driver.

Johnson topped the list by virtue of his series-leading six victories, the last two coming consecutively at California and Richmond as the Race to the Chase drew to a close. Tied with Jeff Gordon at four wins each to that point, Johnson gave himself a huge boost with his recent flurry and started the final 10 races with a 20-point lead on Gordon, thirty over three-time winner Stewart, and 40 ahead of two-time winners Edwards and Kurt Busch.

With one win each, Hamlin, Truex Jr., Kenseth, Kyle Busch, Burton and Harvick all were 50 points down to Johnson going into the final 10 events, while Bowyer, the only driver in the field not to have reached the winner's circle, faced a 60-point deficit as he began the Chase for the NASCAR NEXTEL Cup.

Certainly, any of the 12 were worthy contenders and all possessed the talent and ability to accomplish their goal. But when the checkered flag waved at Homestead-Miami Speedway after 10 more races, only one would be able to claim the title 2007 NASCAR NEXTEL Cup Series Champion.

CHASE FOR THE NASCAR NEXTEL CUP 2007 QUALIFYING FIELD

1 Jimmie Johnson: 5060
Starts: 26 Wins: 6 T-5: 14 T-10: 16 DNF: 4

2 Jeff Gordon: 5040
Starts: 26 Wins: 4 T-5: 15 T-10: 21 DNF: 1

3 Tony Stewart: 5030
Starts: 26 Wins: 3 T-5: 9 T-10: 18 DNF: 3

4 Carl Edwards: 5020
Starts: 26 Wins: 2 T-5: 7 T-10: 11 DNF: 2

5 Kurt Busch: 5020
Starts: 26 Wins: 2 T-5: 5 T-10: 10 DNF: 2

6 Denny Hamlin: 5010
Starts: 26 Wins: 1 T-5: 10 T-10: 15 DNF: 1

7 Martin Truex Jr.: 5010
Starts: 26 Wins: 1 T-5: 5 T-10: 10 DNF: 2

8 Matt Kenseth: 5010
Starts: 26 Wins: 1 T-5: 8 T-10: 16 DNF: 2

9 Kyle Busch: 5010
Starts: 26 Wins: 1 T-5: 6 T-10: 14 DNF: 1

10 Jeff Burton: 5010
Starts: 26 Wins: 1 T-5: 7 T-10: 12 DNF: 2

11 Kevin Harvick: 5010
Starts: 26 Wins: 1 T-5: 4 T-0: 11 DNF: 0

12 Clint Bowyer: 5000
Starts: 26 Wins: 0 T-5: 2 T-10: 12 DNF: 0

Race #	Location	Start	Finish	Status	Points Pos.
1	Daytona	21	39	Accident	37
2	California	23	3	Running	15
3	Las Vegas	23	1	Running	4
4	Atlanta	3	1	Running	4
5	Bristol	6	16	Running	3
6	Martinsville	20	1	Running	3
7	Texas	3	38	Accident	4
8	Phoenix	5	4	Running	4
9	Talladega	8	2	Running	4
10	Richmond	4	1	Running	2
11	Darlington	12	3	Running	2
12	Charlotte	21	10	Running	2
13	Dover	27	15	Running	2
14	Pocono	7	42	Running	4
15	Michigan	2	19	Running	3
16	Infineon Raceway	42	17	Running	5
17	New Hampshire	10	5	Running	4
18	Daytona	4	10	Running	4
19	Chicagoland	8	37	Accident	7
20	Indianapolis	19	39	Accident	9
21	Pocono	7	5	Running	7
22	Watkins Glen	7	3	Running	7
23	Michigan	7	3	Running	6
24	Bristol	9	21	Running	6
25	California	2	1	Running	6
26	Richmond	1	1	Running	4

Jimmie Johnson

Jeff Gordon

Race #	Location	Start	Finish	Status	Points Pos.
1	Daytona	42	10	Running	8
2	California	1	2	Running	3
3	Las Vegas	36	2	Running	2
4	Atlanta	5	12	Running	2
5	Bristol	1	3	Running	1
6	Martinsville	3	2	Running	1
7	Texas	1	4	Running	1
8	Phoenix	1	1	Running	1
9	Talladega	1	1	Running	1
10	Richmond	1	4	Running	1
11	Darlington	10	1	Running	1
12	Charlotte	32	41	Accident	1
13	Dover	6	9	Running	1
14	Pocono	18	1	Running	1
15	Michigan	6	9	Running	1
16	Infineon Raceway	41	7	Running	1
17	New Hampshire	8	2	Running	1
18	Daytona	1	5	Running	1
19	Chicagoland	11	9	Running	1
20	Indianapolis	21	3	Running	1
21	Pocono	11	4	Running	1
22	Watkins Glen	1	9	Running	1
23	Michigan	1	27	Running	1
24	Bristol	18	19	Running	1
25	California	16	22	Running	1
26	Richmond	2	4	Running	1

Tony Stewart

3

Race #	Location	Start	Finish	Status	Points Pos.
1	Daytona	3	43	Accident	39
2	California	11	8	Running	21
3	Las Vegas	25	7	Running	13
4	Atlanta	13	2	Running	6
5	Bristol	4	35	Running	12
6	Martinsville	7	7	Running	8
7	Texas	9	25	Running	9
8	Phoenix	9	2	Running	7
9	Talladega	32	28	Accident	6
10	Richmond	22	8	Running	7
11	Darlington	26	6	Running	6
12	Charlotte	14	6	Running	6
13	Dover	30	40	Accident	7
14	Pocono	6	5	Running	6
15	Michigan	41	3	Running	7
16	Infineon Raceway	5	6	Running	6
17	New Hampshire	14	12	Running	6
18	Daytona	6	38	Running	7
19	Chicagoland	19	1	Running	6
20	Indianapolis	14	1	Running	5
21	Pocono	24	6	Running	5
22	Watkins Glen	5	1	Running	4
23	Michigan	35	10	Running	4
24	Bristol	23	4	Running	2
25	California	22	13	Running	2
26	Richmond	7	2	Running	2

Carl Edwards

4

Race #	Location	Start	Finish	Status	Points Pos.
1	Daytona	14	23	Running	24
2	California	21	29	Running	26
3	Las Vegas	13	6	Running	17
4	Atlanta	14	7	Running	10
5	Bristol	32	12	Running	10
6	Martinsville	9	17	Running	9
7	Texas	10	12	Running	8
8	Phoenix	28	11	Running	8
9	Talladega	16	42	Engine	12
10	Richmond	2	12	Running	11
11	Darlington	4	5	Running	10
12	Charlotte	39	15	Running	8
13	Dover	5	3	Running	6
14	Pocono	32	14	Running	7
15	Michigan	12	1	Running	6
16	Infineon Raceway	15	18	Running	7
17	New Hampshire	22	13	Running	7
18	Daytona	7	4	Running	6
19	Chicagoland	25	3	Running	5
20	Indianapolis	35	18	Running	6
21	Pocono	29	21	Running	6
22	Watkins Glen	6	8	Running	5
23	Michigan	13	7	Running	5
24	Bristol	6	1	Running	5
25	California	19	2	Running	4
26	Richmond	6	42	Engine	6

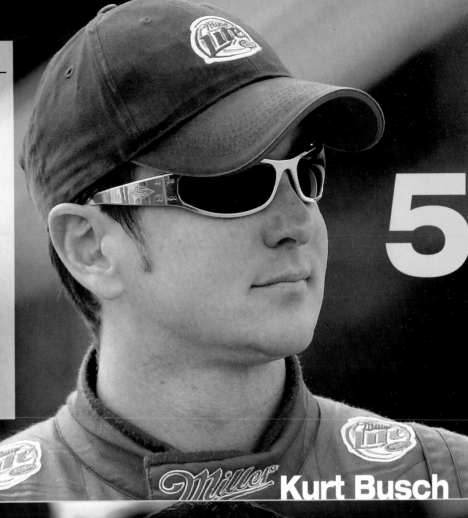

Race #	Location	Start	Finish	Status	Points Pos.
1	Daytona	4	41	Running	36
2	California	18	7	Running	19
3	Las Vegas	10	26	Running	23
4	Atlanta	17	11	Running	20
5	Bristol	42	29	Running	20
6	Martinsville	12	12	Running	17
7	Texas	17	11	Running	15
8	Phoenix	6	18	Running	13
9	Talladega	26	3	Running	10
10	Richmond	33	5	Running	9
11	Darlington	18	12	Running	7
12	Charlotte	2	32	Accident	9
13	Dover	12	42	Parked	17
14	Pocono	27	16	Running	16
15	Michigan	10	25	Running	16
16	Infineon Raceway	14	22	Running	16
17	New Hampshire	2	21	Running	15
18	Daytona	16	3	Running	15
19	Chicagoland	35	6	Running	14
20	Indianapolis	6	11	Running	13
21	Pocono	2	1	Running	12
22	Watkins Glen	13	11	Running	12
23	Michigan	15	1	Running	12
24	Bristol	19	6	Running	12
25	California	1	9	Running	11
26	Richmond	14	9	Running	10

Kurt Busch

5

Denny Hamlin

Race #	Location	Start	Finish	Status	Points Pos.
1	Daytona	9	28	Running	28
2	California	17	11	Running	18
3	Las Vegas	17	3	Running	8
4	Atlanta	30	19	Running	8
5	Bristol	10	14	Running	9
6	Martinsville	1	3	Running	6
7	Texas	7	9	Running	5
8	Phoenix	3	3	Running	5
9	Talladega	3	21	Running	5
10	Richmond	6	3	Running	4
11	Darlington	7	2	Running	4
12	Charlotte	6	9	Running	4
13	Dover	29	4	Running	4
14	Pocono	2	6	Running	3
15	Michigan	7	14	Running	2
16	Infineon Raceway	36	10	Running	2
17	New Hampshire	11	1	Running	2
18	Daytona	2	43	Running	2
19	Chicagoland	13	17	Running	2
20	Indianapolis	10	22	Running	2
21	Pocono	6	3	Running	2
22	Watkins Glen	2	2	Running	2
23	Michigan	8	5	Running	2
24	Bristol	37	43	Engine	3
25	California	9	19	Running	3
26	Richmond	5	6	Running	3

6

Martin Truex Jr.

Race #	Location	Start	Finish	Status	Points Pos.
1	Daytona	13	29	Running	27
2	California	7	42	Engine	38
3	Las Vegas	26	12	Running	27
4	Atlanta	18	8	Running	22
5	Bristol	13	37	Running	25
6	Martinsville	15	29	Running	24
7	Texas	24	7	Running	19
8	Phoenix	7	20	Running	20
9	Talladega	37	10	Running	18
10	Richmond	8	28	Running	20
11	Darlington	25	11	Running	18
12	Charlotte	31	16	Running	16
13	Dover	26	1	Running	12
14	Pocono	3	3	Running	11
15	Michigan	8	2	Running	10
16	Infineon Raceway	18	24	Running	11
17	New Hampshire	9	3	Running	9
18	Daytona	10	13	Running	10
19	Chicagoland	2	39	Engine	11
20	Indianapolis	33	12	Running	11
21	Pocono	13	22	Running	11
22	Watkins Glen	12	6	Running	11
23	Michigan	14	2	Running	11
24	Bristol	25	11	Running	11
25	California	8	6	Running	10
26	Richmond	40	15	Running	11

Matt Kenseth

Race #	Location	Start	Finish	Status	Points Pos.
1	Daytona	10	27	Running	40
2	California	25	1	Running	12
3	Las Vegas	37	4	Running	5
4	Atlanta	21	3	Running	5
5	Bristol	38	11	Running	4
6	Martinsville	33	10	Running	4
7	Texas	4	2	Running	3
8	Phoenix	17	5	Running	3
9	Talladega	17	14	Running	3
10	Richmond	28	10	Running	3
11	Darlington	31	7	Running	3
12	Charlotte	5	12	Running	3
13	Dover	17	5	Running	3
14	Pocono	24	9	Running	2
15	Michigan	26	42	Accident	4
16	Infineon Raceway	27	34	Running	3
17	New Hampshire	30	9	Running	3
18	Daytona	3	8	Running	3
19	Chicagoland	10	2	Running	3
20	Indianapolis	31	10	Running	3
21	Pocono	37	14	Running	3
22	Watkins Glen	3	12	Running	3
23	Michigan	21	4	Running	3
24	Bristol	12	39	Accident	4
25	California	36	7	Running	5
26	Richmond	18	14	Running	5

Kyle Busch

Race #	Location	Start	Finish	Status	Points Pos.
1	Daytona	8	24	Running	23
2	California	12	9	Running	9
3	Las Vegas	12	9	Running	7
4	Atlanta	8	32	Running	14
5	Bristol	20	1	Running	6
6	Martinsville	14	4	Running	5
7	Texas	5	37	Running	7
8	Phoenix	24	7	Running	6
9	Talladega	13	37	Accident	8
10	Richmond	34	2	Running	6
11	Darlington	36	37	Running	11
12	Charlotte	17	30	Running	11
13	Dover	19	17	Running	10
14	Pocono	4	8	Running	10
15	Michigan	3	6	Running	11
16	Infineon Raceway	24	8	Running	10
17	New Hampshire	18	11	Running	10
18	Daytona	11	2	Running	8
19	Chicagoland	6	13	Running	9
20	Indianapolis	18	4	Running	8
21	Pocono	3	12	Running	8
22	Watkins Glen	8	7	Running	8
23	Michigan	6	13	Running	8
24	Bristol	20	9	Running	8
25	California	5	3	Running	8
26	Richmond	3	20	Running	9

Jeff Burton

Race #	Location	Start	Finish	Status	Points Pos.
1	Daytona	7	3	Running	3
2	California	8	4	Running	2
3	Las Vegas	5	15	Running	3
4	Atlanta	32	4	Running	3
5	Bristol	29	2	Running	2
6	Martinsville	19	6	Running	2
7	Texas	2	1	Running	2
8	Phoenix	31	13	Running	2
9	Talladega	42	34	Running	2
10	Richmond	39	43	Engine	5
11	Darlington	34	10	Running	5
12	Charlotte	25	24	Running	5
13	Dover	9	12	Running	5
14	Pocono	10	13	Running	5
15	Michigan	9	24	Running	5
16	Infineon Raceway	6	3	Running	4
17	New Hampshire	26	7	Running	5
18	Daytona	5	16	Running	5
19	Chicagoland	23	7	Running	4
20	Indianapolis	7	8	Running	4
21	Pocono	18	11	Running	4
22	Watkins Glen	4	40	Accident	6
23	Michigan	19	14	Running	7
24	Bristol	10	12	Running	7
25	California	15	4	Running	7
26	Richmond	11	18	Running	7

Kevin Harvick

Race #	Location	Start	Finish	Status	Points Pos.
1	Daytona	34	1	Running	1
2	California	4	17	Running	4
3	Las Vegas	20	27	Running	6
4	Atlanta	36	25	Running	7
5	Bristol	40	4	Running	5
6	Martinsville	6	41	Running	10
7	Texas	11	29	Running	14
8	Phoenix	8	10	Running	11
9	Talladega	41	6	Running	9
10	Richmond	27	7	Running	8
11	Darlington	9	17	Running	8
12	Charlotte	27	21	Running	7
13	Dover	18	20	Running	9
14	Pocono	19	11	Running	9
15	Michigan	19	7	Running	8
16	Infineon Raceway	22	2	Running	8
17	New Hampshire	7	8	Running	8
18	Daytona	8	34	Running	9
19	Chicagoland	14	4	Running	8
20	Indianapolis	20	7	Running	7
21	Pocono	23	17	Running	9
22	Watkins Glen	9	36	Running	10
23	Michigan	28	15	Running	10
24	Bristol	13	16	Running	10
25	California	12	14	Running	12
26	Richmond	13	7	Running	12

Clint Bowyer

Race #	Location	Start	Finish	Status	Points Pos.
1	Daytona	11	18	Running	17
2	California	6	6	Running	6
3	Las Vegas	16	36	Running	18
4	Atlanta	15	6	Running	9
5	Bristol	18	8	Running	8
6	Martinsville	21	11	Running	7
7	Texas	8	16	Running	6
8	Phoenix	12	22	Running	9
9	Talladega	40	35	Running	11
10	Richmond	20	9	Running	10
11	Darlington	1	9	Running	9
12	Charlotte	41	29	Running	10
13	Dover	15	8	Running	8
14	Pocono	5	10	Running	8
15	Michigan	11	16	Running	9
16	Infineon Raceway	10	4	Running	9
17	New Hampshire	20	37	Running	11
18	Daytona	12	7	Running	11
19	Chicagoland	7	10	Running	10
20	Indianapolis	26	13	Running	10
21	Pocono	15	8	Running	10
22	Watkins Glen	11	16	Running	9
23	Michigan	9	17	Running	9
24	Bristol	15	3	Running	9
25	California	24	20	Running	9
26	Richmond	20	12	Running	9

SYLVANIA 300

NEW HAMPSHIRE INTERNATIONAL SPEEDWAY

Clint Bowyer had to be feeling a little left out. Sure, he was in the elite group of 12 who distinguished themselves enough to earn a place in the Chase for the NASCAR NEXTEL Cup. He finished the season's first 26 races in ninth place in the standings, ahead of former champion Kurt Busch, Martin Truex Jr. and his own teammate, veteran Kevin Harvick. He won his first Budweiser Pole Award at, of all places, treacherous Darlington Raceway earlier in the season, and he had proven his ability to run well just about anywhere with top-five finishes at Phoenix, Indianapolis, California, Texas, Infineon Raceway and Bristol over his still-brief career of 63 starts.

Still, with the flurry of media attention surrounding the group of contenders as the Chase for the NASCAR NEXTEL Cup approached, he could not escape the inevitable, haunting, constant reminders that he was the only driver in the field yet to post a victory — a fact that put him alone at the bottom of the standings with a 60-point deficit to overcome.

"I read all the magazines and articles, and it's fuel for the fire," Bowyer said. "It makes you want to win and run up front and prove to the media and everybody that you belong here."

Making matters worse for Bowyer was that only days before, at Richmond International Raceway, he felt he let one get away when his car got out from under him while leading, a momentary glitch that took him from winning contention.

"You ask yourself the same question every time you get close and you make a mistake and come up a little bit short," Bowyer said when asked if he questioned when he would finally win. "It's definitely frustrating."

Bowyer, the quiet, apparently laid-back yet fiercely competitive 28-year-old, carried all that baggage with him to New Hampshire International Speedway, where he led the field under the green flag to begin 300 laps on the flat, 1.058-mile oval. Two hours, 52 minutes and 23 seconds later, Bowyer flung that old baggage away with the veracity of an overworked airline employee after completely thrashing everyone in one of the most heavy-handed smack-downs anyone cared to remember.

So excited — and relieved — was Bowyer that a post-race burnout annihilated what remained of his RCR engine, forcing him to arrive in Victory Lane on foot. No worries. Bowyer had suddenly transformed himself from near afterthought to title contender, fourth in the standings and a mere 15 points away from the No. 1 position in one satisfying afternoon.

The second-year driver of Richard Childress' No. 07 Chevrolet led 222 of the event's 300 laps (74 percent), was never passed on the race track — only while pitting for tires and fuel — and finished a zip code ahead of Jeff Gordon and Tony Stewart with a nearly 6.5-second margin of victory. Both drivers joked afterward that they couldn't catch up to the winner even on the cool-down lap to offer a congratulatory wave before the burnouts began.

"He was dominant. He was so strong," Gordon said admiringly. "Once he got the lead, man, wow. It was incredible. … Today was a real statement for him."

"The only thing that could have beaten us was ourselves," Bowyer said. "I knew I had a car to beat when I came off the first corner. I was loose, but I had the feeling you need here (at New Hampshire).

"This is a big deal, very important to me and a lot of people. … We were the only ones in the Chase that hadn't won … but you can't say that now."

Chase for the NASCAR NEXTEL Cup contenders filled the top seven positions in the finishing order. Gordon's runner-up effort erased the 20-point deficit he had to Jimmie Johnson, leaving the two Hendrick drivers tied at the top of the standings after Johnson finished sixth.

1. **CLINT BOWYER**
   29.206 SEC. 130.4128 MPH

2. **MARTIN TRUEX JR.**
   29.241 SEC. 130.255 MPH

3. **KURT BUSCH**
   29.296 SEC. 130.011 MPH

4. **JIMMIE JOHNSON**
   29.344 SEC. 129.798 MPH

5. **RYAN NEWMAN**
   29.361 SEC. 129.723 MPH

6. **TONY STEWART**
   29.371 SEC. 129.679 MPH

7. **ELLIOTT SADLER**
   29.371 SEC. 129.679 MPH

8. **KEVIN HARVICK**
   29.443 SEC. 129.362 MPH

9. **GREG BIFFLE**
   29.474 SEC. 129.226 MPH

10. **DAVE BLANEY**
    29.488 SEC. 129.164 MPH

"I KNEW I HAD A CAR TO BEAT when I came off the first corner. … This is a big deal, very important to me and a lot of people.

CLINT BOWYER comments on his first NASCAR NEXTEL Cup Series win.

Chase for the NASCAR NEXTEL Cup competitors are positioned side by side in the New Hampshire garage, ready and waiting for a chance to take their battle to the track.

Stewart's third-place result lopped 20 points off of the gap between him and the top position, bringing the two-time champion to within 10 of the Hendrick duo. Behind Bowyer was Kyle Busch, whose fourth-place finish cut his debt from 50 points to 35, with Truex Jr. just five points away from Busch after a strong, fifth-place showing in the race.

(Above) Jimmie Johnson's crew sends him back into action after a quick stop on pit road. Although he started fourth, Johnson was not able to lead in the race and finished sixth, leaving him in a tie with Jeff Gordon at the top of the point standings.

(Right) Clint Bowyer declares victory while his team celebrates behind him. His first NASCAR NEXTEL Cup Series win came in his 64th career start.

(Left) Martin Truex Jr. (1) is chased by Kurt Busch (2) in the early going. Truex qualified on the front row next to pole-winner Clint Bowyer and kept himself in the middle of the championship hunt with a solid fifth-place finish.

RACE RESULTS

SYLVANIA 300

Fin. Pos.	Start Pos.	Car No.	Driver	Team	Laps	Laps Led	Status
1	1	07	Clint Bowyer	Jack Daniel's Chevrolet	300	222	Running
2	18	24	Jeff Gordon	DuPont Chevrolet	300		Running
3	6	20	Tony Stewart	Home Depot Chevrolet	300	39	Running
4	12	5	Kyle Busch	CARQUEST/Kellogg's Chevrolet	300	21	Running
5	2	1	Martin Truex Jr.	Bass Pro Shops/Tracker Chevrolet	300	1	Running
6	4	48	Jimmie Johnson	Lowe's Chevrolet	300		Running
7	30	17	Matt Kenseth	DEWALT Ford	300		Running
8	15	25	Casey Mears	National Guard/GMAC Chevrolet	300	1	Running
9	5	12	Ryan Newman	Mobil 1 Dodge	300	2	Running
10	21	18	J.J. Yeley	Interstate Batteries Chevrolet	300		Running
11	22	26	Jamie McMurray	Crown Royal Ford	300		Running
12	11	99	Carl Edwards	Marriott Vacation Club Ford	300		Running
13	9	16	Greg Biffle	Lumber Liquidators Ford	300		Running
14	13	41	Reed Sorenson	Target Dodge	300	9	Running
15	14	11	Denny Hamlin	FedEx Express Chevrolet	300		Running
16	19	8	Dale Earnhardt Jr.	Budweiser Chevrolet	300	4	Running
17	8	29	Kevin Harvick	Shell/Pennzoil Chevrolet	299		Running
18	23	31	Jeff Burton	AT&T Mobility Chevrolet	299		Running
19	38	6 #	David Ragan	AAA Ford	299		Running
20	25	9	Kasey Kahne	Dodge Dealers/UAW Dodge	299		Running
21	24	96	Tony Raines	DLP HDTV Chevrolet	299		Running
22	26	43	Bobby Labonte	Cheerios/Trix/Lucky Dodge	299		Running
23	31	42 #	Juan Pablo Montoya	Texaco/Havoline Dodge	299		Running
24	17	15 #	Paul Menard	Menards/Sylvania Chevrolet	299		Running
25	3	2	Kurt Busch	Miller Lite Dodge	299		Running
26	20	00 #	David Reutimann	Burger King Toyota	299		Running
27	33	66	Jeff Green	Best Buy Chevrolet	298		Running
28	36	70	Johnny Sauter	Yellow Transportation Chevrolet	298		Running
29	37	78	Joe Nemechek	Furniture Row Chevrolet	298		Running
30	34	21	Ken Schrader	Little Debbie Ford	297	1	Running
31	40	7	Robby Gordon	Jim Beam Ford	297		Running
32	29	10	Scott Riggs	Stanley Tools/Valvoline Dodge	297		Running
33	39	84 #	AJ Allmendinger	Red Bull Toyota	297		Running
34	27	88	Kenny Wallace	Snickers Ford	296		Running
35	10	22	Dave Blaney	Caterpillar Toyota	296		Running
36	16	01	Regan Smith	Principal Financial Chevrolet	296		Running
37	41	45	Kyle Petty	Victory Junction Gang Dodge	296		Running
38	7	19	Elliott Sadler	Dodge Dealers/UAW Dodge	295		Running
39	35	38	David Gilliland	M&M's Ford	295		Running
40	43	98	Boris Said	Valvoline Dodge	292		Running
41	28	4	Ward Burton	State /Lucas Oil Chevrolet	284		Running
42	32	40	David Stremme	Energizer Dodge	273		Running
43	42	83	Brian Vickers	Red Bull Toyota	265		Running

Raybestos Rookie of the Year Contender.

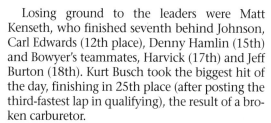

NASCAR NEXTEL CUP SERIES TOP 12

(With 9 Races Remaining)

Pos.	Driver	Points	Behind	Change
1	Jimmie Johnson	5210	—	—
2	Jeff Gordon	5210	—	—
3	Tony Stewart	5200	-10	—
4	Clint Bowyer	5195	-15	+8
5	Kyle Busch	5175	-35	+4
6	Martin Truex Jr.	5170	-40	+1
7	Matt Kenseth	5156	-54	+1
8	Carl Edwards	5147	-63	-4
9	Denny Hamlin	5128	-82	-3
10	Kevin Harvick	5122	-88	+1
11	Jeff Burton	5119	-91	-1
12	Kurt Busch	5108	-102	-7

Losing ground to the leaders were Matt Kenseth, who finished seventh behind Johnson, Carl Edwards (12th place), Denny Hamlin (15th) and Bowyer's teammates, Harvick (17th) and Jeff Burton (18th). Kurt Busch took the biggest hit of the day, finishing in 25th place (after posting the third-fastest lap in qualifying), the result of a broken carburetor.

The point spread among the 12 contenders increased from 60 to 102, but no one had forgotten that one year prior, Johnson's 39th-place finish at New Hampshire was just the first step in his run to the championship.

As for Bowyer, he was not disillusioned regarding his hot start to the Chase for the NASCAR NEXTEL Cup, but there's nothing like getting off on the right foot — and proving you belong.

"It just proves that anybody in the top 12 can win this championship," Gordon said. ⚑

DODGE DEALERS 400

DOVER INTERNATIONAL SPEEDWAY

They don't call it the "Monster Mile" for nothing. Dover International Speedway has a personality all its own. When the Monster gets angry, things happen — bad things. Escape the Monster's wrath, and you might just have a good day. Get caught in it, and a decent effort can get swept away in a Delaware minute. On a beautiful autumn afternoon in Dover, the Monster woke up on the wrong side of the rock, and its grumpy demeanor had a lasting effect on the Chase for the NASCAR NEXTEL Cup.

Conventional wisdom says the best place to be at Dover is in the front, away from accidents that tend to clutter the track. That's where Jimmie Johnson wanted to be, and he made it happen by capturing his second Budweiser Pole Award of the season, a tick faster than Juan Pablo Montoya, who grabbed his third front-row start of the year.

Chase for the NASCAR NEXTEL Cup participants Denny Hamlin, Kurt Busch, Martin Truex Jr., Kevin Harvick and Matt Kenseth joined Johnson in the top 10 to start the race. Jeff Burton and Clint Bowyer were less successful, with Burton 36th and Bowyer 42nd after disappointing qualifying efforts.

Johnson's advantage lasted a little more than a lap before Hamlin, winner of the NASCAR Busch Series event the day before, drove past and began pacing the field. He led 61 of the first 77 laps, settled into the top five and looked well on his way to a strong finish. But as Hamlin was about to lap Kyle Petty near the halfway point, he drove squarely into the back of Petty's Dodge, sending both cars crashing down the frontstretch. Bowyer, running quietly in the top 10, was collected as well.

Petty was done for the day. Hamlin spent 40 laps in the garage for repairs and returned to finish 38th, while Bowyer rallied to finish 12th, gaining 30 positions on the day to lead all drivers.

QUALIFIERS

1. **JIMMIE JOHNSON**
   23.261 SEC. 154.765 MPH

2. **JUAN PABLO MONTOYA**
   23.402 SEC. 153.833 MPH

3. **DENNY HAMLIN**
   23.442 SEC. 153.571 MPH

4. **KURT BUSCH**
   23.450 SEC. 153.518 MPH

5. **MARTIN TRUEX JR.**
   23.497 SEC. 153.211 MPH

6. **SCOTT RIGGS**
   23.540 SEC. 152.931 MPH

7. **KEVIN HARVICK**
   23.548 SEC. 152.879 MPH

8. **BOBBY LABONTE**
   23.616 SEC. 152.439 MPH

9. **GREG BIFFLE**
   23.620 SEC. 152.413 MPH

10. **MATT KENSETH**
    23.628 SEC. 152.362 MPH

(Left) Tony Stewart talks with television analyst Brad Daugherty, a former NBA star and NASCAR team owner, while getting ready to go racing. Stewart had a pretty good day at Dover; his ninth-place finish moved him to second in the standings, just two points away from the top spot.

Carl Edwards (99) takes the green flag on a late-race restart with (in order) Mark Martin, Dale Earnhardt Jr., Greg Biffle and Kyle Busch following in the top five. On the inside, Chase for the NASCAR NEXTEL Cup contenders Jeff Burton, Clint Bowyer and Tony Stewart restart one lap down.

Matt Kenseth was next to assert himself as a potential winner. He led four times for 192 laps in a substantial effort — until his motor let go 26 laps short of the finish line. His first engine failure in two years left Kenseth 35th on the final rundown.

Johnson, a three-time Dover winner, motored safely among the top 10, avoiding trouble in a race that produced a record 13 caution flags. It would not be that easy, as a cut tire on Lap 188 forced an unscheduled pit stop. He returned to the track two laps down in 37th place, was caught in a late-race, multi-car accident and was grateful to finish 14th, two laps off the pace.

Jimmie Johnson (48) and Bobby Labonte (43) circle the track after being caught in a multi-car accident less than 15 laps from the finish. Johnson, who started from the pole, managed to complete the race with a 14th-place finish, the first car two laps down.

(Above) Kevin Harvick's crew jumps into action. They had a busy day, as tire problems plagued the team, causing two unscheduled pit stops under green-flag conditions. Harvick finished four laps off the pace and dropped more points to the leaders in the standings.

(Right) Mark Martin (left) and Casey Mears have a friendly discussion in the Dover garage. Both drivers had good results in the race, with Martin (a four-time Dover winner) taking fourth place and Mears finishing sixth, the last car on the lead lap.

Harvick's experience was similar to Johnson's — only worse. Tire problems dropped him two laps down, twice. He finished in 20th place, four laps short of the 400-lap distance.

Like Johnson, Kurt Busch and Truex Jr. rode carefully among the top 10 all day, and both were poised for good, solid finishes. Not so fast. With 14 laps to go, something snapped on the No. 2 Dodge just as the field was sorting itself out after restart No. 11. Running near the front, Busch careened into the Turn-2 wall and ricocheted across the track, triggering a chain reaction that involved at least 10 cars, Truex Jr. among them.

Busch could not return and was listed 29th. Truex, nursing his damaged car toward the finish, brought out the final caution with six laps to go when debris began falling off of his car. He was eventually black-flagged but still managed to finish 13th, one lap down.

While all that was going on, Edwards established himself at the head of the pack. His advantage was that he had already disbursed of his bad luck, at least during the race. Plagued by a sticking throttle — not something to wish for at Dover — his team

(Left) The Chevrolet of Martin Truex Jr. limps toward pit road after it sustained heavy damage late in the race. Although he would not repeat as a winner at Dover, site of his first win earlier in the year, Truex still managed a 13th-place finish to remain in championship contention.

(Right) Even the winner's trophy hints at how tough the Monster Mile can be.

(Below) Carl Edwards celebrates his third victory of the year on a day that left many competitors licking their wounds. With the win, Edwards remained squarely in the hunt for the NASCAR NEXTEL Cup Series championship.

RACE RESULTS

NASCAR NEXTEL Cup Series Race No. 28 — September 23, 2007
Dover International Speedway

DODGE DEALERS 400

Fin. Pos.	Start Pos.	Car No.	Driver	Team	Laps	Laps Led	Status
1	15	99	Carl Edwards	Office Depot Ford	400	95	Running
2	9	16	Greg Biffle	Nintendo Wii Ford	400	6	Running
3	21	8	Dale Earnhardt Jr.	Budweiser Chevrolet	400		Running
4	31	01	Mark Martin	U.S. Army Chevrolet	400	22	Running
5	22	5	Kyle Busch	Kellogg's/CARQUEST Chevrolet	400		Running
6	17	25	Casey Mears	National Guard/GMAC Chevrolet	400		Running
7	36	31	Jeff Burton	AT&T Mobility Chevrolet	399		Running
8	30	26	Jamie McMurray	IRWIN Ford	399		Running
9	28	20	Tony Stewart	Home Depot Chevrolet	399		Running
10	2	42 #	Juan Pablo Montoya	Texaco/Havoline Dodge	399		Running
11	27	24	Jeff Gordon	DuPont Chevrolet	399		Running
12	42	07	Clint Bowyer	DIRECTV Chevrolet	399		Running
13	5	1	Martin Truex Jr.	Bass Pro Shops/Tracker Chevrolet	399		Running
14	1	48	Jimmie Johnson	Lowe's Chevrolet	398	1	Running
15	43	55	Michael Waltrip	NAPA Auto Parts Toyota	398	1	Running
16	23	83	Brian Vickers	Red Bull Toyota	397		Running
17	12	19	Elliott Sadler	Dodge Dealers/UAW Dodge	397		Running
18	13	00 #	David Reutimann	Dominos.com Toyota	397		Running
19	41	7	Robby Gordon	Jim Beam Black Ford	397		Running
20	7	29	Kevin Harvick	Shell/Pennzoil Chevrolet	396		Running
21	38	15 #	Paul Menard	Menards/Pittsburgh Paints Chev.	396		Running
22	18	78	Joe Nemechek	Furniture Row Chevrolet	396		Running
23	39	88	Kenny Wallace	Snickers Ford	396		Running
24	37	38	David Gilliland	M&M's Ford	395		Running
25	35	6 #	David Ragan	AAA Ford	394		Running
26	26	21	Ken Schrader	U.S. Air Force Ford	394		Running
27	8	43	Bobby Labonte	Cheerios/Betty Crocker Dodge	394		Running
28	24	12	Ryan Newman	Alltel Dodge	386		Accident
29	4	2	Kurt Busch	Miller Lite Dodge	385	20	Accident
30	33	41	Reed Sorenson	Target Dodge	385	2	Accident
31	34	66	Jeff Green	Comcast/Best Buy Chevrolet	384		Accident
32	14	9	Kasey Kahne	Dodge Dealers/UAW Dodge	384		Accident
33	32	18	J.J. Yeley	Interstate Batteries Chevrolet	383		Accident
34	6	10	Scott Riggs	Valvoline/Stanley Tools Dodge	383		Accident
35	10	17	Matt Kenseth	DEWALT Nano Technology Ford	374	192	Engine
36	20	96	Tony Raines	DLP HDTV Chevrolet	360		Accident
37	29	49	John Andretti	Paralyzed Veterans Dodge	358		Accident
38	3	11	Denny Hamlin	FedEx Ground Chevrolet	308	61	Running
39	40	40	David Stremme	Halo 3/Target Dodge	287		Engine
40	16	45	Kyle Petty	Wells Fargo Dodge	200		Accident
41	19	44	Dale Jarrett	UPS Toyota	141		Engine
42	25	70	Johnny Sauter	Haas Automation Chevrolet	11		Accident
43	11	84 #	AJ Allmendinger	Red Bull Toyota	4		Engine

Raybestos Rookie of the Year Contender.

NASCAR NEXTEL CUP SERIES TOP 12
(With 8 Races Remaining)

Pos.	Driver	Points	Behind	Change
1	**Jeff Gordon**	5340	—	+1
2	Tony Stewart	5338	-2	+1
3	Jimmie Johnson	5336	-4	-2
4	Kyle Busch	5330	-10	+1
5	Clint Bowyer	5322	-18	-1
6	Carl Edwards	5312	-28	+2
7	Martin Truex Jr.	5294	-46	-1
8	Jeff Burton	5265	-75	+3
9	Kevin Harvick	5225	-115	+1
10	Matt Kenseth	5224	-116	-3
11	Kurt Busch	5189	-151	+1
12	Denny Hamlin	5182	-158	-3

was able to remedy the problem on Lap 190 and send Edwards on his way.

With his car working properly, Edwards drove to the front and led 95 of the remaining 134 laps, including the final 38 despite five late-race restarts. A four-lap sprint after the last caution went unchallenged, and Edwards picked up his third win of the year, the seventh of his career and the 100th for team owner Jack Roush.

A quick point tally showed Edwards in third place after the race, a scant three points behind leader Gordon, with Stewart second, just two points back. That lasted until post-race inspection, when the rear of Edwards' car measured too low. Ultimately, a 25-point penalty was issued, which dropped Edwards to sixth in the standings, 28 points behind.

Kyle Busch, Burton, Stewart and Gordon had relatively uneventful days that they could consider good, but not great. Busch managed a lead-lap finish in fifth place. Burton was the first car one lap down in seventh. He was followed by Stewart in ninth and Gordon, who was two laps off the pace but still finished 11th and took over the lead in the standings.

Only six cars finished on the lead lap, and one week after all 43 cars finished an event for the first time since 1998 when NASCAR went exclusively to 43-car fields, 16 cars (more than one-third) ended the day in the garage due to accidents or engine failures.

The Monster has spoken. ◢◣◢

LIFELOCK 400

KANSAS SPEEDWAY

NASCAR NEXTEL CUP SERIES

W hen reading or watching assorted media accounts after the race at Kansas Speedway, the adjectives used to describe the event ran the full gamut of possibilities. We'll stick with Jeff Gordon's reaction when he said, "Man, what a crazy race it was."

In a way, the "craziness" started the day before, when Jimmie Johnson — after winning his third Budweiser Pole Award of the season, all in a four-week span — slapped the wall in practice. That forced Johnson to a backup car, which dropped him from first to last on the starting grid. When all was said and done, though, Johnson left the Heartland on top of the standings, having leapfrogged over Clint Bowyer and Jeff Gordon in the process.

That was after Johnson crossed the finish line second behind Bowyer and ahead of Greg Biffle, who won the race. That little twist left more than few people scratching their heads.

Biffle was leading the event, delayed twice by rain for a total of nearly three hours, when Juan Pablo Montoya shredded a tire, leaving chunks of rubber strewn across the track. The caution flew, freezing the running order, and with darkness setting in, it was time to call it a day.

Behind the pace car, Biffle, ready to begin celebrating his first win since the 2006 season finale, dropped to the apron and slowed while removing his gloves and unbuckling his belts. Low on fuel, Biffle shut the car off and coasted, wanting to make sure enough was left to light up the tires on his way to Victory Lane. Bowyer and Johnson took that as a sign that Biffle's tank was dry, passed the No. 16 Ford and crossed the stripe 1-2 behind the pace car.

Various interpretations of the applicable rule were tossed around before NASCAR cleared things up, saying that Biffle maintained a "reasonable pace," which can be slower than that of the pace car. "How much slower?" was the question Bowyer and others asked. Refer to Rule 10-4(A), which states: "Determination of reasonable speed is a judgment call and will be made by NASCAR officials."

Done deal — Biffle wins.

Casey Mears finished fourth ahead of Chase for the NASCAR NEXTEL Cup competitors Jeff Gordon and Kevin Harvick. Gordon dropped to second in the standings, six points behind Johnson, while Harvick picked up four positions and jumped to fifth place, 126 points behind the leader.

At one point, Tony Stewart thought he had bagged his fourth win of the season. Storms on the horizon were quickly moving in, causing many to think that the race would be called shortly after reaching the halfway point at Lap 134. But when it passed without a drop of moisture, teams were suddenly faced with fuel tanks that were about to run dry.

Nine of the top 10 drivers were title contenders, but one by one, they dropped onto pit road for green-flag stops. All except Stewart, who gambled that the rain was imminent, remained on the track and assumed the lead. Two laps later, the sky opened up and the downpour began, leaving those who pitted a lap down and Stewart looking like a genius.

As is often the case on the Plains, however, the storm moved on, the sun reappeared and, a little more than two hours later, the race resumed. Pit road opened before the green flag was shown, allowing Stewart and others to stop for much-needed fuel. He was able to return to the track still holding the lead, but restarted behind a number of cars running on the tail end of the lead lap.

Almost immediately Ken Schrader and Michael Waltrip ran into each other, causing Truex Jr. to get out of the gas. Stewart ran into Truex, inflicting extensive damage to the No. 1 Chevrolet. Kenseth became a victim as well, his Ford battered in the wreckage.

TOP 10 QUALIFIERS

1. **JIMMIE JOHNSON**
   30.846 SEC. 175.063 MPH

2. **MATT KENSETH**
   30.984 SEC. 174.284 MPH

3. **SCOTT RIGGS**
   31.041 SEC. 173.963 MPH

4. **JEFF GORDON**
   31.089 SEC. 173.695 MPH

5. **DENNY HAMLIN**
   31.091 SEC. 173.684 MPH

6. **DALE EARNHARDT JR.**
   31.100 SEC. 173.633 MPH

7. **GREG BIFFLE**
   31.103 SEC. 173.617 MPH

8. **KYLE BUSCH**
   31.127 SEC. 173.483 MPH

9. **MARTIN TRUEX JR.**
   31.132 SEC. 173.455 MPH

10. **CLINT BOWYER**
    31.153 SEC. 173.338 MPH

Kansas Speedway's infield access tunnel offers fans a colorful, artistic look. Kansas hosted its first NASCAR NEXTEL Cup Series race in 2001, the same year Chicagoland joined the annual schedule.

(Far Left) Ryan Newman's crew hurriedly repairs their Dodge, hoping to get it back on the track for the final two laps of the race. Newman had just spun and hit the wall after taking the late-race lead.

Michael Waltrip observes car preparation during downtime at Lowe's Motor Speedway. Waltrip, finding the consistency he had been chasing all season, qualified his car for the fourth straight week and was rewarded with a 10th-place finish in the race, his second top 10 in 12 starts this year.

Then, Johnson made a rare, uncharacteristic and costly mistake. His Chevrolet got out from under him coming off of Turn 2 and sent him spinning down the backstretch. The damage was minimal and he was able to remain on the lead lap, but the mishap dropped Johnson to 30th position with 100 laps to go. His recovery was only good enough for a 14th-place finish.

Gordon ran consistently between 10th and fifth place over the first two-thirds of the race, while he and crew chief Steve Letarte adjusted the chassis of the No. 24 Chevrolet. By the time Johnson spun, Gordon had reached the front, his first lead coming with 126 laps remaining.

Bowyer, who was fast for the entire race after starting 25th, led Laps 225-272 before Gordon reassumed the lead and paced the field for 59 of the final 65 laps.

(Above) Clint Bowyer (07) leads the field on a restart with Kevin Harvick (29) on his left. Bowyer's strong showing, leading three times for 79 laps on the way to a runner-up finish, kept him firmly in the title hunt. Harvick suffered tire problems, fell several laps down and dropped three positions in the standings.

(Right) Dale Earnhardt Jr. prepares to climb aboard his Chevrolet for a long night of racing. Always in the high groove, he hung with the top 10 before fading after halfway, never quite able to hit the setup just right.

(Left) Jimmie Johnson is in for a fresh set of tires after destroying the old ones during a spin down the backstretch. The car sustained only slight damage, but his recovery stalled in 14th place.

A late-race caution, when Johnny Sauter smacked the wall in Turn 4 and dumped oil on the tack, brought out a brief red flag with a handful of laps remaining. Gordon led on the restart, but when he jumped on the accelerator his car hesitated, apparently suffering from vapor lock in the fuel system.

Newman, fourth on the restart, darted to the outside and shot past Bowyer, Kyle Busch and Gordon to take the lead with seven laps left and set sail, gunning for his first win in more than two years — a lead he held for only two laps before his Dodge spun in Turn 2, bringing out the caution and handing the lead back to Gordon.

(Above) Trying to leave after a gas-only stop, Tony Stewart (20) makes contact with Kasey Kahne (9), who was trying to enter his pit. The incident forced Stewart to return to pit road twice more during the caution and cost him valuable track position.

(Right) A very excited Jeff Gordon begins to celebrate as he pulls the race-winning car into Victory Lane at Lowe's Motor Speedway, a place he had not visited in seven years.

(Left) Jeff Gordon (24) brings it home in front of runner-up Clint Bowyer (07) and Kyle Busch (5). Gordon had the lead, lost it, and then got it back again, all over the last handful of laps.

RACE RESULTS

NASCAR NEXTEL Cup Series Race No. 31 — October 13, 2007
Lowe's Motor Speedway

BANK OF AMERICA 500

Fin. Pos.	Start Pos.	Car No.	Driver	Team	Laps	Laps Led	Status
1	4	24	Jeff Gordon	DuPont Chevrolet	337	72	Running
2	25	07	Clint Bowyer	Jack Daniel's Chevrolet	337	79	Running
3	13	5	Kyle Busch	Kellogg's/CARQUEST Chevrolet	337	4	Running
4	27	31	Jeff Burton	AT&T Mobility Chevrolet	337		Running
5	18	99	Carl Edwards	Office Depot Ford	337		Running
6	34	22	Dave Blaney	Caterpillar/CatUsed.com Toyota	337	1	Running
7	29	20	Tony Stewart	The Home Depot Chevrolet	337		Running
8	5	9	Kasey Kahne	Dodge Dealers/UAW Dodge	337		Running
9	28	40	David Stremme	Target Dodge	337		Running
10	19	55	Michael Waltrip	NAPA Auto Parts Toyota	337		Running
11	33	88	Ricky Rudd	Snickers Ford	337		Running
12	3	43	Bobby Labonte	Cheerios/Pink for the Cure Dodge	337		Running
13	39	18	J.J. Yeley	Interstate Batteries Chevrolet	337		Running
14	2	48	Jimmie Johnson	Lowe's/Kobalt Tools Chevrolet	337	95	Running
15	30	84 #	AJ Allmendinger	Red Bull Toyota	337		Running
16	12	01	Mark Martin	U.S. Army Chevrolet	337		Running
17	32	1	Martin Truex Jr.	Bass Pro Shops/Tracker Boats Chev.	337		Running
18	42	45	Kyle Petty	Tire Kingdom Dodge	337	2	Running
19	22	8	Dale Earnhardt Jr.	Budweiser Chevrolet	337		Running
20	11	11	Denny Hamlin	FedEx Kinko's Chevrolet	337		Running
21	9	25	Casey Mears	National Guard/GMAC Chevrolet	336		Running
22	17	15 #	Paul Menard	Menards/Rain-X Chevrolet	336		Running
23	23	70	Johnny Sauter	Yellow Transportation Chevrolet	336		Running
24	6	26	Jamie McMurray	Crown Royal Ford	336	27	Running
25	21	38	David Gilliland	M&M's Ford	335		Running
26	8	2	Kurt Busch	Miller Lite Dodge	335	13	Running
27	10	16	Greg Biffle	3M Ford	334		Running
28	1	12	Ryan Newman	Alltel Dodge	333	11	Accident
29	20	00 #	David Reutimann	Dominos.com Toyota	333		Running
30	26	41	Reed Sorenson	Fuji Film Dodge	333		Running
31	41	96	Tony Raines	DLP/Queen City Appliances Chev.	331		Running
32	37	66	Jeff Green	Best Buy/GARMIN Chevrolet	330		Running
33	24	29	Kevin Harvick	Shell/Pennzoil Chevrolet	330		Running
34	7	17	Matt Kenseth	Carhartt for Women/DEWALT Ford	282	32	Accident
35	35	21	Bill Elliott	Heinz/Ore-Ida Ford	282		Running
36	14	10	Scott Riggs	Stanley Tools/Valvoline Dodge	278		Accident
37	36	42 #	Juan Pablo Montoya	Texaco/Havoline Dodge	273		Accident
38	40	7	Robby Gordon	Motorola Digital Audio Player Ford	270	1	Running
39	38	36	Jeremy Mayfield	360 OTC Toyota	253		Vibration
40	31	6 #	David Ragan	AAA Ford	231		Running
41	16	19	Elliott Sadler	Dodge Dealers/UAW Dodge	228		Running
42	43	49	John Andretti	Paralyzed Veterans Dodge	205		Accident
43	15	4	Ward Burton	State Water Heaters/Lucas Chev.	83		Engine

Raybestos Rookie of the Year Contender.

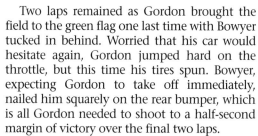

NASCAR NEXTEL CUP SERIES TOP 12

(With 5 Races Remaining)

Pos.	Driver	Points	Behind	Change
1	Jeff Gordon	5880	—	—
2	Jimmie Johnson	5812	-68	—
3	Clint Bowyer	5802	-78	—
4	Tony Stewart	5682	-198	—
5	Carl Edwards	5640	-240	+1
6	Kyle Busch	5600	-280	+2
7	Kurt Busch	5565	-315	—
8	Kevin Harvick	5552	-328	-3
9	Denny Hamlin	5531	-349	—
10	Jeff Burton	5514	-366	+2
11	Martin Truex Jr.	5502	-378	-1
12	Matt Kenseth	5438	-442	-1

Two laps remained as Gordon brought the field to the green flag one last time with Bowyer tucked in behind. Worried that his car would hesitate again, Gordon jumped hard on the throttle, but this time his tires spun. Bowyer, expecting Gordon to take off immediately, nailed him squarely on the rear bumper, which is all Gordon needed to shoot to a half-second margin of victory over the final two laps.

Bowyer finished a strong second to stay well within reach of Gordon in the standings, 78 points behind in third place, and 10 in arrears of Johnson.

Kyle Busch, Jeff Burton and Carl Edwards rounded out the top five. Dave Blaney followed his third-place effort at Talladega with a strong sixth-place finish, one spot ahead of Stewart, who ended a frustrating evening in seventh place.

In a rather bizarre sequence of events, Stewart, who started 29th and had worked his way into the top 10 before the halfway point, opted for a gas-only stop under caution on Lap 177. While pulling away, he collided with the incoming cars of, first, Paul Menard, and then, Kasey Kahne, causing Kahne to spin. Stewart circled the track and returned to pit road to fix the damage, but he slid through his pit box and was forced to make yet another lap before coming in a third time.

When Stewart returned to the track, he was mired in traffic and was forced to play catch-up for the rest of the evening. The net result was an additional 44-point loss to Gordon, leaving Stewart with 198 points to make up over the final five events. 🏁

32

SUBWAY 500

MARTINSVILLE SPEEDWAY

H alfway through the Chase for the NASCAR NEXTEL Cup, Jeff Gordon, Jimmie Johnson and Clint Bowyer had managed to distance themselves from most of the other contenders. Eight of the 12 drivers in the title hunt were already 240 points or more down to Gordon at the top of the standings. Second-place Johnson lost ground at Lowe's Motor Speedway but was still just 68 points behind his teammate, while Bowyer's strong second-place finish in the Bank of America 500 kept him soundly in third, just 10 points behind Johnson and 78 away from Gordon. Any of the three had to be considered likely candidates to emerge with the title after five more events.

Tony Stewart, fourth in the standings and 198 points down to Gordon after his seventh-place finish in Charlotte, desperately needed something positive to happen. Four top 10s in five races was good, but his 39th-place showing at Kansas stuck out like a sore thumb when compared to the top three drivers in the points. Gordon's worst finish over five events was an 11th place at Dover; Johnson had two finishes outside the top 10, both times in 14th place (Dover and Charlotte); while Bowyer's worst included a 12th place at Dover and an 11th at Talladega, which were balanced out by his win at New Hampshire and two runner-up finishes.

Stewart knew he could win at Martinsville — he had done it twice before, in 2000 and 2006 — but overall, his record of six top-five finishes in 17 career starts on the Virginia half-mile was not that stellar. Worse yet for Stewart was the fact that both Gordon and Johnson had proven to be two of the track's hottest and most accomplished competitors.

In this event alone, the pair had split the victories evenly over the past four years. Johnson made it two straight at the track earlier in the season when he out-dueled Gordon over the final laps. And Gordon, already a seven-time winner on the paper-clip-shaped short track, was on fire after winning the last two races to extend his lead in the championship standings.

1. JEFF GORDON
   19.938 SEC. 94.974 MPH

2. MARTIN TRUEX JR.
   19.988 SEC. 94.737 MPH

3. KEVIN HARVICK
   19.999 SEC. 94.685 MPH

4. JIMMIE JOHNSON
   20.013 SEC. 94.619 MPH

5. KASEY KAHNE
   20.020 SEC. 94.585 MPH

6. KYLE BUSCH
   20.025 SEC. 94.562 MPH

7. DALE EARNHARDT JR.
   20.026 SEC. 94.557 MPH

8. J.J. YELEY
   20.039 SEC. 94.496 MPH

9. JAMIE MCMURRAY
   20.050 SEC. 94.444 MPH

10. TONY RAINES
   20.066 SEC. 94.369 MPH

(Far Left) Denny Hamlin (11) fights a tire rub as he ducks inside Juan Pablo Montoya (42) on the frontstretch. Hamlin's race was a see-saw of sorts, repeatedly gaining positions on the track but giving them up in the pits due to repairs. He fought hard for a sixth-place finish, two spots ahead of Montoya, the top-finishing rookie.

Jeff Gordon (24) brings the field to the green flag after winning his seventh Budweiser Pole Award of the season. His closest competition in the point standings, Jimmie Johnson (48), was not far behind in fourth.

Matt Kenseth (17) and Paul Menard (15) demonstrate what close-quarters racing at Martinsville is all about. Kenseth finally broke a horrid, four-race streak of finishes outside the top 25 and placed his Ford fifth, his first top five in the Chase for the NASCAR NEXTEL Cup.

Gordon showed he had no intentions of cooling off by capturing his series-leading seventh Budweiser Pole Award of the season for the Subway 500. Johnson turned a qualifying lap less than four-tenths of a second slower than Gordon's to start fourth, while Bowyer (21st) and Stewart (34th) would have to begin the 500 lapper deep in traffic and hope they could stay clear of trouble that was likely to occur in front of them.

(Left) Jimmie Johnson (48) leads the way with teammate Kyle Busch glued to his rear bumper, while Kevin Harvick closes from behind. All three started in the top six in a race dominated by Hendrick drivers.

(Below) Jimmie Johnson pops out of a sea of reporters to wave the checkered flag for the fans. The win was Johnson's second straight and third overall at Martinsville, and was the eighth for Hendrick Motorsports in the last 10 events at the Virginia short track.

RACE RESULTS

NASCAR NEXTEL Cup Series Race No. 32 — October 21, 2007
Martinsville Speedway

SUBWAY 500

Fin. Pos.	Start Pos.	Car No.	Driver	Team	Laps	Laps Led	Status
1	4	48	Jimmie Johnson	Lowe's Chevrolet	506	147	Running
2	12	12	Ryan Newman	Alltel Dodge	506		Running
3	1	24	Jeff Gordon	DuPont Chevrolet	506	168	Running
4	6	5	Kyle Busch	Kellogg's/CARQUEST Chevrolet	506	106	Running
5	24	17	Matt Kenseth	R&L Carriers/DEWALT Ford	506		Running
6	30	11	Denny Hamlin	FedEx Freight Chevrolet	506		Running
7	37	16	Greg Biffle	Dish Network Ford	506		Running
8	26	42 #	Juan Pablo Montoya	Texaco/Havoline Dodge	506	9	Running
9	21	07	Clint Bowyer	Jack Daniel's Chevrolet	506		Running
10	3	29	Kevin Harvick	Shell/Pennzoil Chevrolet	506		Running
11	20	99	Carl Edwards	Office Depot Ford	506		Running
12	18	31	Jeff Burton	AT&T Mobility Chevrolet	506	51	Running
13	34	20	Tony Stewart	The Home Depot Chevrolet	506		Running
14	10	96	Tony Raines	DLP HDTV Chevrolet	506		Running
15	5	9	Kasey Kahne	Dodge Dealers/UAW Dodge	506		Running
16	32	10	Scott Riggs	Valvoline/Stanley Tools Dodge	506		Running
17	19	00 #	David Reutimann	Dominos.com Toyota	506		Running
18	29	55	Michael Waltrip	NAPA Auto Parts Toyota	506		Running
19	2	1	Martin Truex Jr.	Bass Pro Shops/Tracker Boats Chev.	506		Running
20	22	25	Casey Mears	National Guard/GMAC Chevrolet	506		Running
21	42	45	Kyle Petty	Marathon Motor Oil Dodge	506		Running
22	16	43	Bobby Labonte	Goody's /Cheerios Dodge	506		Running
23	7	8	Dale Earnhardt Jr.	Budweiser Chevrolet	506	24	Running
24	35	15 #	Paul Menard	Menards/Pittsburgh Paints Chevrolet	505		Running
25	40	38	David Gilliland	M&M's Ford	505		Running
26	41	6 #	David Ragan	AAA Ford	505		Running
27	23	88	Ricky Rudd	Combos/Snickers Ford	504		Running
28	31	66	Jeff Green	HAAS CNC/Best Buy Chevrolet	503	1	Running
29	13	70	Johnny Sauter	HAAS CNC/Yellow Chevrolet	503		Running
30	33	44	Dale Jarrett	UPS Toyota	503		Running
31	11	2	Kurt Busch	Miller Lite Dodge	501		Running
32	9	26	Jamie McMurray	Crown Royal Ford	500		Running
33	15	49	John Andretti	Paralyzed Veterans Dodge	492		Trans.
34	43	21	Bill Elliott	Little Debbie Snack Cakes Ford	483		Engine
35	25	84 #	AJ Allmendinger	Red Bull Toyota	474		Running
36	17	22	Dave Blaney	Caterpillar Toyota	439		Running
37	38	40	David Stremme	Target House Dodge	410		Accident
38	36	4	Ward Burton	ITT Night Vision/State Water Chev.	406		Running
39	39	7	Robby Gordon	MAC Tools Ford	390		Running
40	14	19	Elliott Sadler	Dodge Dealers/UAW Dodge	371		Running
41	28	41	Reed Sorenson	Target Dodge	259		Engine
42	8	18	J.J. Yeley	Interstate Batteries Chevrolet	258		Engine
43	27	01	Aric Almirola	U.S. Army Chevrolet	111		Electrical

Raybestos Rookie of the Year Contender.

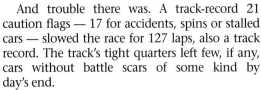

NASCAR NEXTEL CUP SERIES TOP 12
(With 4 Races Remaining)

Pos.	Driver	Points	Behind	Change
1	**Jeff Gordon**	6055	—	—
2	Jimmie Johnson	6002	-53	—
3	Clint Bowyer	5940	-115	—
4	Tony Stewart	5806	-249	—
5	Carl Edwards	5770	-285	—
6	Kyle Busch	5765	-290	—
7	Kevin Harvick	5686	-369	+1
8	Denny Hamlin	5681	-374	+1
9	Jeff Burton	5646	-409	+1
10	Kurt Busch	5635	-420	-3
11	Martin Truex Jr.	5608	-447	—
12	Matt Kenseth	5593	-462	—

And trouble there was. A track-record 21 caution flags — 17 for accidents, spins or stalled cars — slowed the race for 127 laps, also a track record. The track's tight quarters left few, if any, cars without battle scars of some kind by day's end.

Proving that Hendrick Motorsports had Martinsville thoroughly figured out, Gordon, Johnson and teammate Kyle Busch led a combined 424 laps, including every one after the midpoint at Lap 250. Gordon got things started by leading the first 108 laps. Busch dominated the middle portion of the race, leading three times for 106 trips around the tiny oval. And by Lap 300, Johnson found track conditions to his liking and began racking up time at the front of the field.

"The longer the green flag ran and the slicker the track got, the better for me," Johnson explained. "I couldn't go until the track got slick."

To no one's surprise, Johnson and Gordon teamed up as the event wore on, sharing the lead between them exclusively after Lap 355. Only Ryan Newman was able to assert himself as a possible winning contender, fluctuating between second and third place over the final 100 laps.

Johnson seized the lead from Gordon on a restart with 44 laps remaining in the scheduled distance, but six more yellow flags over the remaining laps precluded any extended charge at Johnson and negated a replay of the battle he and Gordon staged in the spring. In fact, Gordon, whose car began to fade just a bit, had his hands full trying to fend off Newman, still bent on grabbing a win before season's end.

Gordon lined up behind Johnson for a restart on Lap 491 and almost immediately got the receiving end of a solid bump-and-run courtesy of Newman. Angered, Gordon tried to return the favor, but before he could repay Newman in kind, the yellow flew for a three-car accident on Lap 497.

Forced into extra laps, Johnson brought the field under green for the final time with Newman still second ahead of Gordon. Before anyone could make a last charge, David Ragan spun in Turn 1, producing the final caution and ending the race on the spot with 506 laps in the books (another track record).

Johnson's 30th career victory cut 15 points into Gordon's lead, which stood at 53 when the checkered flag waved. Bowyer, ninth in the finishing order, dropped 37 points and fell to 115 behind the leader, while Stewart did not have the race he was hoping for, coming home in 13th place. With four races to go, Stewart's deficit grew to 249 points. Considering the pace being set by the teammates from Hendrick Motorsports, Stewart suddenly found himself on the brink of elimination. ✦✦✦

PEP BOYS AUTO 500

ATLANTA MOTOR SPEEDWAY

*E*verything was coming together for Jimmie Johnson. As if it were scripted, Johnson was mounting a late-season charge reminiscent of 2006, when he rallied from seventh place, 146 points behind with five races to go, to grab his first NASCAR NEXTEL Cup Series championship. That charge began with a win at Martinsville, which he followed with three straight runner-up finishes. By the time Johnson started his engine for the season finale at Homestead-Miami Speedway, he had 63 points in hand over his closest competitor, Matt Kenseth. Johnson finished the race in ninth place and captured the title by a comfortable 56-point margin.

This year Johnson was never that far from the top of the order. A deficit of 68 points was the largest he had faced; that, after the fifth race in the Chase for the NASCAR NEXTEL Cup. At that time, Gordon had won two straight, tying Johnson in the win column with six apiece over the season.

It was time to go to work.

When the checkered flag waved at Atlanta — a mere two races later — Johnson's shortfall was all but erased, as he drew to within nine points of Gordon after snatching his second-straight victory, completing season sweeps at Martinsville and Atlanta in the process.

This one, though, was more like a gift.

With the Pep Boys Auto 500 nearing its conclusion, everything came crashing down — literally. Martin Truex Jr., Kyle Busch and Kurt Busch had combined to lead 310 of the event's 329 laps, extended from the scheduled 325-lap distance due to a late-race yellow flag. Truex, who led a race-high 135 laps, finished 31st. Kyle Busch was 20th, and Kurt Busch was listed in eighth place, feeling lucky to do so in a bizarre conclusion to the event.

Johnson led just eight laps — the last eight, of course. Those, after a call by crew chief Chad Knaus for only right-side tires during a stop under caution at Lap 320, a much needed break for those whose fuel tanks were all but empty.

TOP 10 QUALIFIERS

1. **GREG BIFFLE**
   28.807 SEC. 192.453 MPH

2. **KURT BUSCH**
   28.811 SEC. 192.426 MPH

3. **DALE JARRETT**
   28.927 SEC. 191.655 MPH

4. **KASEY KAHNE**
   28.936 SEC. 191.595 MPH

5. **DALE EARNHARDT JR.**
   28.952 SEC. 191.489 MPH

6. **JIMMIE JOHNSON**
   28.996 SEC. 191.199 MPH

7. **DAVID STREMME**
   29.030 SEC. 190.975 MPH

8. **JEFF GORDON**
   29.069 SEC. 190.719 MPH

9. **RYAN NEWMAN**
   29.069 SEC. 190.719 MPH

10. **ELLIOTT SADLER**
    29.071 SEC. 190.706 MPH

(Far Left) Kurt Busch waits for fresh tires and fuel in the Pep Boys Auto 500. Busch led the race four times for 98 total laps and escaped late-race accidents to finish eighth, breaking a two-race slump that dropped him to 10th in the point standings.

Late-day sunlight highlights the cars of Chase for the NASCAR NEXTEL Cup competitors, sitting silently in Atlanta's garage like warriors waiting for battle.

(Above) A flagman in training waves his heroes on as the field charges down the backstretch. Atlanta's racing surface lets drivers pick a groove almost anywhere on the track.

(Left) Martin Truex Jr. blasts through the frontstretch tri-oval, all alone at the head of the pack. Truex led five times for a race-high 135 laps and was poised for a great finish before disaster struck with just three laps to go.

(Right) Mike Patterson, crewman for Matt Kenseth, has some fun entertaining visitors on race morning. His driver had fun on the track, able to end the race in fourth place for his second-straight top-five finish.

Johnson was the fifth car to enter pit road but was the first to leave, beating Dale Earnhardt Jr., Jamie McMurray, Reed Sorenson, Carl Edwards and Jeff Burton, all of whom took two tires in order to gain precious track position. Kyle Busch, Matt Kenseth, Truex Jr. and Kurt Busch, the top four in the running order going into the pits, took four tires each and returned to the track no higher than eighth place.

Everyone lined up behind Denny Hamlin for what was shaping up to be a three-lap sprint to the finish. Hamlin had rolled the dice and remained on the track during the caution, hoping he had enough fuel to squeeze out a good finish on worn tires.

A restart with three laps to go ends in disaster for Denny Hamlin (11), Martin Truex Jr. (1) and Kyle Busch (5). Leading the race, Hamlin's car failed to go when the green flag waved, and Truex had nowhere to go but into the back of Hamlin. Busch almost avoided the incident by darting to the inside but got clipped by Truex and spun.

(Left) Jimmie Johnson celebrates his second-straight win, his eighth of the season and the 31st of his career.

RACE RESULTS

NASCAR NEXTEL Cup Series Race No. 33 — October 28, 2007
Atlanta Motor Speedway

PEP BOYS AUTO 500

Fin. Pos.	Start Pos.	Car No.	Driver	Team	Laps	Laps Led	Status
1	6	48	Jimmie Johnson	Lowe's/KOBALT Tools Chevrolet	329	8	Running
2	16	99	Carl Edwards	Office Depot Ford	329		Running
3	32	41	Reed Sorenson	Target Dodge	329		Running
4	17	17	Matt Kenseth	DEWALT NANO Technology Ford	329		Running
5	28	31	Jeff Burton	AT&T Mobility Chevrolet	329		Running
6	26	07	Clint Bowyer	Jack Daniel's Chevrolet	329		Running
7	8	24	Jeff Gordon	DuPont/Nicorette Chevrolet	329		Running
8	2	2	Kurt Busch	Miller Lite Dodge	329	98	Running
9	4	9	Kasey Kahne	Dodge Dealers/UAW Dodge	329	3	Running
10	14	83	Brian Vickers	Red Bull Toyota	329		Running
11	24	55	Michael Waltrip	NAPA Auto Parts Toyota	329		Running
12	15	25	Casey Mears	National Guard/GMAC Chevrolet	329		Running
13	39	45	Kyle Petty	American Spirit Motor Oil Dodge	329	1	Running
14	10	19	Elliott Sadler	Dodge Dealers/UAW Dodge	329		Running
15	34	29	Kevin Harvick	Shell/Pennzoil Chevrolet	329	1	Running
16	31	84 #	AJ Allmendinger	Red Bull Toyota	329	1	Running
17	38	88	Ricky Rudd	Snickers Ford	329		Running
18	43	21	Bill Elliott	Little Debbie Ford	329		Running
19	3	44	Dale Jarrett	UPS/Toys-for-Tots Toyota	329		Running
20	19	5	Kyle Busch	CARQUEST/Kellogg's Chevrolet	329	77	Running
21	33	7	Robby Gordon	Jim Beam Ford	328		Running
22	1	16	Greg Biffle	Lumber Liquidators Ford	328	1	Running
23	40	96	Tony Raines	DLP HDTV Chevrolet	328		Running
24	18	11	Denny Hamlin	FedEx Express Chevrolet	328	3	Running
25	5	8	Dale Earnhardt Jr.	Budweiser Chevrolet	327		Accident
26	25	26	Jamie McMurray	Crown Royal Ford	327		Accident
27	36	15 #	Paul Menard	Menards/Johns Manville Chevrolet	327	1	Running
28	29	49	John Andretti	Paralyzed Veterans Dodge	327		Running
29	27	10	Scott Riggs	Sears Auto Center Dodge	327		Running
30	30	20	Tony Stewart	The Home Depot Chevrolet	323		Running
31	20	1	Martin Truex Jr.	Bass Pro Shops/Tracker Boats Chev.	322	135	Accident
32	35	70	Johnny Sauter	Radioactive Energy Drink Chevrolet	321		Running
33	37	6 #	David Ragan	AAA Ford	320		Running
34	21	42 #	Juan Pablo Montoya	Texaco/Havoline Dodge	283		Running
35	22	18	J.J. Yeley	Interstate Batteries Chevrolet	275		Running
36	23	78	Joe Nemechek	Furniture Row Chevrolet	268		Accident
37	9	12	Ryan Newman	Mobil 1 Dodge	267		Engine
38	42	22	Dave Blaney	Caterpillar Toyota	263		Running
39	7	40	David Stremme	Coors Light/St. Jude Dodge	250		Accident
40	41	66	Jeremy Mayfield	Best Buy Chevrolet	250		Running
41	11	43	Bobby Labonte	Cheerios/Betty Crocker Dodge	238		Running
42	13	38	David Gilliland	M&M's Ford	64		Accident
43	12	01	Mark Martin	U.S. Army Chevrolet	64		Accident

Raybestos Rookie of the Year Contender.

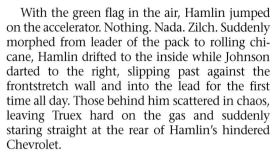

NASCAR NEXTEL CUP SERIES TOP 12

(With 3 Races Remaining)

Pos.	Driver	Points	Behind	Change
1	**Jeff Gordon**	6201	—	—
2	Jimmie Johnson	6192	-9	—
3	Clint Bowyer	6090	-111	—
4	Carl Edwards	5940	-261	+1
5	Tony Stewart	5879	-322	-1
6	Kyle Busch	5873	-328	—
7	Kevin Harvick	5809	-392	—
8	Jeff Burton	5801	-400	+1
9	Kurt Busch	5782	-419	+1
10	Denny Hamlin	5777	-424	-2
11	Matt Kenseth	5753	-448	+1
12	Martin Truex Jr.	5688	-513	-1

With the green flag in the air, Hamlin jumped on the accelerator. Nothing. Nada. Zilch. Suddenly morphed from leader of the pack to rolling chicane, Hamlin drifted to the inside while Johnson darted to the right, slipping past against the frontstretch wall and into the lead for the first time all day. Those behind him scattered in chaos, leaving Truex hard on the gas and suddenly staring straight at the rear of Hamlin's hindered Chevrolet.

In a flash, Truex was finished, having plowed into the back of Hamlin with enough force to end his bid for a second win right then and there. Kyle Busch took evasive action but couldn't avoid the inevitable. He went spinning to the inside after getting tagged by Truex.

There's more.

Hamlin's mishap mandated the second green-white-checkered finish in as many weeks, and like the one at Martinsville seven days earlier, this one didn't last long.

In the first turn under green, the left-rear wheel of Earnhardt Jr.'s Chevrolet, running third at the time, fell completely off the car. Earnhardt spun directly in front of McMurray, who slammed into the red Chevrolet, knocking it into the wall.

"Man, that was a hit," Earnhardt said. "I knew when I was sliding up there it was gonna be big, and it was."

With that, the race was over, leaving Johnson feeling somewhat charmed.

"We didn't have the fastest car," Johnson admitted, "but Chad's call put us in contention to win."

"When that caution (Lap 320) came out, we knew we didn't have a car capable of winning the race at that point," Knaus said. "But usually late in the race when cautions come out, cautions breed cautions, so track position was going to be important."

Johnson summed it up, saying, "Today was a great day on a lot of fronts, in so many ways."

Sure it was, for Johnson, who whacked another 44 points off of Gordon's lead, now measured in single digits.

"I'm just happy to have a points lead now after the day we had," Gordon said after somehow finishing in seventh place.

Gordon ran in the middle of the pack for most of the day before adjustments finally took hold and allowed a late-race rally.

"We were too far behind at that point," Gordon continued. "If we hadn't gotten better late, it would have been much, much worse. We made something out of not much."

Carl Edwards finished second and moved into fourth place in the standings, displacing Stewart, who finished in the 30th position. Reed Sorenson finished in third place, a career best and his third top five of the season, while Clint Bowyer came home in sixth place, one spot in front of Gordon, to keep his title hopes alive. ▪▪▪

DICKIES 500

TEXAS MOTOR SPEEDWAY

1. MARTIN TRUEX JR.
27.964 SEC. 193.105 MPH

2. JEFF GORDON
28.063 SEC. 192.424 MPH

3. JUAN PABLO MONTOYA
28.064 SEC. 192.417 MPH

4. KEVIN HARVICK
28.090 SEC. 192.239 MPH

5. AJ ALLMENDINGER
28.090 SEC. 192.239 MPH

6. KURT BUSCH
28.101 SEC. 192.164 MPH

7. DENNY HAMLIN
28.106 SEC. 192.130 MPH

8. JIMMIE JOHNSON
28.115 SEC. 192.068 MPH

9. CASEY MEARS
28.139 SEC. 191.904 MPH

10. MARK MARTIN
28.183 SEC. 191.605 MPH

In Jimmie Johnson's first win in the Chase for the NASCAR NEXTEL Cup, at Martinsville, he merely needed to hold his position at the front, while a flurry of late-race cautions stymied any serious challenge to take it away. At Atlanta, Johnson stole some late-race track position with a two-tire stop, and when Denny Hamlin's Chevrolet turned into a sitting duck, Johnson shot past everyone and led the final eight laps.

But at Texas, Johnson had to race his way to victory. And it was by no means easy. Up against one of the very best in Matt Kenseth, Johnson fought tooth and nail for every grain of Texas asphalt. Three times he measured his competition and struck. Twice foiled, he regrouped, planned and struck again as the final laps evaporated in the dry night air.

Johnson had something to gain, sure, but he had everything to loose. Go for broke and risk losing the car could easily end in disaster with a championship hanging in the balance. But back off and settle for a sure second place? No way. Not Jimmie Johnson. It was time to race, and race for the win.

So there he was with Kenseth, fender to fender, door to door at 190 mph, sliding in tandem off the corners over a 10-lap stretch that had all 180,000+ fans on their feet.

(Far Left) Crew chief Chad Knaus, once again, made the right call on pit road. This time the decision for four tires instead of two, gave his driver what he needed to win.

Carl Edwards' Ford sits idly on pit road, hood raised for crewmen trying to solve suspension problems. Edwards, who clinched the NASCAR Busch Series championship the day before, never quite got his car sorted out in this one and was three laps down at the finish.

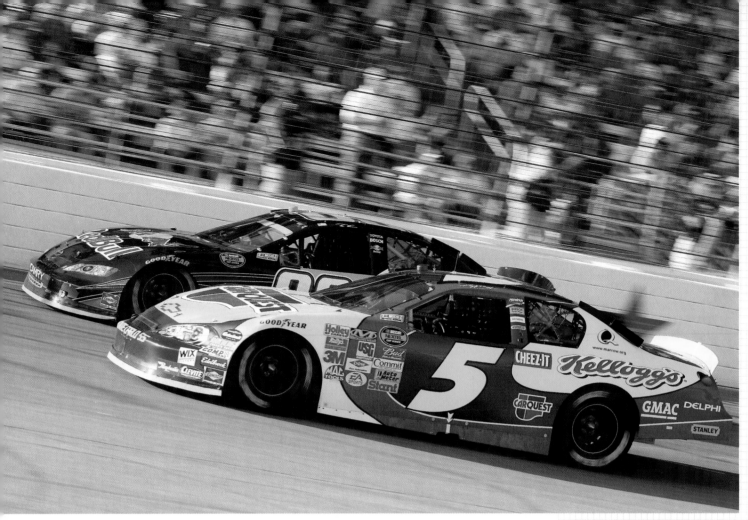

Twice they crossed the start/finish line in a literal a dead heat, the timing and scoring system — accurate to one ten-thousandth of a second — measuring the gap between them with nothing but zeros. Finally, with three laps to go in the race, Johnson gained enough of an edge to pull in front of Kenseth and close the door. Kenseth, riding on worn tires, had had enough by then and backed off slightly to allow Johnson to finish with nearly a one-second margin of victory.

(Above) Kyle Busch (5) slips past Brian Vickers on the inside. Busch led more laps than anyone by far, totaling 153 during the race while leading six different times, but he could not find the speed he needed in the closing laps and finished fourth.

(Right) Budweiser Pole Award winner Martin Truex Jr. (1) takes the green flag to begin the Dickies 500 with second-fastest qualifier Jeff Gordon on his right. Truex broke a five-race string of disappointing results with a third-place finish at Texas.

(Left) Matt Kenseth waits for new tires and a load of fuel during a green-flag stop. Kenseth led four times for 44 of the final 117 laps in the race, but didn't have enough to hold off Jimmie Johnson at the finish.

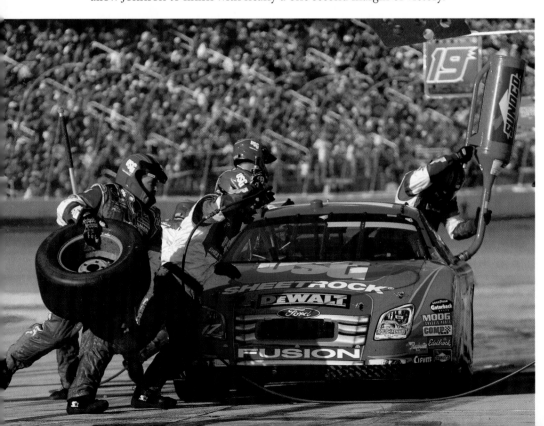

(Above) Jimmie Johnson's crew was perfect on his final stop of the race, fitting the Chevrolet with four fresh tires and sending him out ahead of all others who did the same. He lined up for the final restart behind three drivers who took two tires each and beat them all.

(Left) Jimmie Johnson (48) and Matt Kenseth (17) remain side by side on the frontstretch during one of the finest battles for a win staged during the season. They fought this way for 10 laps until Johnson finally prevailed with less than three laps remaining.

"It was evident how close our cars were and how much both of us wanted that win," Johnson said. "At times, I thought about the points, but I knew I needed every one I could get. Every spot counts, so you have to go for it. That's what I was doing."

And when the points were counted, Johnson came out on top. His third straight win combined with Jeff Gordon's seventh-place finish boosted the reigning champion to the top of the standings with a 30-point margin over his friend and teammate.

RACE RESULTS

NASCAR NEXTEL Cup Series Race No. 34 — *November 4, 2007*
Texas Motor Speedway

DICKIES 500

Fin. Pos.	Start Pos.	Car No.	Driver	Team	Laps	Laps Led	Status
1	8	48	Jimmie Johnson	Lowe's/KOBALT Chevrolet	334	9	Running
2	18	17	Matt Kenseth	USG Ford	334	44	Running
3	1	1	Martin Truex Jr.	Bass Pro Shops/Tracker Chevrolet	334	16	Running
4	17	5	Kyle Busch	CARQUEST/Kellogg's Chevrolet	334	153	Running
5	11	12	Ryan Newman	Alltel Dodge	334	4	Running
6	27	31	Jeff Burton	AT&T Mobility Chevrolet	334		Running
7	2	24	Jeff Gordon	DuPont Chevrolet	334	20	Running
8	6	2	Kurt Busch	Miller Lite Dodge	334	10	Running
9	24	26	Jamie McMurray	Crown Royal Special Reserve Ford	334		Running
10	4	29	Kevin Harvick	Shell/Pennzoil Chevrolet	334		Running
11	15	20	Tony Stewart	Home Depot Chevrolet	334		Running
12	19	19	Elliott Sadler	Dodge Dealers/UAW Dodge	334		Running
13	20	10	Scott Riggs	Proto/Stanley Tools/Valvoline Dodge	334		Running
14	12	8	Dale Earnhardt Jr.	Budweiser Chevrolet	334	12	Running
15	39	88	Ricky Rudd	Snickers Ford	334	10	Running
16	13	43	Bobby Labonte	Cheerios Spoonful of Stories Dodge	334		Running
17	38	18	J.J. Yeley	Interstate Batteries Chevrolet	333		Running
18	25	9	Kasey Kahne	Dodge Dealers/UAW Dodge	332		Running
19	29	07	Clint Bowyer	Jack Daniel's Chevrolet	332	1	Running
20	40	96	Tony Raines	DLP HDTV Chevrolet	332		Running
21	32	22	Dave Blaney	Caterpillar Toyota	332		Running
22	36	66	Jeremy Mayfield	Best Buy Chevrolet	332		Running
23	22	83	Brian Vickers	Red Bull Toyota	332		Running
24	14	36	Mike Skinner	360 OTC Toyota	331		Running
25	3	42 #	Juan Pablo Montoya	Texaco/Havoline Dodge	331	10	Running
26	21	99	Carl Edwards	Office Depot Ford	331		Running
27	42	70	Johnny Sauter	FleetPride Chevrolet	330		Running
28	34	38	David Gilliland	M&M's Ford	330		Running
29	7	11	Denny Hamlin	FedEx Kinko's Chevrolet	324	45	Running
30	16	15 #	Paul Menard	Menards/Moen Chevrolet	322		Running
31	9	25	Casey Mears	National Guard/GMAC Chevrolet	302		Running
32	41	7	Robby Gordon	Menards/MAPEI Ford	300		Running
33	23	16	Greg Biffle	Jackson Hewitt Ford	295		Oil Cooler
34	10	01	Mark Martin	U.S. Army Chevrolet	278		Running
35	35	78	Joe Nemechek	Furniture Row Chevrolet	275		Brakes
36	30	21	Bill Elliott	Delimex Ford	248		Running
37	33	6 #	David Ragan	AAA Insurance Ford	222		Accident
38	26	44	Dale Jarrett	UPS Toyota	217		Accident
39	5	84 #	AJ Allmendinger	Red Bull Toyota	151		Accident
40	31	41	Reed Sorenson	Target Dodge	143		Accident
41	28	40	David Stremme	HomeLife Communities Dodge	136		Accident
42	37	45	Kyle Petty	National Tire & Battery Dodge	129		Accident
43	43	00 #	David Reutimann	Burger King Toyota	90		Engine

Raybestos Rookie of the Year Contender.

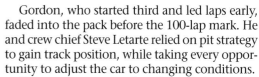

NASCAR NEXTEL CUP SERIES TOP 12

(With 2 Races Remaining)

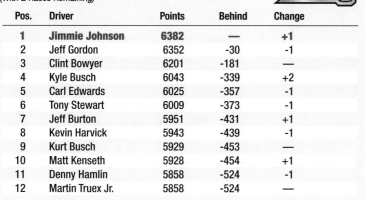

Pos.	Driver	Points	Behind	Change
1	**Jimmie Johnson**	**6382**	—	+1
2	Jeff Gordon	6352	-30	-1
3	Clint Bowyer	6201	-181	—
4	Kyle Busch	6043	-339	+2
5	Carl Edwards	6025	-357	-1
6	Tony Stewart	6009	-373	-1
7	Jeff Burton	5951	-431	+1
8	Kevin Harvick	5943	-439	-1
9	Kurt Busch	5929	-453	—
10	Matt Kenseth	5928	-454	+1
11	Denny Hamlin	5858	-524	-1
12	Martin Truex Jr.	5858	-524	—

Gordon, who started third and led laps early, faded into the pack before the 100-lap mark. He and crew chief Steve Letarte relied on pit strategy to gain track position, while taking every opportunity to adjust the car to changing conditions.

"We got our car good at the end, but it was too late," Gordon said, echoing his comments of one week earlier at Atlanta.

Overall, Gordon was actually keeping a better pace than the one that put him on top of the standings for 22 straight races leading up to the Chase for the NASCAR NEXTEL Cup. His average finish of 8.2 over the first 26 events looked anemic compared to his 4.6 average over the last eight. But a third place at Martinsville followed by a pair of seventh-place finishes paled to Johnson's three straight wins.

"He's smooth and smart and doesn't make mistakes," Kenseth said of Johnson. "So one little slip and Jeff will be right there. But Jimmie and Chad (Knaus) are better right now."

Indeed, crew chief Chad Knaus was making all the right moves at all the right times. A call for two tires at Atlanta put Johnson in position to win. At Texas, Knaus opted for four new tires during the 12th caution of the race with 29 laps to go. The team did their part as well, sending Johnson back to the track as the first car with fresh rubber all around.

Ryan Newman, Kenseth and Jamie McMurray each took two tires and lined up in front of Johnson, who made quick work of McMurray and Newman as soon as the race went green. In the end, his four fresh tires compared to Kenseth's two was the edge Johnson needed to track down Kenseth and make the final pass.

Bowyer, third in points, worked his way up to sixth place after starting back in 29th. But any thoughts he had of challenging for the win disappeared when a loose wheel forced him onto pit road for an unscheduled stop. It got worse when crew chief Gil Martin guessed wrong, electing to change right-side tires and sending Bowyer back to the action. The vibration persisted, and Bowyer had to return to the pits for left sides as well.

Laps lost dropped Bowyer to a 19th-place finish, increased his deficit to new-leader Johnson to 181 points and effectively ended his chances of winning the championship.

With only two races to go, it looked like the title fight would come down to Johnson and Gordon.

"I've made up 39 points in the last two races," Johnson said. "And it's possible I can lose that many the next two races. … Jeff and those guys aren't going to give it away this late in the season. I'm just happy to be in this position. I just hope this ride we're on stays for a while." ⬛⬛⬛

CHECKER AUTO PARTS 500

PHOENIX INTERNATIONAL RACEWAY

Jimmie Johnson (48) leads Martin Truex Jr. (1) and Matt Kenseth (17) in the late afternoon at Phoenix. He led twice for 55 laps, including the final 24, on the way to his fourth straight win and a commanding lead in the championship standings.

Too much can be made of the whole momentum thing, and often is. On the other hand, it can not be ignored, especially with a championship on the line. Clearly, Jimmie Johnson, crew chief Chad Knaus and the entire No. 48 team had momentum — tons of it. Three straight wins had vaulted them from 68 points behind to 30 ahead in the standings, a swing of 98 points against one of the best in the business in Jeff Gordon.

Gordon had momentum after winning two straight, at Talladega and Charlotte, but Johnson and Company snatched it away the following week at Martinsville and were keeping it for themselves. With only two chances left to win his elusive fifth title, Gordon needed to get it back.

In the Checker Auto Parts 500 at Phoenix, Johnson continued to show that he and his team had lost nothing, running effortlessly in the top three after starting sixth. At the same time, Gordon, who started third, again was struggling, fighting to maintain a place among the top 10 in the running order.

Something had to be done. So when Dale Earnhardt Jr. hit the wall and brought out the fifth caution on Lap 120, crew chief Steve Letarte took action and called Gordon to pit road. Few others pitted, as expected, which put Gordon out of sequence with the leaders.

"It was pretty crystal clear that the car wasn't going to be good enough to run in the top two or three," Letarte said. "It became evident that the only chance we had was to get out of sequence and get a lucky finish out of it."

The plan was simple but risky. The way to profit from being out of sequence is to hope that the leaders would have to pit under green, and thereby fall a lap down. Then, the yellow flag would have to appear at the right time, keeping them a lap down.

"We were going to have to have the miraculous caution," Letarte continued. "That was the only chance we had."

Funny thing about momentum: When you're on a roll, these things seem to fall your way. When you're not, they rarely do. Such was the case for Gordon, who spent the rest of the day mired in traffic, fighting for every position until eventually salvaging a 10th-place finish.

There were 10 lead changes in the race, shared among six drivers. Carl Edwards, winner of the Budweiser Pole Award, led the first 87 laps before pitting on the day's second caution. His car immediately developed engine troubles, though, and eventually failed completely after 125 laps, leaving Edwards ahead of only Earnhardt Jr. in the finishing order.

Martin Truex Jr., who started on the front row for the third time in his last four starts, led three times for 72 laps, but was listed fifth when the last of 10 cautions flew with 42 laps to go. Taking a gamble for late-race track position, he remained on the track while others pitted. Truex was able to hold his lead for 14 laps after the restart, but he was no match for those with fresher tires and fell to seventh place over the remaining distance.

"If we pitted, I don't think we could have won," Truex said, "so we stayed out and tried to do what we could do. ... We were a sitting duck at the end."

The other dominant driver was Matt Kenseth, on a roll of his own with three straight top-five finishes. Kenseth led three times for a race-high 93 laps and was in front when the final caution appeared on Lap 270.

Kenseth left pit road first and lined up behind Truex Jr. and Johnny Sauter, who also elected not to pit, with Tony Stewart and Johnson behind him for the restart with 38 laps to go.

Fans get a panoramic view of the one-mile Arizona oval from the top of the hillside bordering Turns 3 & 4. Inside the speedway, more than 100,000 fill the grandstands for the season's penultimate event.

It took less than two laps for Johnson to move into second behind Truex, with Kenseth hounding him from behind in third. Two laps later, Kenseth passed Johnson for second place, but when he encountered the lapped car of Aric Almirola, Johnson seized the opportunity and slipped past Kenseth to take over second place once again.

(Above) Crew chief Steve Letarte intently talks with driver Jeff Gordon during a practice session at Phoenix. Although Gordon qualified with the third-fastest lap, the No. 24 team was never quite able to obtain the speed needed to challenge the frontrunners during the race.

(Left) In Victory Lane, Jeff Gordon (left) congratulates teammate Jimmie Johnson on his 10th win of the season. Gordon knew full well that Johnson had all but sewn up his second consecutive NASCAR NEXTEL Cup Series crown.

(Right) Greg Biffle (16) leads Martin Truex Jr. (1) with Ryan Newman trailing from a distance. Biffle adjusted his setup throughout the race and finally hit it right, allowing a late-race charge to a runner-up finish.

RACE RESULTS

NASCAR NEXTEL Cup Series Race No. 35 — November 11, 2007
Phoenix International Raceway

CHECKER AUTO PARTS 500

Fin. Pos.	Start Pos.	Car No.	Driver	Team	Laps	Laps Led	Status
1	6	48	Jimmie Johnson	Lowe's Chevrolet	312	55	Running
2	7	16	Greg Biffle	Dish Network Ford	312		Running
3	18	17	Matt Kenseth	DEWALT NANO Technology Ford	312	93	Running
4	21	20	Tony Stewart	Home Depot Chevrolet	312		Running
5	13	12	Ryan Newman	Alltel Dodge	312	4	Running
6	34	29	Kevin Harvick	Shell/Pennzoil Chevrolet	312		Running
7	2	1	Martin Truex Jr.	Bass Pro Shops/Tracker Boats Chev.	312	72	Running
8	38	5	Kyle Busch	Kellogg's/CARQUEST Chevrolet	312		Running
9	12	31	Jeff Burton	AT&T Mobility Chevrolet	312		Running
10	3	24	Jeff Gordon	DuPont Chevrolet	312		Running
11	20	07	Clint Bowyer	Jack Daniel's Chevrolet	312		Running
12	9	2	Kurt Busch	Miller Lite Dodge	312		Running
13	11	25	Casey Mears	National Guard/GMAC Chevrolet	312		Running
14	4	18	J.J. Yeley	Interstate Batteries Chevrolet	312		Running
15	5	70	Johnny Sauter	Yellow Transportation Chevrolet	312		Running
16	15	11	Denny Hamlin	FedEx Ground Chevrolet	312		Running
17	14	42 #	Juan Pablo Montoya	Texaco/Havoline Dodge	312		Running
18	32	43	Bobby Labonte	Cheerios/Betty Crocker Dodge	312		Running
19	25	41	Reed Sorenson	Target Dodge	312	1	Running
20	37	40	David Stremme	Wrigley's Juicy Fruit Dodge	312		Running
21	22	83	Brian Vickers	Red Bull Toyota	312		Running
22	19	15 #	Paul Menard	Menards/Johns Manville Chevrolet	312		Running
23	23	26	Jamie McMurray	IRWIN Ford	312		Running
24	39	7	Robby Gordon	Menards/MAPEI Ford	312		Running
25	29	09	Sterling Marlin	Miccosukee Resorts Chevrolet	311		Running
26	28	01	Aric Almirola	U.S. Army Chevrolet	311		Running
27	16	19	Elliott Sadler	Siemens Dodge	311		Running
28	42	38	David Gilliland	M&M's Ford	311		Running
29	36	45	Kyle Petty	Wells Fargo Dodge	311		Running
30	26	06	Sam Hornish Jr.	Mobil 1 Dodge	310		Running
31	17	22	Dave Blaney	Caterpillar Toyota	310		Running
32	41	6 #	David Ragan	AAA Insurance Ford	310		Running
33	24	10	Patrick Carpentier	Valvoline/Sears Auto Center Dodge	310		Running
34	43	21	Bill Elliott	Ore-Ida/Heinz Ford	310		Running
35	33	88	Ricky Rudd	Pedigree Ford	309		Running
36	30	36	Johnny Benson	360 OTC Toyota	308		Running
37	8	96	Tony Raines	DLP HDTV Chevrolet	291		Running
38	31	78	Joe Nemechek	Furniture Row Chevrolet	241		Accident
39	40	66	Jeremy Mayfield	Haas Automation Chevrolet	212		Engine
40	10	9	Kasey Kahne	Dodge Dealers/UAW Dodge	147		Accident
41	27	27	Jacques Villeneuve	UNICEF Toyota	136		Accident
42	1	99	Carl Edwards	Office Depot Ford	125	87	Engine
43	35	8	Dale Earnhardt Jr.	Budweiser Chevrolet	118		Accident

Raybestos Rookie of the Year Contender.

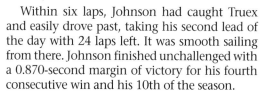

NASCAR NEXTEL Cup Series TOP 12
(With 1 Race Remaining)

Pos.	Driver	Points	Behind	Change
1	**Jimmie Johnson**	**6,572**	—	—
2	Jeff Gordon	6,486	-86	—
3	Clint Bowyer	6,331	-241	—
4	Kyle Busch	6,185	-387	—
5	Tony Stewart	6,169	-403	+1
6	Matt Kenseth	6,103	-469	+4
7	Kevin Harvick	6,093	-479	+1
8	Jeff Burton	6,089	-483	-1
9	Carl Edwards	6,067	-505	-4
10	Kurt Busch	6,056	-516	-1
11	Martin Truex Jr.	6,009	-563	+1
12	Denny Hamlin	5,973	-599	-1

Within six laps, Johnson had caught Truex and easily drove past, taking his second lead of the day with 24 laps left. It was smooth sailing from there. Johnson finished unchallenged with a 0.870-second margin of victory for his fourth consecutive win and his 10th of the season.

Combined with Gordon's 10th-place result, Johnson's lead ballooned to 86 points going into the final race of the season.

Greg Biffle mounted a late-race charge after making the right adjustments to his car and finished second in front of Kenseth. With his fourth consecutive top-five finish, Kenseth jumped from 10th to sixth in the point standings, but could only shake his head in wonderment at Johnson and his team.

"They're just unbelievably good," Kenseth said. "I don't know how you can put yourself in position to win every week like that. It's just amazing."

Or maybe it's momentum.

FORD 400

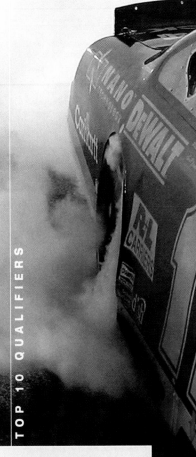

T he final event in any season has many storylines, and this year was no exception. Of course, the biggest one surrounded Jimmie Johnson and Jeff Gordon, both still in the running for the championship that would be decided when the checkered flag fell to end the Ford 400.

Gordon would start the race 86 points behind his teammate, a daunting but not insurmountable task. After all, two years ago Johnson was caught up in an accident in the final race of the season while Gordon finished ninth, the result being a 100-point spread between the two at the finish. The incident also dropped Johnson from having a legitimate shot at his first championship to fifth place in final point standings.

But that was two years ago. This time Johnson was the defending champion, he was riding a tidal wave of positive energy after four straight wins, and he knew he needed only to finish in the top 20 for the title to be his, no matter what Gordon did in the race. For Johnson and crew chief Chad Knaus, winning the championship was Job One, and, as Johnson stated before the race, if the opportunity to win his fifth in a row presented itself, it would be a great way to finish off the season.

Johnson's confidence was bolstered even further when he positioned himself at the front of the field by winning his fourth Budweiser Pole Award of the season (all of them in the last 11 races) for the start of the race. Clearly with a fast car and in front of potential trouble at the start of the race, Johnson's prospects looked good, indeed.

For others, the season finale represented pure opportunity. Other than Johnson and Gordon, Chase for the NASCAR NEXTEL Cup drivers viewed the race as a chance to improve their position in the final point standings, a factor having significant impact on the size of their bonus checks at the end of the season.

Still others saw the Ford 400 as one final shot to snap a haunting winless streak and end the year on a high note. Ryan Newman last won in September 2005 but had recently scored four top-five finishes in his last six starts. Newman increased his chances by qualifying on the front row, one position ahead of Kasey Kahne. This was Kahne's last chance to extend his personal streak of winning in each of the last two seasons and also continue a six-year winning streak for his team owner, Ray Evernham. He could think of no better way to end his disappointing season than with a win.

Dale Earnhardt Jr., who last went to Victory Lane 61 races earlier, in May 2006 at Richmond, was about to end an era in his final race with Dale Earnhardt Inc. Forever grateful to the members of his team, Earnhardt wanted desperately to win once more and give them the victory he felt they so richly deserved.

Then there was Matt Kenseth. Four straight finishes outside the top 25 had taken him out of title contention before the halfway point in the Chase for the NASCAR NEXTEL Cup. But Kenseth rallied, stringing together finishes of fifth, fourth, second and third over the last four races in a brilliant show of strength and consistency. The only thing missing in his late-season flurry was a win. After it was announced that crew chief Robbie Reiser would step down from the pit box after the race to become general manager at Roush Fenway Racing, Kenseth had extra incentive to give his longtime partner a going-away present.

It took Kenseth, who started fourth, slightly more than three laps to power past Kahne, Johnson and Newman to take his first lead of the day. It was nearly over at that point, as Kenseth led seven more times for 214 of the 267-lap distance in a dominant performance. A 1.6-second lead in the waning laps was cancelled by the seventh and final caution flag when Tony Stewart spun with 13 laps to go. But Kenseth somehow rocketed away from everyone on the restart and finished convincingly with nearly a one-second advantage over second-place Kurt Busch at the finish.

TOP 10 QUALIFIERS

1. **JIMMIE JOHNSON**
   30.545 SEC. 176.788 MPH

2. **RYAN NEWMAN**
   30.583 SEC. 176.569 MPH

3. **KASEY KAHNE**
   30.621 SEC. 176.350 MPH

4. **MATT KENSETH**
   30.669 SEC. 176.074 MPH

5. **KURT BUSCH**
   30.692 SEC. 175.942 MPH

6. **MARK MARTIN**
   30.708 SEC. 175.850 MPH

7. **DAVID RAGAN**
   30.708 SEC. 175.850 MPH

8. **KEVIN HARVICK**
   30.733 SEC. 175.707 MPH

9. **JEFF BURTON**
   30.741 SEC. 175.661 MPH

10. **CARL EDWARDS**
    30.792 SEC. 175.370 MPH

With the nose of his race-winning Ford against the frontstretch wall, Matt Kenseth smokes the tires to celebrate his second victory of the season. The win capped a five-race stretch during which he finished in every top-five position and rocketed from 12th to fourth in the point standings.

In the championship fight, Johnson got off to a good start, while Gordon, who qualified 11th, began carving his way through traffic toward the front of the field. Everything looked fine for Johnson until the first caution flew when Earnhardt and Kyle Busch got together at the entrance to pit road. Johnson had just pitted under green and suddenly found himself one lap down when the yellow flag flew.

At the tail end of the lead lap on the restart, he got an instant break when Jeff Burton and Earnhardt collided as soon as the green flag flew, which allowed Johnson to circle around to the back of the lead-lap pack. Having avoided a possible catastrophe, the rest of Johnson's day was uneventful, resulting in a seventh-place finish and his second NASCAR NEXTEL Cup Series crown.

Matt Kenseth (17) leads Ryan Newman and Jimmie Johnson in the early laps of the Ford 400. Kenseth took his first lead four laps into the race and stayed in front for 214 of the 267-lap distance (80 percent), leaving little doubt that he was the man to beat.

(Above) Kurt Busch gets a set of fresh tires and a full tank of fuel under one of seven cautions in the race. Busch had to fight back after falling a lap down and rallied to a second-place finish.

(Right) Ryan Newman (12) and David Ragan (6) run together in the late laps. Newman qualified on the front row and was fast early on, but spun near the halfway point and could not regain lost ground. Ragan capped his rookie season with a solid 10th-place finish.

Gordon finished the race in fourth place, falling 77 points shy in his quest for a fifth title. He remained upbeat however, saying, "We have a lot to be proud of and happy about this year. It's been a great year.

"Jimmie and Chad and all those guys did a phenomenal job. … He and his team are the best out there and they deserve [the championship]."

RACE RESULTS

NASCAR NEXTEL Cup Series Race No. 36 — November 18, 2007
Homestead-Miami Speedway

FORD 400

Fin. Pos.	Start Pos.	Car No.	Driver	Team	Laps	Laps Led	Status
1	4	17	Matt Kenseth	DEWALT NANO Technology Ford	267	214	Running
2	5	2	Kurt Busch	Miller Lite Dodge	267	17	Running
3	32	11	Denny Hamlin	FedEx Express Chevrolet	267	19	Running
4	11	24	Jeff Gordon	DuPont Chevrolet	267		Running
5	10	99	Carl Edwards	Office Depot Ford	267		Running
6	15	1	Martin Truex Jr.	Bass Pro Shops/Tracker Chevrolet	267	3	Running
7	1	48	Jimmie Johnson	Lowe's Chevrolet	267	1	Running
8	9	31	Jeff Burton	AT&T Mobility Chevrolet	267		Running
9	6	01	Mark Martin	U.S. Army Chevrolet	267		Running
10	7	6 #	David Ragan	AAA Insurance Ford	267	1	Running
11	30	40	David Stremme	Target Dodge	267		Running
12	23	22	Dave Blaney	Caterpillar Toyota	267	2	Running
13	37	16	Greg Biffle	Dish Network Ford	267		Running
14	25	26	Jamie McMurray	Crown Royal Ford	267	1	Running
15	33	42 #	Juan Pablo Montoya	Texaco/Havoline Dodge	267		Running
16	21	25	Casey Mears	National Guard/GMAC Chevrolet	267	1	Running
17	26	44	Dale Jarrett	UPS Toyota	266		Running
18	2	12	Ryan Newman	Alltel Dodge	266	7	Running
19	8	29	Kevin Harvick	Shell/Pennzoil Chevrolet	266		Running
20	18	5	Kyle Busch	Kellogg's/CARQUEST Chevrolet	266	1	Running
21	38	88	Ricky Rudd	Snickers Ford	266		Running
22	27	41	Reed Sorenson	Target Dodge	266		Running
23	36	43	Bobby Labonte	Cheerios/Betty Crocker Dodge	266		Running
24	3	9	Kasey Kahne	Dodge Dealers/UAW Dodge	265		Running
25	35	00 #	David Reutimann	Burger King Toyota	265		Running
26	34	66	Jeremy Mayfield	Best Buy Chevrolet	265		Running
27	41	7	Robby Gordon	Camping World Ford	264		Running
28	43	21	Bill Elliott	Motorcraft Ford	264		Running
29	42	96	Tony Raines	DLP HDTV Chevrolet	264		Running
30	14	20	Tony Stewart	Home Depot Chevrolet	264		Running
31	24	18	J.J. Yeley	Interstate Batteries Chevrolet	263		Running
32	12	38	David Gilliland	M&M's Ford	263		Running
33	16	09	Sterling Marlin	Miccosukee Resorts Chevrolet	263		Running
34	40	45	Kyle Petty	Marathon Motor Oil Dodge	263		Running
35	39	15 #	Paul Menard	Menards/Johns Manville Chevrolet	262		Running
36	13	8	Dale Earnhardt Jr.	Budweiser Chevrolet	261		Running
37	29	06	Sam Hornish Jr.	Mobil 1 Dodge	254		Running
38	31	19	Elliott Sadler	Dodge Dealers/UAW Dodge	250		Running
39	19	07	Clint Bowyer	Jack Daniel's Chevrolet	242		Running
40	28	10	Patrick Carpentier	Valvoline/Stanley Tools Dodge	225		Running
41	22	70	Johnny Sauter	Yellow Transportation Chevrolet	157		Accident
42	17	83	Brian Vickers	Red Bull Toyota	154		Accident
43	20	36	Johnny Benson	360 OTC Toyota	73		Engine

Raybestos Rookie of the Year Contender.

NASCAR NEXTEL Cup Series TOP 12

(Final Standings)

Pos.	Driver	Points	Behind	Change
1	**Jimmie Johnson**	6723	—	—
2	Jeff Gordon	6646	-77	—
3	Clint Bowyer	6377	-346	—
4	Matt Kenseth	6298	-425	+2
5	Kyle Busch	6293	-430	-1
6	Tony Stewart	6242	-481	-1
7	Kurt Busch	6231	-492	+3
8	Jeff Burton	6231	-492	—
9	Carl Edwards	6222	-501	—
10	Kevin Harvick	6199	-524	-3
11	Martin Truex Jr.	6164	-559	—
12	Denny Hamlin	6143	-580	—

REFLECTIONS

Crew members take a rare moment to catch a nap in the garage at New Hampshire International Speedway. The 38-race season schedule (including non-points events) tests the strength and stamina of every team member.

FedEx
RACING
EVERY DAY
IS RACE DAY SM
Coca-Cola
JOE
GIBBS
RACING
11

Dale Earnhardt Jr. captured more attention during the 2007 season than perhaps at any time in his career. On the track, strong efforts were consistently confounded by accidents and engine failures, while his contract status dominated conversation off the track.

(Left) Kevin Harvick ponders what's ahead at Dover in September. A win in the Daytona 500 and a victory in the NASCAR NEXTEL All-Star Challenge were high points in a season that put Harvick in the Chase for the NASCAR NEXTEL Cup for the second year in a row.

(Above) Plans to build on an extremely successful 2006 season never materialized for Kasey Kahne. Six DNFs, five due to accidents, contributed to a frustrating year for the popular young star. His outlook for the future includes a new sponsor, as Budweiser announced it would back him in 2008 and beyond.

(Left) Teammates Denny Hamlin (left) and Tony Stewart had their share of different opinions during the 2007 season, but both drivers won races and made the Chase for the NASCAR NEXTEL Cup. Before the year was over, their team announced it would switch to Toyotas in 2008.

(Right) Juan Pablo Montoya made quite a splash during his run for 2007 Raybestos Rookie of the Year, highlighted by a win at Infineon Raceway and a runner-up finish in the Allstate 400 at the Brickyard.

(Below) Martin Truex Jr. joined the first-time-winners' club with a dominating victory at Dover in early June. He followed his win with six more top-five finishes and joined the Chase for the NASCAR NEXTEL Cup.

Fans at Bristol Motor Speedway are always willing to take part in pre-race activities, especially when it involves showing their patriotism. This crowd, on hand in late March, also witnessed the debut of the Car of Tomorrow.

Heavy hearts were evident when the NASCAR NEXTEL Cup Series visited Phoenix International Raceway in April. In the garage, Virginia native Ward Burton (above) recognized those affected by the shootings on the campus of Virginia Tech. (Left) Up on the hillside, fans constructed their own tribute to two fallen NASCAR champions, Benny Parsons and Bobby Hamilton.

AUTOGRAPHS